Lecture Notes in Artificial Intelligence 13786

Subseries of Lecture Notes in Computer Science

More information about this subseries at https://link.springer.com/bookseries/1244

Ana Paula Rocha · Luc Steels ·
Jaap van den Herik (Eds.)

Agents and Artificial Intelligence

14th International Conference, ICAART 2022
Virtual Event, February 3–5, 2022
Revised Selected Papers

Springer

Editors
Ana Paula Rocha
LIACC/FEUP
Porto, Portugal

Luc Steels
ICREA, Institute of Evolutionary Biology
Barcelona, Spain

Jaap van den Herik
Leiden Institute of Advanced
Computer Science
Leiden, The Netherlands

ISSN 0302-9743   ISSN 1611-3349 (electronic)
Lecture Notes in Artificial Intelligence
ISBN 978-3-031-22952-7   ISBN 978-3-031-22953-4 (eBook)
https://doi.org/10.1007/978-3-031-22953-4

LNCS Sublibrary: SL7 – Artificial Intelligence

This Springer imprint is published by the registered company Springer Nature Switzerland AG
The registered company address is: Gewerbestrasse 11, 6330 Cham, Switzerland

Preface

The present book includes extended and revised versions of a set of selected papers from the 14th International Conference on Agents and Artificial Intelligence (ICAART 2022), that was exceptionally held as an online event, due to the COVID-19 pandemic, during February 3–5, 2022.

ICAART 2022 received 302 paper submissions from 53 countries, of which 3% were included in this book.

The papers were selected by the event chairs and their selection is based on a number of criteria that include the classifications and comments provided by the Program Committee members, the session chairs' assessment, and also the program chairs' global view of all papers included in the technical program. The authors of selected papers were then invited to submit revised and extended versions of their papers having at least 30% innovative material.

The purpose of the International Conference on Agents and Artificial Intelligence is to bring together researchers, engineers, and practitioners interested in the theory and applications in the areas of agents and artificial intelligence. Two simultaneous related tracks were held, covering both applications and current research work in these two areas.

The papers selected to be included in this book contribute to the understanding of relevant trends of current research on agents and artificial intelligence, including deep learning, multi-agent systems, machine learning, hybrid intelligent systems, evolutionary computing, uncertainty in AI, distributed problem solving, explainable artificial intelligence, constraint satisfaction, and big data.

We would like to thank authors for their contributions. Moreover, we are grateful to the reviewers who helped ensure the quality of this publication.

February 2022

Ana Paula Rocha
Luc Steels
Jaap van den Herik

Organization

Conference Chair

Jaap van den Herik   Leiden University, The Netherlands

Program Co-chairs

Ana Paula Rocha   University of Porto, Portugal
Luc Steels   ICREA and Institute of Evolutionary Biology,
     Spain

Program Committee

Vicki Allan	Utah State University, USA
Klaus-Dieter Althoff	German Research Center for Artificial Intelligence and University of Hildesheim, Germany
Frédéric Amblard	IRIT - Université Toulouse 1 Capitole, France
Ilze Andersone	Riga Technical University, Latvia
Alla Anohina-Naumeca	Riga Technical University, Latvia
Marcelo Armentano	ISISTAN Research Institute, CONICET-UNICEN, Argentina
Jean-Michel Auberlet	IFSTTAR, France
Farshad Badie	Berlin School of Business and Innovation, Germany
Montserrat Batet	Universitat Rovira i Virgili, Spain
Carole Bernon	University of Toulouse III, France
Stefano Bistarelli	University of Perugia, Italy
Carlos Bobed Lisbona	University of Zaragoza, Spain
Lars Braubach	City University of Hamburg, Germany
Joerg Bremer	University of Oldenburg, Germany
Paolo Bresciani	Fondazione Bruno Kessler, Italy
Daniela Briola	Università degli Studi di Milano-Bicocca, Italy
Aleksander Byrski	AGH University of Science and Technology, Poland
Giacomo Cabri	Università di Modena e Reggio Emilia, Italy
Patrice Caire	Independent Consultant, Luxembourg
Valérie Camps	IRIT - Université Toulouse III, France
Javier Carbó Rubiera	Universidad Carlos III de Madrid, Spain

Henrique Lopes Cardoso	Universidade do Porto, Portugal
Cristiano Castelfranchi	Institute of Cognitive Sciences and Technologies - National Research Council, Italy
Wen-Chung Chang	National Taipei University of Technology, Taiwan, Republic of China
Davide Ciucci	Università degli Studi di Milano-Bicocca, Italy
Stéphanie Combettes	IRIT - Université Toulouse III, France
Flavio Correa da Silva	University of Sao Paulo, Brazil
Paulo Cortez	University of Minho, Portugal
Matteo Cristani	University of Verona, Italy
Erzsébet Csuhaj-Varjú	Eötvös Loránd University, Hungary
Riccardo De Benedictis	National Research Council, Italy
Fernando de Souza	Universidade Federal de Pernambuco, Brazil
Bruno Di Stefano	Nuptek Systems Ltd., Canada
Michel Dojat	Université Grenoble Alpes, France
Francisco Domínguez Mayo	University of Seville, Spain
Viktor Eisenstadt	University of Hildesheim, Germany
Thomas Eiter	Technische Universität Wien, Austria
Christophe Feltus	Luxembourg Institute of Science and Technology, Belgium
Edilson Ferneda	Catholic University of Brasilia, Brazil
Alexander Ferrein	FH Aachen University of Applied Sciences, Germany
Roberto Flores	Christopher Newport University, USA
Agostino Forestiero	ICAR-CNR, Italy
Claude Frasson	University of Montreal, Canada
Katsuhide Fujita	Tokyo University of Agriculture and Technology, Japan
Leonardo Garrido	Tecnológico de Monterrey, Mexico
Benoit Gaudou	Université Toulouse 1 Capitole, France
Luciano H. Tamargo	Universidad Nacional del Sur, Argentina
James Harland	RMIT University, Australia
Hisashi Hayashi	Advanced Institute of Industrial Technology, Japan
Vincent Hilaire	UTBM, France
Hanno Hildmann	TNO, The Netherlands
Rolf Hoffmann	Darmstadt University of Technology, Germany
Sviatlana Höhn	University of Luxembourg, Luxembourg
Wei-Chiang Hong	Asia Eastern University of Science and Technology, Taiwan, Republic of China
Ales Horak	Masaryk University, Czech Republic
Marc-Philippe Huget	University of Savoie Mont-Blanc, France

Dieter Hutter	German Research Centre for Artificial Intelligence, Germany
Agnieszka Jastrzebska	Warsaw University of Technology, Poland
Michael Jenkin	York University, Canada
Norihiro Kamide	Teikyo University, Japan
Geylani Kardas	Ege University, Turkey
Petros Kefalas	CITY College, Greece
Matthias Klusch	German Research Center for Artificial Intelligence, Germany
Mare Koit	University of Tartu, Estonia
Pavel Kral	University of West Bohemia, Czech Republic
Daniel Ladley	University of Leicester, UK
Divesh Lala	Kyoto University, Japan
Marc Le Goc	Polytech Marseille, France
Agapito Ledezma	Carlos III University of Madrid, Spain
Ladislav Lenc	University of West Bohemia, Czech Republic
Letizia Leonardi	Università di Modena e Reggio Emilia, Italy
Churn-Jung Liau	Academia Sinica, Taiwan, Republic of China
Jianyi Lin	Università Cattolica del Sacro Cuore, Italy
Stephane Loiseau	LERIA, University of Angers, France
António Lopes	Instituto Universitário de Lisboa, Portugal
Audrone Lupeikiene	Vilnius University, Lithuania
Lorenzo Magnani	University of Pavia, Italy
Jerusa Marchi	Universidade Federal de Santa Catarina, Brazil
Philippe Mathieu	University of Lille, France
Toshihiro Matsui	Nagoya Institute of Technology, Japan
Marjan Mernik	University of Maribor, Slovenia
Raul Monroy	Tecnológico de Monterrey, Mexico
Manuela Montangero	Università di Modena e Reggio Emilia, Italy
Maxime Morge	Université de Lille, France
Gildas Morvan	Université d'Artois, France
Bernard Moulin	Université Laval, Canada
Muhammad Marwan Muhammad Fuad	Coventry University, UK
Juan Carlos Nieves	Umeå Universitet, Sweden
Antoine Nongaillard	Lille University, France
Luis Nunes	Instituto Universitário de Lisboa and Instituto de Telecomunicações, Portugal
Michel Occello	Université Grenoble Alpes, France
Andrei Olaru	Politehnica University of Bucharest, Romania
Joanna Isabelle Olszewska	University of the West Scotland, UK
Stanislaw Osowski	Warsaw University of Technology, Poland

Lena Valavani	Massachusetts Institute of Technology, USA
Leo van Moergestel	HU Utrecht University of Applied Sciences, The Netherlands
Harko Verhagen	Stockholm University, Sweden
Emilio Vivancos	Universitat Politecnica de Valencia, Spain
Wojciech Waloszek	Gdansk University of Technology, Poland
Frank Wang	University of Kent, UK
Jianshu Weng	AI Singapore, Singapore
Bozena Wozna-Szczesniak	Jan Dlugosz University in Czestochowa, Poland
Chung-Hsing Yeh	Monash University, Australia

Additional Reviewers

Kholud Alghamdi	Florida Institute of Technology, USA
Akram Alghanmi	Florida Institute of Technology, USA
Remis Balaniuk	Catholic University of Brasilia, Brazil
Lorenzo Baraldi	Università degli Studi di Modena e Reggio Emilia, Italy
Thales Bertaglia	Maastricht University, The Netherlands
Giovanni Ciatto	University of Bologna, Italy
Paula De Toledo	Universidad Carlos III de Madrid, Spain
Hércules do Prado	Catholic University of Brasília, Brazil
Viktor Eisenstadt	German Research Center for Artificial Intelligence and University of Hildesheim, Germany
Jose Iglesias	Universidad Carlos III de Madrid, Spain
Gonçalo Leão	INESC TEC, Portugal
Jesus Llano Garcia	Tecnologico de Monterrey, Mexico
Ascensión Lopez	Universidad Carlos III de Madrid, Spain
Antoine Louis	Maastricht University, The Netherlands
Ben Mathew	Florida Institute of Technology, USA
Corrado Mio	Khalifa University of Science and Technology, UAE
Josias Moukpe	Florida Institute of Technology, USA
Quentin Pouvreau	IRIT, France
Guiseppe Russo	ETH Zurich, Switzerland
Sophia Schlosser	ETH Zurich, Switzerland
Jakob Schoenborn	University of Hildesheim and German Research Center for Artificial Intelligence, Germany
Jose Simmonds	Universidad Carlos III de Madrid, Spain
Carlo Taticchi	University of Perugia, Italy
Joaquin Taverner	Universitat Politècnica de València, Spain

Invited Speakers

Michael Beetz	University of Bremen, Germany
Jan Seyler	Festo SE & Co. KG, Germany
Catherine Pelachaud	CNRS, Sorbonne University, France

Contents

Agents

Efficient Visual Sign Assignment for Crowd Evacuation Guidance Considering Risks and Multiple Objectives

Akira Tsurushima$^{(\boxtimes)}$ (ID)

Intelligent Systems Laboratory, SECOM Co., Ltd., Tokyo, Japan
a-tsurushima@secom.co.jp

Abstract. Numerous studies conducted on crowd evacuation have illustrated the effectiveness of using evacuation guidance systems with visual evacuation signage. The efficient arrangement of signage on the premises is crucial for the optimal use of these systems; however, to determine the optimal assignment of visual signs is challenging because of several factors, such as complex crowd behaviors, multiple conflicting objectives in evacuations, randomness, and situation uncertainties. Blackbox optimization techniques with multiagent simulations as objective functions have been applied to evaluate the outcome of visual sign arrangements in evacuation studies. They explore an efficient arrangement of evacuation signs achieving a swift and safe crowd evacuation. However, the randomness and complexity involved in the problem causes significant variances in the outcomes of the solutions, increasing the risk that the satisfactory solution explored during the design phase may result in significantly different severe consequences during actual implementation. Here, we formulated this problem as a stochastic multi-objective optimization problem with two objectives: maximizing the number of agents who select the correct exit, and minimizing the total evacuation time. The average value at risk (AVaR) used as a risk measure in finance and economics was employed to evaluate the risks involved in the solutions. NSGA-II algorithms incorporating simulations with the evacuation decision model have been used to explor solutions satisfying both expected values and AVaRs.

Keywords: Evolutionary multi-objective optimization · Black-box optimization · Visual evacuation signage assignment problem · Average values at risk · NSGA-II

1 Introduction

Numerous studies have been conducted on crowd evacuation to mitigate loss of life during a disaster [7,8]. In these studies, visual evacuation signage proved to be practical and efficient; hence, evacuation guidance systems using visual signage were developed. The proper arrangement of visual signs within premises is crucial for these systems to achieve the appropriate effects. We have conducted studies to explore the optimal arrangement of visual evacuation signs. However, achieving an optimal arrangement is challenging because of the following several factors.

The crowd behavior of evacuees is a complex system often unpredictable and uncontrollable. The cognitive characteristics of evacuees are the prime factors causing

A. P. Rocha et al. (Eds.): ICAART 2022, LNAI 13786, pp. 3–26, 2022.
https://doi.org/10.1007/978-3-031-22953-4_1

complex crowd behaviors. Herd behavior, the tendency of an individual to follow other people's behaviors or decisions, is one of those well-studied characteristics in crowd evacuation; however, it still remains unclear [10,27]. Herd behaviors during evacuation cause substantial variance in evacuation results and the consequences of evacuation guidance is unpredictable. This is particularly true if the evacuation process includes some evacuation decisions, such as choosing the evacuation route or exit [9,19]. Asymmetry of exit choice is a well-known and intriguing phenomenon during evacuations [12,14,30–32]. Multiagent simulations are frequently employed to model this issue and explore suitable arrangements of signage.

Certain properties of the problem also make this task challenging, such as large decision spaces, computationally expensive evaluation methods, noisy objective functions, lack of efficient search methods, and multiple conflicting objectives. Black-box optimizations that employ simulations as the objective functions often address this issue. However, the high computational costs resulting from the large search spaces and simulations employed to evaluate the solution candidates are often infeasible for most architectural projects.

Furthermore, the risk of outcomes between the design and the real situation might differ significantly because the stochastic nature of the problem is another crucial, albeit hardly pointed out, issue. The risk-avoidance feature of human decision-making transforms the original problem into a decision problem, which is more challenging to manage and may require human subjective judgments rather than purely objective assessments. This is because a simple expected value cannot represent human decision-making; expected utilities have to be considered to properly evaluate the solution candidates.

We addressed these issues in the visual signage arrangement problem for crowd evacuations by considering it a stochastic multi-objective problem. We also formulated this problem and named it the visual evacuation signage assignment problem (VESAP) [34]. This study analyzed an instance of a VESAP where the environment has two exits: a correct (safe) exit and an incorrect (dangerous) exit. Thus, the evacuees in our problem have to decide which one should be selected to egress. This problem maximizes the number of evacuees that determine the correct exit (f_1). However, maximizing f_1 causes another unfavorable issue, which is a long total evacuation time. This is because assigning visual signage in front of an incorrect exit is an optimal solution to the problem. However, evacuees move to the incorrect exit first and then after assessing the signage head to the correct exit, resulting in unnecessarily long evacuation routes. Thus, by introducing another objective, minimizing the total evacuation time (f_2), we formulated the VESAP as a multi-objective optimization problem.

To address the aforementioned risk issue, we also consider the VESAP as a mean risk model, a stochastic optimization model that deals with risk aversion problem [20]. We introduce the notion of the average value at risk (AVaR), which is a risk measure employed in economics and finance, to incorporate risk-averse decisions in our model.

Previously, we only investigated the VESAP with a single visual evacuation sign case and analyzed it in terms of the Pareto-efficiency and the risks associated with these solutions [34]. However, guiding a crowd using a single visual sign is unrealistic in most real cases. Moreover, we assumed a discrete decision space and conducted brute-force approaches for all candidate positions in the assigned visual signs to analyze

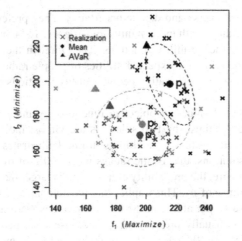

Fig. 1. Motivating example [36].

Pareto-optimal solutions, which may be inapplicable in practical problems because of the computational cost.

This study investigates the VESAP with multiple visual signs for discrete and continuous decision spaces. The combinatorial property of the problem results in a large decision space and costly computations, rendering the brute-force approach inapplicable. We employed a black-box optimization technique to explore the optimum through simulations as objective functions for searching large decision spaces. We also applied multi-objective optimization techniques to explore the Pareto frontiers and employed AVaR to estimate the risks involved in the solutions. This study is an extended version of our previous study [36]. The main difference between these two studies is that only continuous decision spaces were analyzed previously. In this study, we also analyzed discrete decision spaces for multiple visual signage cases.

2 Motivating Example

Figure 1 shows the objective space of the VESAP for f_1 and f_2 with three example solutions, p_1, p_2, and p_3, are indicated in black, green, and red, respectively. In this figure, the bottom right corner shows the most preferable solution and the top-left corner is the least preferable solution because we are looking to maximize f_1 and minimize f_2. Twenty-four simulations were conducted for each solution and the realization of each solution were indicated in $\times$ with the associated colors with each solution in space. The means of 24 realizations, which are often considered to be representations of solid circles also indicate these realizations with colors is associated with each solution. However, the realizations of each solution were distributed differently due to the effects of herd behaviors and random property of the problem. The mean of these realizations disregards the spread of these values in space. This makes it difficult to specify the coordinates of points which represents the outcomes of the solutions on the objective space.

Most people are risk-averse and dislike uncertainty. They prefer random variables with less variance over those with more significant variance. To be precise, most human decision-makers have concave utility functions. Therefore, in the VESAP, the quantity to be optimized should be the expected utilities of people rather than the expected values of outcomes. However, estimating people's utility functions can be difficult and sometimes impossible.

In Fig. 1, the expected values of objective functions p_2 and p_3 are close to each other for both f_1 and f_2; thus, the two solutions are almost indistinguishable if we consider only the expected values. The ellipses in Fig. 1 illustrates a 50% probability ellipses of the three solutions, that is, the ranges where 50% of these realizations are located inside. In the figure, the probability ellipse of p_2 is larger than that of the p_3 and includes almost the ellipse of p_3. This implies that the outcomes of p_2 are more unpredictable than the those of p_3, although the expected values were almost equal. Here, human decision-makers usually prefer p_3 to p_2 because most people are risk-averse and dislike unpredictability. Because risks are major factors in evacuation problems, the risk attitude of decision-makers is crucial and should be considered for the evacuation protocol analysis. Numerical risk measures that appropriately represent this type of risk involved in the solutions are desirable.

3   Preliminaries

In the previous example, two factors determined that even a partial ordering of solutions difficult: risks (distribution of realizations), and multiple objectives (f_1 and f_2).

Let F and G be the cumulative distribution functions of the random variable $x \in X$, and $a \succeq b$ denotes a decision maker who weakly prefers a to b. A stochastic order between F and G such that $F \succeq G$, is determined if

$$\int u(x)dF \geq \int u(x)dG,$$

where $u(\cdot)$ denotes a utility function and dF and dG indicate Stieltjes integrals. Stochastic dominance determines the partial order between random variables without estimating the explicit utility function.

Definition 1 (First Order Stochastic Dominance). *[17] F first-order stochastically dominates G if the decision-maker weakly prefers F to G under any non-decreasing utility function u, which is equivalent to*

$$\forall x, \ F(x) \leq G(x).$$

First-order stochastic dominance determines the partial order between random variables, assuming a risk-neutral decision-maker. However, most people are risk-averse and have concave utility functions, which are not considered in first-order stochastic dominance. Second-order stochastic dominance addresses this issue.

Definition 2 (Second Order Stochastic Dominance). *[17] F second-order stochastically dominates G if the decision-maker weakly prefers F to G under any nondecreasing concave utility function, which is equivalent to*

$$\forall x, \int_{-\infty}^{x} F(z)dz \le \int_{-\infty}^{x} G(z)dz.$$

In the modern portfolio theory, Markowitz introduced the mean-risk model, which is a stochastic optimization model that addresses risk aversion by introducing a risk measure ρ; the variance was employed as risk measure in Markowitz's model. Thus, the mean risk model transforms a stochastic optimization problem into a bi-objective optimization problem that maximizes the expected values f and minimizes the risk measures ρ rather than calculating all non-stochastically dominated solutions. However, there are several deficiencies, such as disregarding profit and loss, and considering only the differences, have been pointed out by employing the variance as a risk measure to represent human attitudes toward risks.

The average value at risk (AVaR), which is a common risk measure in many fields, including economics and finance, it is currently considered a coherent risk measure consistent with the maximum expected utility principle and second-order stochastic dominance [6,21]. AVaR satisfies several desired properties, including monotonicity, positive homogeneity, subadditivity, and translation invariance. It is defined based on the value at risk (VaR), which is another risk measure employed before AVaR [23].

Definition 3 (Value at Risk: VaR). *Value at risk of random outcome X at the level* $\alpha(0 < \alpha \le 1)$ *is the* $\alpha-quantile,$[1] *of the random variable X, that is,*

$$VaR_{\alpha}(X) = F_X^{-1}(\alpha).$$

Definition 4 (Average Value at Risk: AVaR). *AVaR of random outcome X at level* $\alpha(0 < \alpha \le 1)$ *is defined as (See footnote 1):*

$$AVaR_{\alpha}(X) = \frac{1}{\alpha} \int_0^{\alpha} VaR_p(X)dp \tag{1}$$
$$= \mathbf{E}[X|X \le VaR_{\alpha}(X)]. \tag{2}$$

The triangles in Fig. 1 depicts the coordinates of $(AVaR_{0.3}(f_1), AVaR_{0.3}(f_2))$ of p_1, p_2, and p_3 in black, red, and green, respectively.

Because Fig. 1 has two objectives f_1 and f_2, it is difficult or impossible to set the order of the expected values of p_1, p_2, and p_3 (three filled circles), without using subjective preferences because one may have a better value for one objective function than those of the others while having a worse value for the other objective functions. These solutions are called Pareto-optimal solutions in multi-objective optimizations [6].

Definition 5 (Pareto-optimal). *A solution x is non-dominated, Pareto-efficient, or Pareto-optimal, if no solution* $y \ne x$ *dominates x. A solution y is said to dominate x if a solution y satisfies*[2]

---

[1] The financial field defines VaR as negative α-quantile of random variable X because X is the return value, which can be negative or positive, but not the outcome itself. However, for simplicity, we used this definition (outcome).

[2] We assume f_i is maximized.

1. $\forall h : f_h(y) \geq f_j(x)$
2. $\exists g : f_g(y) > f_g(x)$.

If x is a Pareto-optimal solution, then the image of x, $f(x)$, is called Pareto-optimal point and the set of Pareto-optimal points on the objective space is called the Pareto-frontier.

For instance, p_2 and p_3 are Pareto-optimal points with respect to expected values. However, p_2 is dominated by p_3 with respect to the risks, because p_3 has better values for both $AVaR_{0.3}(f_1)$ and $AVaR_{0.3}(f_2)$ than for p_2. By considering AVaRs, we can conclude that p_3 is a better solution than p_2 because p_3 has smaller risks than p_2, even though the expected values of the two were almost equivalent.

4 Related Works

Numerous studies have been conducted on multi-objective optimization. Many researchers have developed methods based on an evolutionary multi-objective (EMO) algorithm, which holds a set of solutions and iteratively approximates them to a Pareto-frontier, is intriguing and promising. Deb et al. (2002) proposed the NSGA-II algorithm [1], which is one of the most representative and widely used EMO algorithms. Following NSGA-II, the other EMO algorithms are introduced as follows: MOEA/D [38], MSOPS [13], and NSGA-III [2]. Promising approaches for solving real-world multi-objective problems with computationally expensive objective functions are CMA-ES. [11] and MOTPE [22].

Several researchers have addressed EMO algorithms with fitness functions that are contaminated by noise. Siegmund et al. (2015) proposed dynamic resampling strategies based on evolutionary generations, Pareto rankings, and distances to the reference points to mitigate noise [28]. Implicit sampling techniques using a large population as a substitute for explicit sampling were proposed in [29]. Sano and Kita (2002) proposed a method using a history of search results to reduce fitness evaluations [25]. Goh and Tan (2007) adopted experimental learning-directed perturbation strategy for noise-tolerant search [5]. Probabilistic dominance has been proposed for robust selection operations against noise in evolutionary optimization [4]. All of these approaches address the issues of obtaining quality solutions with lower costs; the issues of risks between the real and expected outcomes were not considered.

Saadatseresht et al. (2009) formulated a crowd evacuation guidance problem as follows: as a multi-objective optimization problem and solved using NSGA-II for developing evacuation plans [24]. Dubey et al. (2020) developed an interactive design support system (AUTOSIGN) to develop an optimal signage system with multiple objectives: random weight genetic algorithm (MO-RWGA) was applied to address these objectives in this system [3]. Li et al. (2010) developed a method for achieving an optimal evacuation route assignments with three objectives; NSGA-II was employed to solve this problem [18]. However, none of these approaches consider the risks or uncertainties involved for the problem in the solution procedure.

León et al. (2020) analyzed a stochastic multi-objective problem using AVaR, assuming that decision-makers are risk-averse [16]. Schantz et al. (2021) formulated

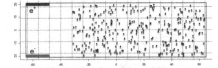

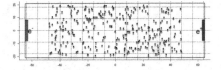

Fig. 2. S_1 [36] (Color figure online)   **Fig. 3.** S_2 [36] (Color figure online)

the evacuation-planning problem as follows: a multi-objective optimization problem with AVaR as a risk measure [26]. This study considers AVaR as one of the objectives to be minimized and formulated the problem as a bi-objective optimization problem with expected value, and AVaR as objective functions.

5 Visual Evacuation Signage Assignment Problem

This section presented an instance of a VESAP with 300 agents. The 300 agents $A = \{a_1, \ldots, a_{300}\}$ are randomly located on the two-dimensional Euclidean space $S \in \mathbb{R}^2$ with two exits e^+ and e^-. Exit e^+ is assumed to be the correct exit, which will lead agents to safe evacuations; however, e^- will not. Therefore, in the VESAP, the objective is to maximize the number of agents who choose e^+ to flee from S. However, this single objective often leads to an unpreferable solution: which is the position in front of e^-; this will likely cause unnecessarily long travel distance. In this solution, many agents first move to the position in front of e^- and obtain information on the correct exit through visual evacuation signage k. They then change their headings to e^+ and move again to the correct exit. The results are evacuations with a long total evacuation time, which is another serious problem in most evacuation scenarios. These two objectives were evaluated using multiagent simulations whose outcomes are contaminated with noise caused by randomness and herd behaviors of the agents. Thus, we formulated VESAP as stochastic multi-objective problems [34].

$$max \quad f_1(k, \omega) \tag{3}$$

$$max \quad -f_2(k, \omega) \tag{4}$$

$$s.t. \quad k \in \mathcal{K}, |k| \leq L, \omega \in \Omega.$$

Here, $k = \{(x, y), \ldots\}$ represents the set of visual sign coordinates of S, $\mathcal{K}$ represents the solution space, and L is the maximum number of visual signs. assigned to S, ω is a stochastic scenario, and Ω is the sample space. Let f_1 and f_2 be the two objective functions of the VESAP referring to the number of agents selecting the correct exit e^+ and the total evacuation times, respectively. As we aim to minimize the total evacuation time, $-f_2$ is maximized. This study examines two example spaces with differing exit arrangements, S_1 and S_2, as shown in Figs. 2 and 3. Both S_1 and S_2 are $x \in [-65, 65], y \in [-21, 21]$ units with different layouts of e^+ (blue exit) and e^- red exit), respectively. The intersections of the dashed lines indicate candidate positions. Furthermore, we denote $\mathcal{P}_C$ as a VESAP with a continuous solution space and $\mathcal{P}_D$ as discrete.

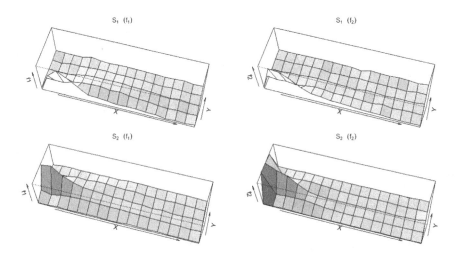

Fig. 4. Landscapes of S_1 (upper) and S_2 (lower). The figures on the left show f_1 on the right show f_2 [36].

Futhermore, we have investigated VESAP with a single visual evacuation sign case $L = 1$ [34] and multiple visual evacuation signs case $L \geq 2$ for a continuous decision space [36]. We also investigated the VESAP with multiple visual evacuation sign for a discrete decision space. The evacuation decision model [30], which represents the herd behavior of evacuees, was incorporated into each agent. However, the social force model [12] was not employed, owing to the computational cost. We also assumed that the visual field of an agent was fan-shaped with a radius of 10 units and angle of $20°$ [33, 35].

6   Baseline

This section introduces and examines a VESAP with a discrete decision space. We assumed the candidate positions of the visual signs to be $x = \{-64, -56, -48, -40, -32, -24, -16, -8, 0, 8, 16, 24, 32, 40, 48, 56, 64\}$ and $y = \{-18, -9, 0, 9, 18\}$, 85 candidate positions are introduced on S as shown in Figs. 2 and 3. We now examine VESAP with one and two visual signs by brute-force approaches for this space. The results are considered baselines.

6.1   One Evacuation Sign

First, we investigated this space using a single evacuation sign case [34]. We conducted 250 simulations, with visual signs assigned to each the candidate positions for both S_1 and S_2. The results of the analysis are presented in Fig. 4 as fitness landscapes of both f_1 (left figs) and f_2 (right figs). The results indicate that the optimal solutions are in front of the incorrect exits e^- for f_1 and f_2 for both S_1 and S_2. The landscapes of these objective functions are almost smooth and the values of f_1 and f_2 are mostly correlated in both cases.

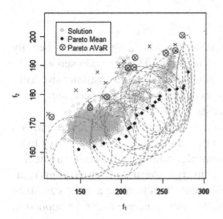 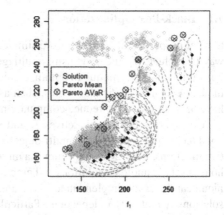

Fig. 5. Baseline with $L = 2$ for S_1 generated through brute-force approach.

Fig. 6. Baseline with $L = 2$ for S_2 generated through brute-force approach.

6.2 Two Evacuation Signs

Second, we investigated this space using two visual evacuation signs. Here, the decision space has a combination of two 85 candidate positions (3570 combinations). We conducted 24 simulation runs for each combination. Expected values and $AVaR_{0.3}$ are estimated for both f_1 and f_2.

Figures 5 and 6 show the simulation results for S_1 and S_2. As we aim to maximize f_1 and minimize f_2, the lower-right corner of the figure shows the most preferable solution and the upper-left solution, the least preferable solutions for these spaces. The small gray circles show the means of f_1 and f_2 for all the solutions (3570 combinations of candidate positions) and solid black circles indicate the Pareto-optimum of these solutions. The ellipses with red dashed lines show the 50% probability ellipses of the Pareto-optimum solutions. The blue ×s depict the $AVaR_{0.3}$s of f_1 and f_2 associated with Pareto-optimal solutions, blue ⊗s indicate that these points are Pareto-optimal for $AVaR_{0.3}$. The number of Pareto optimas explored were 20 and 24 for S_1 and S_2, respectively. The number of Pareto optimas for $AVaR_{0.3}$, which are also Pareto optimas for the expected values were 9 and 14 for S_1 and S_2, respectively.

7 Method

In Sect. 6.2, 85,680 simulation runs were performed to obtain the Pareto-optima because 24 simulations were conducted for all possible combinations of the two signs assigned to candidate positions. However, this brute-force approach is unrealistic and inapplicable in general cases because of its high computational cost. A total of 2,370,480 simulations were required with three visual signs. An efficient method to obtain Pareto-optima is required to solve the VESAP.

7.1 Black-Box Optimization

Several properties of VESAP make simple formulas for evaluating solutions, the only way to evaluate f_1 and f_2 is using multiagent simulations. Thus, we adopted a black-box optimization technique to optimize noisy objectives, which is a cost-intensive technique. Several heuristic algorithms, such as simulated annealing or genetic algorithms have been employed to reduce computational costs.

Considering the two objectives f_1 and f_2 in our problem, the EMO algorithm, is a good technique applicable to multi-objective optimization problems using noisy objective functions. The EMO algorithm is a multi-point algorithm search meta-heuristic that holds a set of candidate solutions and gradually converges to Pareto-frontiers. This technique can be easily implemented in the a parallel algorithm because a set of candidate solutions is mutually independent. Particularly, parallel simulations can be applied to evaluate these solutions.

Theoretically, VESAP has four objective functions: expected values, and AVaRs of f_1 and f_2, respectively. However, multi-objective problems with many objectives result in numerous Pareto-optimas that is difficult to handle. The analysis in Sect. 6.1 reveals that the landscapes of both f_1 and f_2 are smooth and highly correlated for both S_1 and S_2. These spaces do not require a sophisticated EMO algorithm. However, they will be handled by most EMO algorithms. Previously, we analyzed the correlations between the expected values and AVaRs, and found that these two are highly correlated for both f_1 and f_2 (Observation 8 in [34]). This observation suggests that VESAP can be reduced to a bi-objective optimization problem, which is easier to handle than a four-objective problem with the expected values of f_1 and f_2. Because the expected values and AVaRs were highly correlated, AVaRs of f_1 and f_2 can be treated after the expected values of the Pareto-optima of f_1 and f_2 are obtained.

NSGA-II [1] is a commonly applied evolutionary algorithm that solves multi-objective optimization problems. The fast nondominated sorting algorithm in NSGA-II can efficiently generate a series of ranked nondominated frontiers with $O(MN^2)$ computational complexity. Here, N is the population size, and M is the number of objectives. Crowding distances are also used in NSGA-II to keep individuals in a diverse population to represent the entire Pareto-frontier properly. NSGA-II is a good algorithm for problems with fewer objective functions.

7.2 Discretization

In many real-world evacuation guidance problems, the number of available positions for visual evacuation signs is often constrained. Evacuation protocol designers must choose positions from the available candidate positions instead of determining them freely on the premises. Here, the decision space of VESAP is discrete. However, NSGA-II was initially designed for multi-objective problems with continuous decision variables. The algorithm must be modified to deal with discrete decision space. The proper coding rule for VESAP and crossover operation for a coding representation must be designed.

Consider a VESAP with n visual signs: The solution to this problem can be represented as an ordered list of $2n$ elements $c = (x_1, x_2, \ldots, x_n, y_1, y_2, \ldots, y_n)$, where x_i represents x-coordinate of the i th sign ($x_i \in x$), y_i, y-coordinate ($y_i \in y$), a simple one-point crossover operation may be applicable to this representation to generate offspring.

Kondo et al. (2016) studied the impact of discretizing decision variables on real-coded genetic algorithms (e.g., NSGA-II), and revealed that the representation of the chromosome affects the search efficiency; and the convergence and diversity of the set of Pareto optima often conflict [15]. Combination of the above representation and a simple one-point crossover operation leads to solutions with many redundant chromosomes. The diversity of the solutions was rapidly lost. Therefore, we adopted a customized crossover operation for this representation to mitigate diversity loss, as shown in Algorithm 1. With two chromosomes c^0 and c^1, Algorithm 1 generates new offspring c^*. An example of the problem for Algorithm 1 is given in Table 1.

Algorithm 1. Customized Crossover.

Input: c^0, c^1
Output: c^*
1: Generate masks $M^+ = (m_1, m_2, \ldots, m_{2n})$ where $m_i = 0$ if $c_i^0 = c_i^1$, $m_i = 1$ othewise and $M^- = 1 - M^+$
2: Generate masks $R^+ = (r_1, r_2, \ldots, r_{2n})$ where r_i is randomly set to 0 or 1 and $R^- = 1 - R^+$.
3: $\widehat{c^0} = c^0 M^+ R^+$, $\widehat{c^1} = c^1 M^+ R^-$, $\widehat{c^*} = \widehat{c^0} + \widehat{c^1}$
4: $c^* = c^0 M^- + \widehat{c^*}$

Table 1. Example of customized crossover.

	x_1	x_2	x_3	x_4	x_5	y_1	y_2	y_3	y_4	y_5
c^0	−64	−48	−48	−56	−56	−18	−9	−9	0	0
c^1	−64	−56	−48	−64	−48	−18	−18	−9	0	0
M^+	0	1	0	1	1	0	1	0	0	0
M^-	1	0	1	0	0	1	0	1	1	1
R^+	0	1	1	0	0	1	1	0	1	0
R^-	1	0	0	1	1	0	0	1	0	1
$\widehat{c^0}$	0	−48	0	0	0	0	−9	0	0	0
$\widehat{c^1}$	0	0	0	−64	−48	0	0	0	0	0
$\widehat{c^*}$	0	−48	0	−64	−48	0	−9	0	0	0
c^*	−64	−48	−48	−64	−48	−18	−9	−9	0	0

7.3 Expected Value Pareto-Optimum and AVaR Pareto-Optimum

Previously, we introduced two new concepts to evaluate the solutions of the VESAP, namely, the expected value Pareto-optimum (EVPO) and AVaR Pareto-optimum (AVOP) [34].

Definition 6 (EVOP: $\mathcal{E}$). *$\mathcal{E}$ denotes a set of expected Pareto-optimum solutions. for the current population as follows:*

$$\mathcal{E} = \{k \in \mathcal{K} | \neg(\exists z \in \mathcal{K}, \ \mathbb{E}(f_1(z)) \geq \mathbb{E}(f_1(k)) \wedge \mathbb{E}(-f_2(z)) \geq \mathbb{E}(-f_2(k)),$$
$$\mathbb{E}(f_1(z)) > \mathbb{E}(f_1(k)) \vee \mathbb{E}(-f_2(z)) > \mathbb{E}(-f_2(k)))\}$$

Definition 7 (AVPO: $\mathcal{A}$). $\mathcal{A}$ *is a set of AVaR Pareto-optimum solutions for current population as:*

$$\mathcal{A} = \{k \in \mathcal{K} | \neg (\exists z \in \mathcal{K},\ AVaR_\alpha(f_1(z)) \geq AVaR_\alpha(f_1(k)) \wedge AVaR_\alpha(-f_2(z)) \geq AVaR_\alpha(-f_2(k)),$$
$$AVaR_\alpha(f_1(z)) > AVaR_\alpha(f_1(k)) \vee AVaR_\alpha(-f_2(z)) > AVaR_\alpha(-f_2(k)))\}$$

EVPO is a set of good solutions for expected values and AVOP is a set of good solutions with respect to risks. Then, we consider the expected value and AVaR Pareto-optimum solutions: which can be considered as a set of good solutions with fewer risks, as follows:

Definition 8 (Expected Value and AVaR Pareto-Optimum Solutions: Q).

$$Q = \mathcal{E} \cap \mathcal{A}$$

In the following analysis, we explore the expected value and AVaR Pareto-optimum solutions Q for several instances of the VESAP.

7.4   Analysis Scheme

This study formulated VESAP as a bi-objective optimization problem with the expected values of f_1 and f_2 as objective functions. We then employ the NSGA-II algorithm to obtain a set of Pareto-optimal solutions $\mathcal{E}$. Because the outcome of a solution is evaluated through simulation, numerous simulations required to estimate the expected values of the solution. Determining the number of simulations to estimate the expected value is debatable because the solutions are not reliable if the number is small. However, if the number is large, the result is accurate but computationally expensive. Let ε be a small value. We conduct ε simulations to estimate the expected values for each solution using the NSGA-II search procedure. Thus, to obtain $\mathcal{E}$, we require εNG simulations in a single NSGA-II run with N population size and G generations.

However, the number ε may be excessively small to explore a good set of Pareto-optima that precisely represents the true Pareto-frontiers. Therefore, a two-phase approach was adopted. First, we explored a set of Pareto-optima $\mathcal{E}$ using NSGA-II with ε simulations, respectively. Second, 100 simulations were reconducted for the Pareto-optima obtained in the first phase to calculate the expected values for $\acute{\mathcal{E}}$ and AVaRs for $\acute{\mathcal{A}}$. Some Pareto-optima obtained in the first phase may degenerate in the second phase. The procedure is summarized as follows:

1. Phase1: Generate $\mathcal{E}$ using NSGA-II with ε simulations.
2. Phase2: Conduct 100 simulations for each of $\mathcal{E}$ and obtain $\acute{\mathcal{E}}$ and $\acute{\mathcal{A}}$.
3. Obtain $Q = \acute{\mathcal{E}} \cap \acute{\mathcal{A}}$

We conducted simulations with $\varepsilon = 16$ for discrete problems and $\varepsilon = 24$ for continuous problems.

In this study, *NetLogo 6.0.2* [37] is used to implement the crowd evacuation simulator using an evacuation decision model. The entire procedure is implemented in *R x64 3.5.1* as follows: libraries: *nsga2R* for the NSGA-II algorithm and *parallel* for the parallel execution of the simulations and *RNetLogo* for the connection for *R* and *NetLogo*. Simulations and optimizations were executed on a machine with *Intel Core i7-6700* CPU.

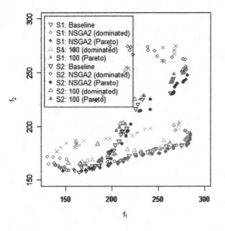

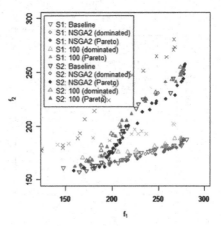

Fig. 7. $\mathcal{P}_{\mathcal{D}}$ with 2 signs.   **Fig. 8.** $\mathcal{P}_C$ with 2 signs.

8 Performance Analysis

8.1 Baseline and NSGA-II

This analysis aimed to examine whether our analysis scheme discussed in Sect. 7.4 can explore a reasonably good Pareto-frontiers by comparing it with the true Pareto-frontiers explored through brute-force approaches in the two-sign discrete case, presented in Sect. 6.2. The coordinates of the ith visual sign were chosen as $x_i \in x$ and $y_i \in y$ for $\mathcal{P}_{\mathcal{D}}$; and $x_i \in [-65, 65]$ and $y_i \in [-21, 21]$ for $\mathcal{P}_C$. NSGA-II algorithms with 56 populations and 40 generations were applied to explore the Pareto optima for the $\mathcal{P}_{\mathcal{D}}$ and 48 populations and 50 generations were applied to the $\mathcal{P}_C$. Sixteen simulations were conducted to obtain expected values during the search in $\mathcal{P}_{\mathcal{D}}$, and 24 simulations, $\mathcal{P}_C$.

Figure 7 shows the results for the $\mathcal{P}_{\mathcal{D}}$ and Fig. 8 shows the results for the $\mathcal{P}_C$. The red and blue triangles depict the Pareto optima explored using the brute-force approaches in Sect. 6.2 for S_1 and S_2, respectively. The red and blue circles represent solutions explored through NSGA-II for S_1 and S_2; the red and blue filled circles represent $\mathcal{E}$ for S_1 and S_2. The green and violet triangles depict the results of 100 simulations of $\mathcal{E}$ reconducted for the validation purposes for S_1 and S_2; respectively, and the green and violet-filled triangles depict $\acute{\mathcal{E}}$ of the solutions. Thus, NSGA-II first explored 29 and 29 Pareto optima for S_1 and S_2 respectively, for $\mathcal{P}_{\mathcal{D}}$; and 28 and 36 Pareto optima for S_1 and S_2, for $\mathcal{P}_C$. However, in the validation simulations with 100 repetitions, the size of the sets of Pareto optima decrease to 14 and 18 for S_1 and S_2 in $\mathcal{P}_{\mathcal{D}}$, and 11 and 26 in $\mathcal{P}_C$. Thus, in our approach, NSGA-II first explored Pareto-optima, which appears to cover the true Pareto-frontiers explored through the brute-force approach reasonably well. However, the number of solutions is decreased in the validation simulations. Finally, green and violet × depict the AVaRs at a level of 0.3, corresponding to 100 simulation results. Number of Pareto-optima satisfying both EVPO and AVPO (Q) were 7 and 9 for $\mathcal{P}_{\mathcal{D}}$ and 8 and 18 for $\mathcal{P}_C$.

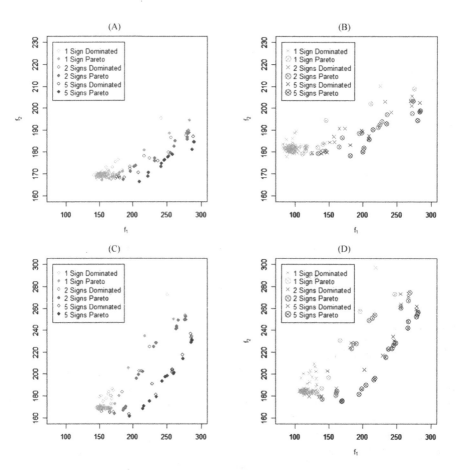

Fig. 9. 1, 2, and 5 sign cases for $\mathcal{P}_{\mathcal{D}}$. (A) $\acute{E}$ for S_1 and (B) $\acute{A}$ for S_1. (C) $\acute{E}$ for S_2, and (D) $\acute{A}$ for S_2.

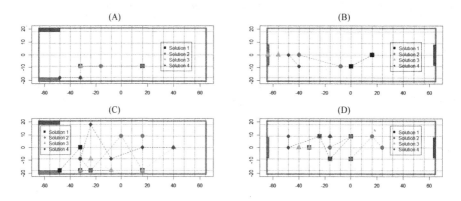

Fig. 10. Four representative solutions for $\mathcal{P}_{\mathcal{D}}$. (A) Two signs for S_1 (B) Two signs for S_2, (C) five signs for S_1, and (D) five signs for S_2

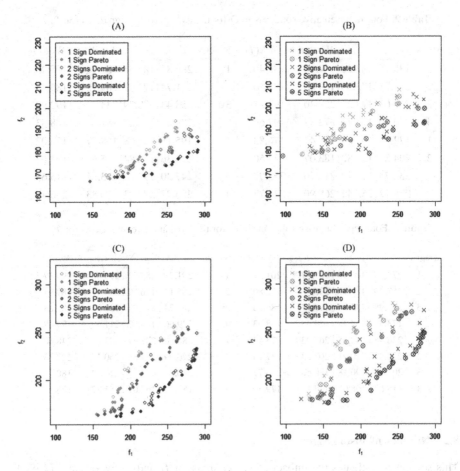

Fig. 11. 1, 2, and 5 sign cases for $\mathcal{P}_C$. (A) $\acute{E}$ for S_1 and (B) $\acute{A}$ for S_1. (C) $\acute{E}$ for S_2 and (D) $\acute{A}$ for S_2 [36]

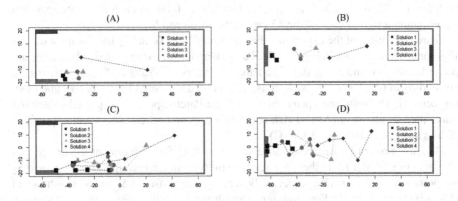

Fig. 12. Four representative solutions for $\mathcal{P}_C$. (A) Two signs for S_1 (B) Two signs for S_2; (C) five signs for S_1; and (D) five signs for S_2 [36].

Table 2. Four representative solutions in Q for the two- and five-sign cases for $\mathcal{P}_\mathcal{D}$.

2 signs		$\bar{f}_1$	$\bar{f}_2$	$AVaR(f_1)$	$AVaR(f_2)$	5 signs	$\bar{f}_1$	$\bar{f}_2$	$AVaR(f_1)$	$AVaR(f_2)$
S_1	1	185.35	167.20	144.36	180.40	1	289.83	184.51	283.30	198.23
	2	201.71	173.26	169.80	186.40	2	241.74	173.17	209.10	185.87
	3	252.63	178.24	222.40	191.27	3	258.43	178.79	234.73	192.93
	4	280.10	185.71	272.37	197.60	4	209.88	166.27	181.20	178.33
S_2	1	172.31	163.64	140.43	176.83	1	195.15	161.08	168.77	175.07
	2	204.83	195.82	183.07	223.50	2	234.36	178.84	215.60	194.67
	3	233.75	228.18	217.70	253.90	3	247.30	197.20	233.37	215.63
	4	278.12	252.42	268.90	274.77	4	286.77	230.93	280.83	256.40

Table 3. Four representative solutions in Q for the two- and five-sign cases for $\mathcal{P}_C$.

2 signs		$\bar{f}_1$	$\bar{f}_2$	$AVaR(f_1)$	$AVaR(f_2)$	5 signs	$\bar{f}_1$	$\bar{f}_2$	$AVaR(f_1)$	$AVaR(f_2)$
S_1	1	274.67	186.63	267.07	201.33	1	291.73	184.73	285.53	199.77
	2	257.40	180.92	236.40	192.80	2	265.12	176.99	243.37	189.97
	3	217.98	173.04	197.37	186.50	3	256.74	174.23	236.87	185.83
	4	173.97	167.38	124.63	178.93	4	229.66	169.82	211.50	179.40
S_2	1	276.43	249.65	267.93	273.40	1	288.80	230.47	283.87	248.60
	2	220.80	210.91	202.23	237.73	2	270.09	204.85	260.40	222.33
	3	203.74	190.28	180.63	213.77	3	230.21	173.12	214.00	188.53
	4	175.62	166.07	147.10	179.50	4	187.04	162.09	155.87	175.37

8.2   Number of Visual Signs

This section investigates the impact of visual signs on f_1 and f_2 by varying $|L|$ by 1, 2, and 5 for S_1 and S_2 and for $\mathcal{P}_\mathcal{D}$ and $\mathcal{P}_C$. Population size, generations, and simulation repetitions of NSGA-II for each case are summarized in Table 4. In this table, the results with $L = 1$ in $\mathcal{P}_\mathcal{D}$ for S_1 and S_2 are given not by NSGA-II but by the brute-force approach by assigning a sign to each of the 85 candidate positions [34].

Pareto frontiers of the expected values and AVaRs of S_1 and S_2 for $\mathcal{P}_\mathcal{D}$ are shown in Fig. 9 and $\mathcal{P}_C$, as shown in Fig. 11. The Pareto frontiers of the expected values of S_1 are presented as (A): and S_2, in (C). The Pareto frontiers of AVaRs of S_1 are presented in (B) and S_2 in (d). The cases with signs 1, 2, and 5 are colored in green, red, and blue, respectively. The solid and open circles represent Pareto optima of expected values and dominated solutions in (A) and (C), respectively. $\otimes$ and $\times$ represent Pareto optima of AVaRs and dominate the (B) and (C).

We also present four representative solutions of Q for each case of $\mathcal{P}_\mathcal{D}$ and $\mathcal{P}_C$, as shown in Fig. 10 and 12. In these figures, the solutions of the two sign cases of S_1 and S_2 are presented in (A) and (B), respectively, with five sign cases of S_1 and S_2 are shown in (C) and (D), respectively. Four solutions were drawn using different colors and symbols. The expected values and AVaRs of these solutions were summarized in Table 2 and 3 for $\mathcal{P}_\mathcal{D}$ and $\mathcal{P}_C$, respectively. In these tables, $\bar{f}_1$ and $\bar{f}_2$ denote the expected values of f_1

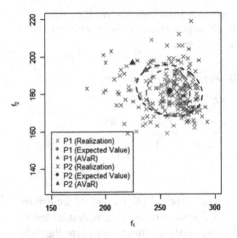

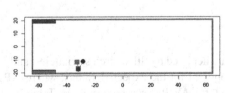

Fig. 13. Two example solutions: P1 and P2. [36].

Fig. 14. Two example solutions: P1 and P2. [36].

and f_2 and $AVaR(f_1)$ and $AVaR(f_2)$ indicate $AVaR_{0.3}$ of f_1 and f_2, respectively, for each representative solution.

Table 4 presents a summary of the analyses in this section. The parameters of NSGA-II used to explore $\mathcal{E}$ are summarized as follows: whereas the size of $\mathcal{E}$, $\acute{\mathcal{E}}$, $\acute{\mathcal{A}}$ and Q explored during the analysis were are also provided in the table.

Table 4. Summary of the analysis in Sect. 8.2 for S_1 and S_2. The column labels represent the following: L, number of signs; Pop, population size in NSGA-II; Gen, the number of generations in NSGA-II; Rep, the number of simulation repetition. $|\mathcal{E}|$, $|\acute{\mathcal{E}}|$, $|\acute{\mathcal{A}}|$, and $|Q|$ denote the sizes of $\mathcal{E}$, $\acute{\mathcal{E}}$, $\acute{\mathcal{A}}$, and Q, respectively.

		L	Pop	Gen	Rep	$|\mathcal{E}|$	$|\acute{\mathcal{E}}|$	$|\acute{\mathcal{A}}|$	$|Q|$			L	Pop	Gen	Rep	$|\mathcal{E}|$	$|\acute{\mathcal{E}}|$	$|\acute{\mathcal{A}}|$	$|Q|$
S_1	$\mathcal{P}_D$	1	–	–	–	–	11	8	5	S_2	$\mathcal{P}_D$	1	–	–	–	–	7	11	6
		2	56	40	16	29	14	13	7			2	56	40	16	29	18	13	9
		5	56	40	16	18	11	9	8			5	56	40	16	25	14	17	13
	$\mathcal{P}_C$	1	48	50	24	37	17	14	10		$\mathcal{P}_C$	1	48	50	24	34	22	16	15
		2	48	50	24	28	11	10	8			2	48	50	24	36	26	21	18
		5	100	100	24	20	13	7	6			5	100	100	24	49	24	22	18

8.3 Illustrative Example

This section presents example solutions to highlight advantage of AVaR to explore an exemplary assignment of visual signs with minimal risks. Figures 13 and 14 show two example solutions, P1 and P2, obtained using VESAP with two visual signs for S_1 in the objective and decision spaces. Table 5 summarizes the expected values and AVaRs of these solutions. In Fig. 13, the expected values, $AVaR_{0.3}$, and the realizations of f_1 and f_2

Table 5. Two example solutions: P1 and P2. The column 'Pareto' indicates *yes* if the solution is Pareto-optimal for AVaR; *no* otherwise. A cell with a blue background shows a better value. The bottom row shows the p-values of the Wilcoxon rank-sum test.

	$\bar{f}_1$	$\bar{f}_2$	$AVaR(f_1)$	$AVaR(f_2)$	Pareto
P1	257.40	180.92	236.40	192.80	*yes*
P2	258.30	181.79	224.33	196.60	*no*
p-value	0.50	0.68	0.00	0.53	

are depicted by filled circles, triangles, and '×,' respectively. Both P1 and P2 are Pareto-optimal for the expected values, whereas P1 is a Pareto-optimum, P2 is dominated by P1 for AVaRs (see blue cells in Table 5). The two dashed ellipses illustrate the 50% probability ellipses of P1 and P2 which reveals that P2 has more risk than P1, whereas the expected values of the two are almost equivalent because the red- and blue-filled circles in Tabel 13 almost overlap each other. This is because the probability ellipse of P1 is included in that of P2. The realizations of P2 were distributed more broadly than those of P1 in Fig. 13, which implies that P2 will more likely produce unexpectedly bad outcomes if adopted as a solution.

Moreover, we conducted a Wilcoxon rank sum test to examine statistically significant differences among the 100 samples for P1 and P2 used to estimate the expected values, and the worst 30% of samples to estimate $AVaR_{0.3}$s. The p-values of the tests for $\bar{f}_1$, $\bar{f}_2$, $AVaR(f_1)$, and $AVaR(f_2)$ were 0.50, 0.68, 0.00, and 0.53, respectively, (Bottom row in Table 5) indicating that the results for $AVaR(f_1)$ are statistically significant.

Figure 14 shows P1 and P2 for the decision space. The figure illustrates that these two solutions are similar and almost sharing one position $(-31, -17)$ and the other positions also being close. This example highlights the advantage of AVaR in that subtle differences in the decision space produces a solution that can reduce the risk significantly.

9   Discussion

This study formulated the VESAP as a stochastic multi-objective optimization problem with two objective functions: maximizing the number of agents selecting the correct exit (f_1) and minimizing the total evacuation time (f_2) and analyzed this problem with multiple visual evacuation signs for both discrete and continuous decisions spaces from the perspective of the expected outcomes and risks involved in the solutions. NSGA-II, a multi-objective evolutionary optimization algorithm was applied to explore Pareto-optimal solutions and the Pareto-frontiers of the two objective functions were obtained for cases with one, two, and five visual signs for the two exit layouts. (S_1 and S_2) and for discrete and continuous decision spaces ($\mathcal{P}_D$ and $\mathcal{P}_C$.) To reduce computational effort, we first explored Pareto-optima with a relatively small sampling size ε and then reconducted 100 simulations based on the Pareto-optima obtained using the first trials to obtain more accurate results. Solutions satisfying the Pareto-optimal for both expected values and AVaRs were obtained in all cases (one, two, and five signs; two layouts: S_1 and S_2; and two decision spaces: $\mathcal{P}_D$ and $\mathcal{P}_C$).

Figures 7 and 8 shows that NSGA-II can explore Pareto-frontiers that are reasonably close to those obtained by brute-force approaches. However, NSGA-II with a small sample size will lead to somewhat inaccurate results because the Pareto-frontiers obtained by NSGA-II are located in the lower-right regions than those obtained using the brute-force approach. This implies that NSGA-II outperforms the brute-force approaches, which is unrealistic. NSGA-II with small simulations seems to lead to inaccurate solutions that are unrealistically optimistic. This indicates the necessity to reconduct simulations with a large sample size.

Simulations with different numbers of visual signs (Figs. 9 and 11) revealed that having many visual signs constantly leads to better solutions. This is especially true if both objective values are distant from extreme points (i.e., minimum or maximum). Figures 9 and 11 show the difference between the two Pareto-frontiers with a small and a large number of visual signs are significant in the middle of the Pareto-front. Figure 9 (A) and (B) should be considered exceptions, because the Pareto optima of the two and five signs become close at the middle of the Pareto frontier. This may be because the number of feasible arrangements of the visual signs is more limited in the discrete case than in the continuous case. For instance, in a previous study, it was found that assigning a single sign in a specific position can lead almost all agents to e^+; an optimal solution for maximizing f_1. Thus, if a solution with two signs has significant performance, adding three more signs in limited positions may not affect the positive outcomes. However, in general, if more visual signs are introduced, better solutions are obtained, whereas a problem with many signs require massive computational resources. The trade-off between computational cost and solution quality warrants further investigation.

This study conducted additional experiments using the VESAP for discrete decision space, respectively. This is crucial because the baseline experiments were conducted using brute-force approaches on discrete decision space with two visual signs. We then compared the results between the baseline and those obtained using the approach presented in Sect. 7.4. The results of the continuous cases can be analyzed indirectly using compared with the results of this case. In the baseline analysis, the brute-force approach was first used to explore 20 and 24 Pareto optimas for the expected values of S_1 and S_2, respectively; thereafter, it was used to explore 9 and 14 Pareto optimas for both expected values and AVaRs (Sect. 6.2). These Pareto optimas can be considered as true Pareto frontiers. In our approach, NSGA-II first explored 29 Pareto optima for the S_1 and S_2; however, this number was reduced to 14 and 18, respectively, in the validation simulations. Therefore, our approach explores fewer Pareto optima than the brute-force approach. Our approach then explored Pareto optima for expected values and AVaRs were seven and nine for S_1 and S_2, respectively (Table 4), which indicates that our approach explores fewer Pareto optima than the true Pareto optima. Table 6 summarizes all the Pareto optima explored with both the brute-force approach and the proposed approach. This table shows the coordinates of the first and second visual signs and the outcomes of the corresponding visual sign assignments. The blue cells in the table highlight the common solutions explored using both approaches. Only two and three solutions are common for S_1 and S_2, respectively. This suggests that our approach can explore a few true Pareto optima. Most solutions found by our approach were approximately solutions of the true Pareto optima.

Our research had some limitations and open problems. Some may consider our results inaccurate because of insufficient computational resources. Had we conducted more simulation runs, employed more populations, and more generations in NSGA-II, or incorporate a more sophisticated physical model (e.g., the social force model) in the simulations, we could have obtained more accurate results. Some sophisticated approaches can be used to generate Pareto-optimal solutions efficiently at lower costs, as discussed in Sect. 4, can be applied for this purpose. We also assumed that the two objective functions were independent and employed a logical conjunction of the two AVaRs $(AVaR(f_1) \wedge AVaR(f_2))$ to test Pareto efficiency. This may be inappropriate if the two objectives are negatively correlated. Here, one objective produces a better outcome, whereas the other will have worse value; both objectives producing worse outcomes simultaneously rarely occur. The logical conjunction of two AVaRs that may overestimate risk is difficult to achieve; a different approach is required to address this issue. We will address these problems in future work.

10   Conclusion

This study formulated a visual evacuation signage assignment scheme problem as a stochastic bi-objective optimization problem and explored Pareto optima with fewer risks. We explored Pareto optima using NSGA-II with a few simulations and reconducted more simulations to obtain more accurate results. Solutions satisfying Pareto efficiency for both the expected values and AVaRs were obtained using our approach. This set of solutions is an approximate solution with a few true Pareto optimal solutions.

Acknowledgments. The author is grateful to Mr. Kei Marukawa for his helpful discussions. Comments on the manuscript. The author also would like to thank Editage (www.editage.com) for English language editing.

A   Appendix

Table 6. Summary of Q explored by the brute-force approach and our approach. The blue cells indicate solutions common to the both approaches.

		x_1	y_1	x_2	y_2	$\mathbb{E}(f_1)$	$\mathbb{E}(f_2)$	$AVaR(f_1)$	$AVaR(f_2)$
		-48	-18	-32	-18	280.79	187.54	273.83	200.25
		-48	-18	-16	-18	275.75	182.79	265.92	195.17
		-40	-18	-40	-9	267.42	181.83	254.28	194.22
		-32	-18	-24	-9	241.38	177.17	215.81	189.36
	S_1	-32	-18	-24	0	245.67	178.04	208.25	189.11
		-32	-18	-16	-9	247.21	179.29	216.81	192.69
		-16	-9	0	-9	209.63	168.21	182.47	178.97
		-8	-18	8	0	206.13	165.45	162.08	175.28
		-8	18	32	9	166.96	161.88	115.00	172.11
Brute-force approach (Baseline)		-64	0	-56	0	276.00	250.63	266.14	268.06
		-56	0	-48	0	265.96	244.46	255.86	265.00
		-56	0	-32	-9	263.25	230.88	251.39	256.75
		-48	0	-32	-9	233.00	224.92	214.47	246.50
		-48	0	-24	9	228.25	220.46	215.14	246.69
		-48	0	-8	9	225.54	216.17	207.36	234.14
	S_2	-40	0	-32	-9	215.83	197.96	200.36	219.69
		-40	0	-24	9	209.71	192.67	185.47	213.17
		-40	0	-16	-9	211.46	195.88	194.92	214.39
		-32	0	-24	9	203.67	182.42	176.50	205.31
		-24	0	-8	-9	195.88	169.25	175.83	185.64
		-16	0	0	9	181.04	160.92	156.83	172.08
		0	9	8	-9	172.41	158.21	136.97	168.72
		56	0	64	9	164.58	157.21	131.94	176.67
		-48	-18	-32	-18	280.10	185.71	272.37	197.60
		-40	-18	-16	-18	260.65	182.62	235.20	197.10
		-32	-9	-32	-18	252.63	178.24	222.40	191.27
	S_1	-32	-9	-24	-18	232.10	177.08	198.10	188.63
		8	-9	-32	-9	196.86	171.04	165.13	182.40
		16	-9	-32	-9	185.35	167.20	144.37	180.40
		16	-9	-16	-9	201.71	173.26	169.80	186.40
Our approach		-64	0	-56	0	278.12	252.42	268.90	274.77
		-56	0	-48	0	264.94	242.87	256.43	260.20
		-40	-9	-48	0	233.75	228.18	217.70	253.90
		-40	0	-40	-9	214.45	202.03	190.10	227.90
	S_2	-40	0	-8	-9	204.83	195.82	183.07	223.50
		-24	-9	-48	0	230.48	224.78	213.87	250.83
		-24	0	-8	-9	186.36	168.40	161.70	184.50
		-8	-9	-24	0	185.82	166.84	160.20	180.47
		0	-9	16	0	172.31	163.64	140.43	176.83

References

1. Deb, K., Pratap, A., Agarwal, S., Meyarivan, T.: A fast and elitist multiobjective genetic algorithm: NSGA-II. IEEE Trans. Evol. Comput. **6**(2), 182–197 (2002). https://doi.org/10.1109/4235.996017

2. Deb, K., Jain, H.: An evolutionary many-objective optimization algorithm using reference-point-based nondominated sorting approach, Part I: Solving problems with box constraints. IEEE Trans. Evol. Comput. **18**(4), 577–601 (2014). https://doi.org/10.1109/TEVC.2013.2281535

3. Dubey, R.K., Khoo, W.P., Morad, M.G., Hölscher, C., Kapadia, M.: AUTOSIGN: a multi-criteria optimization approach to computer aided design of signage layouts in complex buildings. Comput. Graph. **88**, 13–23 (2020). https://doi.org/10.1016/j.cag.2020.02.007

4. Fieldsend, J.E., Everson, R.M.: Multi-objective optimisation in the presence of uncertainty. In: 2005 IEEE Congress on Evolutionary Computation, vol. 1, pp. 243–250. IEEE (2005). https://doi.org/10.1109/CEC.2005.1554691

5. Goh, C.K., Tan, K.C.: An investigation on noisy environments in evolutionary multiobjective optimization. IEEE Trans. Evol. Comput. **11**(3), 354–381 (2007). https://doi.org/10.1109/TEVC.2006.882428

6. Gutjahr, W.J., Pichler, A.: Stochastic multi-objective optimization: a survey on non-scalarizing methods. Ann. Oper. Res. **236**(2), 475–499 (2013). https://doi.org/10.1007/s10479-013-1369-5

7. Haghani, M.: Empirical methods in pedestrian, crowd and evacuation dynamics: Part I. Experimental methods and emerging topics. Saf. Sci. **129**, 104743 (2020). https://doi.org/10.1016/j.ssci.2020.104743

8. Haghani, M.: Empirical methods in pedestrian, crowd and evacuation dynamics: Part II. Field methods and controversial topics. Saf. Sci. **129**, 104760 (2020). https://doi.org/10.1016/j.ssci.2020.104760

9. Haghani, M., Sarvi, M.: Human exit choice in crowd built environments: investigating underlying behavioural differences between normal egress and emergency evacuations. Fire Saf. J. **85**, 1–9 (2016)

10. Haghani, M., Sarvi, M., Shahhoseini, Z., Bolts, M.: How simple hypothetical-choice experiments can be utilized to learn humans' navigational escape decisions in emergencies. PLoS ONE **11**(11), e0166908 (2016). https://doi.org/10.1371/journal.pone.0166908

11. Hansen, N., Ostermeier, A.: Adapting arbitrary normal mutation distributions in evolution strategies: the covariance matrix adaptation. In: Proceedings of IEEE International Conference on Evolutionary Computation, pp. 312–317 (1996). https://doi.org/10.1109/ICEC.1996.542381

12. Helbing, D., Farkas, I., Vicsek, T.: Simulating dynamical features of escape panic. Nature **407**(28), 487–490 (2000)

13. Hughes, E.: Evolutionary many-objective optimisation: many once or one many? In: 2005 IEEE Congress on Evolutionary Computation, vol. 1, pp. 222–227 (2005). https://doi.org/10.1109/CEC.2005.1554688

14. Ji, Q., Xin, C., Tang, S., Huang, J.: Symmetry associated with symmetry break: revisiting ants and humans escaping from multiple-exit rooms. Phys. A Stat. Mech. Appl. **492**, 941–947 (2017)

15. Kondoh, T., Tatsukawa, T., Oyama, A., Watanabe, T., Fujii, K.: Effects of discrete design-variable precision on real-coded genetic algorithm. In: 2016 IEEE Symposium Series on Computational Intelligence (SSCI), pp. 1–8 (2016). https://doi.org/10.1109/SSCI.2016.7850230

16. León, J., Puerto, J., Vitoriano, B.: A risk-aversion approach for the multiobjective stochastic programming problem. Mathematics **8**(11), 2026 (2020). https://doi.org/10.3390/math8112026
17. Levy, H.: Stochastic Dominance. Springer, Cham (2016). https://doi.org/10.1007/978-3-319-21708-6
18. Li, Q., Fang, Z., Li, Q., Zong, X.: Multiobjective evacuation route assignment model based on genetic algorithm. In: 2010 18th International Conference on Geoinformatics, pp. 1–5 (2010). https://doi.org/10.1109/GEOINFORMATICS.2010.5567485
19. Lovreglio, R., Fonzone, A., dell'Olio, L., Ibeas, A.: The role of herding behaviour in exit choice during evacuation. Procedia. Soc. Behav. Sci. **160**, 390–399 (2014)
20. Markowitz, H.: Portfolio selection*. J. Financ. **7**(1), 77–91 (1952). https://doi.org/10.1111/j.1540-6261.1952.tb01525.x
21. Ogryczak, W., Ruszczynski, A.: Dual stochastic dominance and related mean-risk models. SIAM J. Optim. **13**(1), 60–78 (2002). https://doi.org/10.1137/S1052623400375075
22. Ozaki, Y., Tanigaki, Y., Watanabe, S., Onishi, M.: Multiobjective tree-structured parzen estimator for computationally expensive optimization problems. In: Proceedings of the 2020 Genetic and Evolutionary Computation Conference, pp. 533–541. GECCO 2020, Association for Computing Machinery, New York (2020). https://doi.org/10.1145/3377930.3389817
23. Rachec, S.T., Stoyanov, S.V., Fabozzi, F.J.: Advanced stochastic models, risk assessment, and portfolio optimization: the ideal risk, uncertainty, and performance measures. Wiley (2008)
24. Saadatseresht, M., Mansourian, A., Taleai, M.: Evacuation planning using multiobjective evolutionary optimization approach. Eur. J. Oper. Res. **198**, 305–314 (2009). https://doi.org/10.1016/j.ejor.2008.07.032
25. Sano, Y., Kita, H.: Optimization of noisy fitness functions by means of genetic algorithms using history of search with test of estimation. In: Proceedings of the 2002 Congress on Evolutionary Computation. CEC 2002 (Cat. No. 02TH8600), vol. 1, pp. 360–365 (2002). https://doi.org/10.1109/CEC.2002.1006261
26. von Schantz, A., Ehtamo, H., Hostikka, S.: Minimization of mean-CVaR evacuation time of a crowd using rescue guides: a scenario-based approach. Collective Dyn. **6** (2021). https://doi.org/10.17815/CD.2021.112
27. Sieben, A., Schumann, J., Seyfried, A.: Collective phenomena in crowds—where pedestrian dynamics need social psychology. PLoS ONE **12**(6), e0177328 (2017). https://doi.org/10.1371/journal.pone.0177328
28. Siegmund, F., Ng, A.H.C., Deb, K.: Hybrid dynamic resampling for guided evolutionary multi-objective optimization. In: Gaspar-Cunha, A., Henggeler Antunes, C., Coello, C.C. (eds.) EMO 2015. LNCS, vol. 9018, pp. 366–380. Springer, Cham (2015). https://doi.org/10.1007/978-3-319-15934-8_25
29. Tan, K., Lee, T., Khor, E.: Evolutionary algorithms with dynamic population size and local exploration for multiobjective optimization. IEEE Trans. Evol. Comput. **5**(6), 565–588 (2001). https://doi.org/10.1109/4235.974840
30. Tsurushima, A.: Modeling herd behavior caused by evacuation decision making using response threshold. In: Davidsson, P., Verhagen, H. (eds.) MABS 2018. LNCS (LNAI), vol. 11463, pp. 138–152. Springer, Cham (2019). https://doi.org/10.1007/978-3-030-22270-3_11
31. Tsurushima, A.: Validation of evacuation decision model: an attempt to reproduce human evacuation behaviors during the great east Japan earthquake. In: Proceedings of the 12th International Conference on Agents and Artificial Intelligence (ICAART 2020), vol. 1, pp. 17–27 (2020). https://doi.org/10.5220/0008874300170027
32. Tsurushima, A.: Herd behavior is sufficient to reproduce human evacuation decisions during the great east Japan earthquake. In: Rocha, A.P., Steels, L., van den Herik, J. (eds.) ICAART

2020. LNCS (LNAI), vol. 12613, pp. 3–25. Springer, Cham (2021). https://doi.org/10.1007/978-3-030-71158-0_1

33. Tsurushima, A.: Reproducing evacuation behaviors of evacuees during the great east Japan earthquake using the evacuation decision model with realistic settings. In: Proceedings of the 13th International Conference on Agents and Artificial Intelligence (ICAART 2021), vol. 1, pp. 17–27. INSTICC, SciTePress (2021). https://doi.org/10.5220/0010167700170027

34. Tsurushima, A.: Scochastic multi-objective decision analysis for crowd evacuation guidance using a single visual signage. In: 2021 IEEE International Conference on Systems, Man, and Cybernetics (SMC), pp. 360–367 (2021). https://doi.org/10.1109/SMC52423.2021.9658866

35. Tsurushima, A.: Simulation analysis of tunnel vision effect in crowd evacuation. In: Rutkowski, L., Scherer, R., Korytkowski, M., Pedrycz, W., Tadeusiewicz, R., Zurada, J.M. (eds.) ICAISC 2021. LNCS (LNAI), vol. 12854, pp. 506–518. Springer, Cham (2021). https://doi.org/10.1007/978-3-030-87986-0_45

36. Tsurushima, A.: Multi-objective risk analysis for crowd evacuation guidance using multiple visual signs. In: Proceedings of the 14th International Conference on Agents and Artificial Intelligence (ICAART 2022), vol. 1, pp. 71–82. INSTICC, SciTePress (2022). https://doi.org/10.5220/0010886400003116

37. Wilensky, U.: NetLogo. Center for Connected Learning and Computer-Based Modeling, Northwestern University, Evanston, IL (1999)

38. Zhang, Q., Li, H.: MOEA/D: a multiobjective evolutionary algorithm based on decomposition. IEEE Trans. Evol. Comput. **11**(6), 712–731 (2007). https://doi.org/10.1109/TEVC.2007.892759

Negotiation Protocol with Learned Handover of Important Tasks for Planned Suspensions in Multi-agent Patrol Problems

Sota Tsuiki[⊠], Keisuke Yoneda, and Toshiharu Sugawara[iD]

Department of Computer Science and Communications Engineering, Waseda University, Shinjuku-ku, Tokyo 169-8050, Japan
{s.tsuiki,k.yoneda}@isl.cs.waseda.ac.jp, sugawara@waseda.jp

Abstract. In this study, we propose a negotiation protocol for task handovers in the multi-agent cooperative patrol problem (MACPP) to alleviate temporary performance degradation due to planned suspension. In recent years, thanks to improvements in the performance of computers and the spread of technologies such as AI and IoT, systems with multiple agents such as autonomous robots or self-driving machines have been widely adopted to perform tasks on behalf of humans. To prevent sudden breakdowns, planned suspensions for periodic inspections and replacements are mandatory. However, if the agents stop without any prior action in the MACPP, performance rapidly worsens at least temporarily, which may be unacceptable in a number of applications. Meanwhile, in such a planned suspension, information on the agents to be suspended is given in advance, and the performance degradation can be reduced by using this information by transferring the important tasks to others in advance. The proposed novel negotiation method between agents is designed for this purpose based on the existing method for MACPP and can reduce the performance degradation caused by planned suspensions. A comparison with the conventional method shows that the proposed approach can mitigate performance degradation during planned suspension and transition periods.

Keywords: Multi-agent cooperative patrolling problem · Task handover · Negotiation protocol · Cooperation and coordination · Scheduled suspension · Periodic inspection

1 Introduction

In recent years, with progressive improvements in the performance of computer hardware and the spread of technologies such as artificial intelligence (AI) and the Internet of Things (IoT), agents such as autonomous robots with intelligent sensors and/or actuators have been networked and used to perform hazardous and complex tasks that would otherwise be handled by humans. Furthermore, in large environments or more complicated tasks, multiple agents need to complete these tasks together to achieve a common or individual goal. While there are many tasks that require cooperation and coordination among agents, one abstract model of this type of multi-agent problems is the *multi-agent*

© The Author(s), under exclusive license to Springer Nature Switzerland AG 2022
A. P. Rocha et al. (Eds.): ICAART 2022, LNAI 13786, pp. 27–47, 2022.
https://doi.org/10.1007/978-3-031-22953-4_2

cooperative patrol problem (MACPP), in which multiple agents patrol a given environment and coordinate/cooperate with one another to achieve the system's objectives. Examples of this problem include security patrols [4], cleaning up large or dangerous spaces [3,28], egg collection [12,27], and environmental monitoring [19,33].

In an environment where multiple autonomous agents act simultaneously, although agents must determine their own actions individually to accomplish their assigned goals based only on the information obtained from their local observations, agents are likely to interfere or conflict with one another, leading to errors such as collisions and resource conflicts, which lower the overall efficiency of the system. To resolve this issue, cooperative behavior among agents is required, for example, to prevent overlapping of work with other agents. Unfortunately, designing and implementing cooperative behaviors among agents in advance is difficult owing to the many factors to be considered, such as temporal and spatial constraints and the performance of individual agents. Therefore, a learning method must be developed in which each agent autonomously chooses its own actions by considering its own performance and that of other agents, as well as the characteristics of the environment and the positions and actions of other agents.

Two main approaches to the study of cooperation and coordination among agents in MACPP have mainly been considered in the relevant literature. One approach involves partitioning the entire environment to assign each partitioned subarea to an agent either statically in advance or dynamically through learning and negotiation. Then, the agents patrol within an assigned subarea for which they are responsible [1,2,6,9,11,29,32]. Elor and Bruckstein [6], for example, proposed a partitioning algorithm to balance the size of subareas assigned to agents using a model inspired by the pressure in a balloon. However, because the complexity of the shape of the environment and the presence of obstacles require divisions based only on the size imbalanced workload, Kato and Sugawara [11] extended their method to a fair division by considering these factors. Xie et al. [29] proposed a maritime area patrol system using multiple cooperative unmanned surface vehicles by hierarchically partitioning the area with a centralized partition algorithm and by generating paths using *particle swarm optimization* (PSO).

The second approach is that the individual agents determine their own patrol strategies by using information available from their local viewpoint with additional data provided by the environment or the system without prior partitioning of the entire environment into subareas [5,10,16,17,20,23,24,31]. Sampaio, Ramalho, and Tedesco [20] proposed a patrol strategy called the *gravitational strategy*, in which the locations that have been unvisited by agents for a long time are assigned higher values of gravity and are likely to be able to attract agents, although they need a central monitor of the environment to calculate gravity. Sugiyama et al. [23] proposed *an adaptive meta-target decision strategy with learning of event probabilities to enhance divisional cooperation* (AMTDS/EDC), in which agents independently determine an appropriate patrol strategy from a predefined set of patrol algorithms through reinforcement learning. They also introduced a lightweight negotiation protocol to enhance the division of labor and balance the workloads of the agents.

Meanwhile, assuming that agents are robots or machines that operate by themselves, they require periodic inspections or replacements to prevent sudden failures or unexpected stoppages. Hence, agents must be halted at a certain cycle for this purpose.

Compared to the relatively short periodic stops required for battery recharging, etc., this has a larger impact on the degradation of the overall performance of the system. In the case of security patrols, in particular, a sudden performance degradation may cause serious albeit perhaps only temporary problems. However, conventional methods cannot be applied to this issue directly. For example, in the first approach, if a few agents leave the system for a relatively long period of time for inspection, the partitions need to be recomputed from scratch to ensure that certain regions are not omitted from the patrol. Even in the second approach, the learned division of labor does not operate correctly if some agents are suspended, which also results in a sudden performance degradation, as shown in experiments performed by Sugiyama et al. [23]. However, information on such inspections is often known in advance, such as the scheduled time of the stops, their duration, and the agents to be stopped. In this study, such a periodic stop the information of which is given in advance is called a *planned suspension*. We consider that temporary but rapid performance degradation can be mitigated using the advanced information on planned suspensions by appropriately and gradually reassigning the parts of patrolling tasks through negotiation between agents.

To address this issue, we propose a negotiation method with which agents that are going to stop for inspection can hand over their important tasks to other agents to prevent sudden degradation due to planned suspension by extending AMTDS/EDC [23]. In our method, agents individually identify which tasks in their environment are important and autonomously take responsibility for the identified tasks. By assuming that communications are available only when two agents are close each other, agents that are scheduled to stop at the next planned suspension hand over some of their important tasks until the suspension to other agents that are not expected to stop because neglecting these important tasks may result in considerable performance degradation. Of course, the agents to which the tasks are delegated may not be able to perform all these tasks successfully if they are already overloaded or have more important tasks. In this case, the agents to which the tasks are delegated would hand over portions of their tasks to other agents to balance their workload and maintain efficiency.

We conducted experiments for the two MAPP applications, including cleaning/sweeping and security surveillance, in which several agents cooperatively patrol in environments that consists of a number of rooms that were required to be visited with different frequencies. We then evaluated our proposed method by comparing the experimental results with those by using the conventional method AMTDS/EDC. Although we already proposed the method called *AMTDS with task handover for scheduled suspension* (AMTDS/TH) [25] for the issue addressed here, the method involved a shortcoming that the performance was considerably reduced during the *transition period*, which is the period from when the agents start handing over the important tasks for which they were responsible to the schedule suspension time. To compensate for this shortcoming, Tsuiki et al. [26] added an ability to estimate the number of negotiation chances to improve the effectiveness of task handover. In contrast, in the present work, we conducted additional experiments and extensively analyzed the features of agents' patrolling behaviors generated by our proposed method to understand the total effectiveness.

2 Related Work

As mentioned in the previous section, much of the research aiming to enable agents to produce cooperative and coordinating activities for MACPP has considered one of these two approaches. In another study on the first approach, Ahmadi and Stone proposed a method of dividing the work area by negotiation into subareas of responsibility for individual agents to balance their workload in an environment where, as in our case, the frequency of events and task occurrences may be disparate and uneven, and thus agents should visit those places with different frequencies [2]. Meanwhile, in the second approach, Elmaliach et al. [5] proposed a centralized method in which the patrol paths were constructed for all agents and assigned to them.

Several recent studies have used learning techniques [16,17,32] and bio-inspired optimization algorithms [29] to enable multiple agents to patrol an environment in a cooperative manner [16,17,29,32]. For example, Othmani-Guibourg et al. [17] introduced a model of a varying environment based on a classical patrol model and on an edge-Markovian evolving graph, and compared two different strategies of agents, including a *conscientious reactive strategy* and a *heuristic pathfinder cognitive coordinated strategy* in this environment. Subsequently, Othmani-Guibourg et al. [16] proposed training a decentralized multi-agent patrolling strategy by using a *long short-term memory* (LSTM) neural network embedded in each agent and trained based on artificial data generated in a simulated environment. They showed that the network could navigate the agents in an environment to be patrolled by providing the next movement. Zhou et al. [32] modeled MACPP as a Bayes-adaptive transition-decoupled partially observable Markov decision process and introduced a decentralized online learning algorithm using the Monte Carlo tree search method. However, these studies did not consider the significant degradation caused by suspensions of some agents.

In contrast, a number of studies discussed planned suspension and stoppages using multi-agent models. Panteleev et al. [18] and Ghita et al. [8] proposed methods to construct operational plans for the periodic maintenance and inspection and for repair of technical equipment in agent-based simulation environments. However, these studies differed from the present work in that they aimed to create work plans that took scheduled furloughs into account to reduce the workload of human employees. For example, in another research field, Gavranis and Kozanidis [7] developed an automated method for the flight maintenance (FM) problem. Seif and Andrew [21] extended their method to find solutions for the operation and maintenance planning problem, which is a generalized version of the FM problem. Moradi and Shadrokh [14] developed a robust trust-based scheduling system by using a heuristic algorithm for efficient resource allocation to ensure the reliability of the system for planned maintenance activities with unknown activity durations. However, these methods require centralized control and, to the best of our knowledge, no works in the relevant literature have considered methods for agents to independently prepare for planned suspensions in a cooperative manner.

3   Problem Description

In this section, we describe the model of MACPP and the issue addressed in the present work. However, because these descriptions are almost identical to those in the previous studies [23,25], please refer to them for details.

3.1   Problem Environment

The environment in which agents patrol is a graph $G = (V, E)$ which can be embedded in a two-dimensional Euclidean space where $V = \{v_1, \ldots, v_n\}$ and E are the sets of nodes and edges, respectively. Node v_i in V corresponds to a location in the environment and edge $e_{i,j} \in E$ corresponds a direct link connecting nodes v_i and v_j in V. An agent, an *event*, and an obstacle exist at node $v \in V$. Only a single agent can be at a given node and no agent can be in the nodes where an obstacle exists; otherwise, we consider a collision to occur. Similarly, two agents cannot cross on a link at the same time. Note that the meaning of an event in our model differs across applications. For example, in a patrol system for security surveillance, the number of events at a location might correspond to the alert level at the location, and an accumulation of events would indicate a rising alert level. In a cleaning application, an event might represent that some amount of dirt has accumulated in a location and a task to vacuum up the dirt has been assigned. Similarly in an application for egg collection, an event could indicate that a chicken has spawned in a certain area in a free-range farm, and the task might be to collect the eggs [12].

Let us introduce a discrete time with the unit of *timestep*. We assume that the length of all the edges is one without the loss of generality by adding dummy nodes as needed, and agents can move to one of neighboring nodes along an edge in a timestep. For any two nodes $v, v' \in V$, we define that *path*, $\mathbf{p}_{v,v'}$ from v to v' is the sequence of edges $e_{1,2}, e_{2,3}, \ldots, e_{l-1,l}$ and the *path length* as the number of edges $l-1$ in the path, where $v = v_1$, $v' = v_l$ and $e_{i,j} \in E$. We denote the distance $d(v, v')$ between v, v' which is defined as the shortest path length between them (i.e., the minimum number of edges between two nodes). We also define *metric* $m(v, v')$ as the Euclidean distance between them when G is embedded in two-dimensional space.

We define the *event occurrence probability* $p(v)$ at $\forall v \in V$ ($0 \leq p(v) \leq 1$) to describe the occurrence of an event; at each timestep t, the cumulative number of events $L_t(v)$ for v is updated as follows.

$$L_t(v) = \begin{cases} L_{t-1}(v) + 1 & \text{(with probability } p(v)\text{, i.e., if an event occurs)} \\ L_{t-1}(v) & \text{(with probability } 1 - p(v)\text{, i.e., if no event occurs)} \end{cases} \tag{1}$$

However, when any agent reaches v, all events accumulated on v are dealt with by the execution of the corresponding task, and then $L_t(v)$ is set to 0. This definition indicates that the node with a high probability is important and agents must visit there more frequently to avoid leaving many events unprocessed. Thus, we also refer to $p(v)$ as the *node importance value* of v.

3.2 Estimation of Node Importance Value and Behaviors of Agents

We denote the set of n agents as $A = \{1, \ldots, n\}$. We assume that agent $\forall i \in A$ has a finite battery capacity and must return to its charging base periodically before its battery is drained. We introduce two assumptions; first, agents can identify their location in the environment using the global positioning system (GPS) or an indoor mapping system. Second, agents can see the history of other agents' locations; this can be accomplished, for example, by communicating with a central server on a regular basis or only when returning to the charging base, or by communicating between agents when agents are close to each other. Agent i estimates $p(v)$ for $\forall v \in V$. The estimated value, which is denoted by $p^i(v)$, is obtained from the number of events processed by agent i. More specifically, $p^i(v)$ is initialized as 0, and when i process the task in v at t, it is updated, regardless of the value of $L_t(v)$, which is the number of events accumulated in v, as

$$p^i(v) = (1 - \alpha) \cdot p^i(v) + \alpha \cdot \frac{1}{t - t_{vis}(v)}, \tag{2}$$

where α ($0 < \alpha \leq 1$) is the learning rate and $t_{vis}(v)$ is the time when node v is most recently visited by a certain agent. We also refer to the estimated probability $p^i(v)$ as the *estimated node importance value* of v in i. Agent i updates the estimated node importance value when it has reached v or it returns to the charging base using the history data. Because agents individually estimate $p^i(v)$, they are likely to exhibit different values for the same node v, so each agent is likely to learn that different locations are important. This estimation of the environment was introduced in AMTDS/EDC [23]; readers are referred to that work for further information.

Agent i cannot directly access the number of the accumulated events $L_t(v)$ before reaching v, and i can calculate the estimated number of events $E[L_t^i(v)]$ for node $\forall v$ at t using the estimated probability $p^i(v)$ by

$$E[L_t^i(v)] = (t - t_{vis}(v)) \cdot p^i(v). \tag{3}$$

Agents patrol the environment and attempt to maintain $E[L_t^i(v)]$ at small values.

3.3 Patrol Strategy

Agent i moves along the path generated by the following planning activity. First, i selects the destination node v_{dst}^i through a *target decision strategy* (TDS). Second, it constructs a path to v_{dst}^i using the *path-planning algorithm*. When i arrives at v_{dst}^i, it selects the next destination node by TDS and thereafter repeats the cycle of the planning and execution. In AMTDS/EDC, agents select the next destination on the basis of the values of $E[L_t^i(v)]$ to maintain them at a low levels. TDSs include, for example, random selection, *probabilistic greedy selection* (PGS) (in which, nodes with higher $E[L_t^i(v)]$ are likely to be selected), *prioritized unvisited intervals* (in which nodes that have been left unvisited for a long time are preferentially selected) and *balanced neighbor-preferential selection* (in which if there exists a node v with high values of $E[L_t^i(v)]$ in a given neighborhood, it is selected first. Otherwise, i adopts PGS). Then, i generates a path to the selected target. A detailed description of path-planning algorithms is not provided here, because it is beyond the scope of this study. However, because there are many algorithms to generate collision-free paths for the *multi-agent path finding* (MAPF) problem [13, 15, 22, 30], any of them can be used. Furthermore, i must return to the charging base before its battery runs out. Please refer to Sugiyama et al. [23] for the methods of the selection of the destination nodes, the path-planning, and the decision of returning to charge they adopted.

3.4 Exchange of Node Importance Values

The basic concept of our proposed method is that agents exchange their node importance values, $p^i(v)$ for $\forall v \in V$, with other agents through a negotiation to delegate nodes, i.e., tasks that process the events on the nodes. For improved load balancing, compensation by coordinated behavior between the agents, and to enhance robustness against changes in the environment including the number of agents, they exchange and delegate (or are delegated) a certain ratio of the (estimated) node importance values through negotiation when they come sufficiently close to one another. We assume that for $\forall i, j \in A$, when $m(v^i, v^j) < d_{co}$ i and j are in *communications range* and so are able to start the negotiation, where v^i and v^j are the current locations of i and j, and parameter $d_{co} (> 0)$ is the size of the communications range. Moreover, to eliminate redundant negotiation, we introduce the *minimum communication interval B*, which is a positive real number, that is, agents i and j store the last time they negotiated with one another $t^{i,j}_{lst}$, and do not negotiate before $t^{i,j}_{lst} + B$.

Agent i maintains its own *responsible node set* $V^i_R \subset V$, which is the set of N^i_R (> 0) nodes in order of the node importance values. Initially, we set $V^i_R = V$ and $N^i_R = |V|$. Then, when i returns to its charging base, V^i_R and N^i_R are updated. The agents adopt two kinds of negotiation, including negotiation for balancing task workloads and negotiation for exchanging responsibility to update $p^i(v)$, V^i_R, and N^i_R. For more details on the two types of negotiations and how $p^i(v)$, V^i_R, and N^i_R are updated, please refer to [23].

4 Proposed Method

We propose the *AMTDS with task handover for scheduled suspension based on the estimated negotiable chances* (AMTDS/THE), as an extension of AMTDS/EDC [23] designed to mitigate performance degradation during periods of planned suspension and transition periods for task handovers before the planned suspension. Because agents can begin the negotiation only when they encounter/come close one another, i.e., when they are in communications range, they record the number of times that they have negotiated from their own (re)start time. Note that the (re)start time is defined as when the system was launched or when the agent returned from the previous scheduled suspension. The agents that are already scheduled for their next planned suspension estimate the number of possible negotiation chances until the suspension by using the number of past communication chances. They then determine the number of nodes that should be delegated to other agents during the transition period, i.e., the period until the planned suspension. This estimation can reduce the efficiency loss not only during the planned suspension but also during the transition period before the planned suspension [26].

4.1   Estimated Number of Negotiable Chances

Agent i counts the number of negotiations $N_{Neg}^i(t)$ from the most recent start time or the return time from inspection to the current time t, and uses it to estimate the number of possible negotiable chances until the next planned suspension time. Note that i does not negotiate with another agent $j \in A$ for B timesteps since the last negotiation with j to prevent unnecessary communication.

The planned suspension S for replacement or periodic inspection is described as a tuple $S = (A_S, T_{sp}, T_{rs}, D_{tp})$, where $A_S(\subset A)$ is the set of agents that participate a suspension that extends from the start time T_{sp} to the return time T_{rs}. Parameter D_{tp} is the transition period length. Therefore, at the latest, the scheduled suspension must be announced to all agents by $T_{sp} - D_{tp}$. When S is announced at t, agent i estimates the number of chances for negotiation $\mu^i(t)$ between $T_{sp} - D_{tp}$ and T_{sp} as follows.

$$\mu^i(t) = N_{Neg}^i(t) \times \frac{T_{sp} - t}{t - T_{start}} \times \frac{|A_S|}{|A| - 1}, \tag{4}$$

where T_{start} is the time when i started to count $N_{Neg}^i(t)$ after its initialization. Thus, $T_{sp} - t$ is the remaining time until the planned suspension. Note that $\mu^i(t)$ is an estimated value and therefore usually differs from those of other agents; this difference is reasonable because they usually work in their areas which they determine are important.

4.2   Negotiation for Handover of Important Nodes

When agents $i, j \in A_S$ or $i, j \in A \setminus A_S$ have a chance to communicate, they begin negotiation with one another during a transition period by using the conventional negotiation [23] to improve workload balance and to enhance coordinated behavior between agents. Otherwise, i.e., when $i \in A_S$ and $j \in A \setminus A_S$, they perform the proposed negotiation for unidirectional and indirect task delegation from i to j. This is realized when i transfers to j a certain ratio of the node importance values of nodes that should not be neglected and thus j should increase the number of the responsible nodes.

Agent $i \in A_S$ first selects the top κ_g^i nodes from V_R^i in descending order of their node importance values from V_R^i, where κ_g^i is a positive integer set by individual agents as described below. Then, agent i delegates these nodes to other agents, by transferring ratio δ_c of the node importance values, $p^i(v)$, of the selected nodes to j through the proposed negotiation. Therefore, the node importance values of v for i and j are updated as follows.

$$p^j(v) \leftarrow p^j(v) + p^i(v) \times \delta_c \tag{5}$$
$$p^i(v) \leftarrow p^i(v) \times (1 - \delta_c), \tag{6}$$

where δ_c $(0 < \delta_c < 1)$ is the *ratio of node importance value passed*. This means that i does not completely ignore the delegated nodes, but rather induces j to expand its work scope. Thus, j cannot visit these nodes sufficiently. However, in this case, i also visits the nodes that it has delegated and reverts some of them to V_R^i if necessary.

The number of nodes κ_g^i that agent i transfers to another agent is determined using the estimated number of chances for negotiation $\mu^i(t)$ by the following formula.

$$\kappa_g^i = \left\lfloor \frac{N_R^i}{\max(1, \mu^i(t))} \right\rfloor, \tag{7}$$

where the max in the denominator in Eq. (7) prevents division by zero. $N_R^i > 0$, which is the maximal number of nodes that are to be delegated, is updated in both i and j as

$$N_R^i \leftarrow N_R^i - \kappa_g^i \tag{8}$$

$$N_R^j \leftarrow \min(|V|, N_R^j + \kappa_g^i). \tag{9}$$

Note that after the node importance values are updated, the sets of responsible nodes, V_R^i and V_R^j, are also recalculated when they have returned to the charging bases.

4.3 Metrics for Evaluation

We use two types of evaluation metrics depending on the applications envisioned. The first evaluation metric is the *maximum number of unprocessed events* for all the nodes. For example, no single location should be left unmonitored in timed security patrols. Therefore, all agents must maintain the maximum number of unprocessed events (i.e., time left unvisited) across all nodes in the environment and should visit nodes whose security level is high (so $p(v)$ is high) more frequently to ensure that a preset alert level is not exceeded. This type of evaluation metric U_{t_s,t_e} between time t_s and t_e can be defined as

$$U_{t_s,t_e} = \max_{v \in V, t_s \leq t \leq t_e} L_t(v), \tag{10}$$

where $t_s < t_e$. A smaller value of U_{t_s,t_e} indicates a more efficient and effective patrol.

The second metric is the *cumulative timesteps in which the events are left unprocessed* for event collection. For example, in cleaning and/or egg collection applications, the number of unprocessed events (pieces of dust not collected by the vacuum cleaner or uncollected eggs) remaining in the environment in which dust or eggs are accumulated. Therefore, the group of agents should minimize the cumulative time periods that they remain relatively idle. This evaluation metric D_{t_s,t_e} between time t_s and t_e ($t_s < t_e$) can be denoted by

$$D_{t_s,t_e} = \sum_{v \in V} \sum_{t=t_s+1}^{t_e} L_t(v). \tag{11}$$

A smaller value of D_{t_s,t_e} also indicates a more effective patrol. We denote U_{t_s,t_e} and D_{t_s,t_e} as $U(s)$ and $D(s)$, respectively, for simplicity, by omitting t_s and t_e if these intervals are obvious. We aim to maintain $U(s)$ and $D(s)$ lower even if several agents stop for their scheduled suspension.

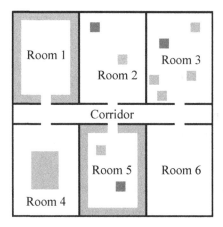

Fig. 1. Experimental environment.

Table 1. Experimental parameters.

Description	Parameter	Value
Number of agents	$|A|$	20
Communication range	d_{co}	5
Minimum communication interval	B	10800
Ratio of importance values passed	δ_c	0.5
Data collection interval	$t_e - t_s$	3600
Learning rate for importance value	α	0.1

5   Experiments and Discussion

5.1   Experimental Setup

We compared the proposed AMTDS/THE method with the conventional AMTDS/EDC [23] and AMTDS/TH [25] methods through an experiment (Fig. 1) to show that AMTDS/THE can ease performance degradation with the proposed task handover from the agents being suspended during the transition period and during the suspension of a number of agents for inspection. For this purpose, we analyzed $U(s)$ for the timed security patrol application and $D(s)$ for the cleaning application. We then introduced different lengths of the transition period leading up to the suspension to show that the proposed method is effective in various situations of the MACPP. We also confirmed whether agents really covered the entire environment after some agents stopped by investigating the number of important nodes of all agents. At the same time, we also indicate that the numbers of important nodes were quite different depending on the agents' behavioral strategies and considerably varied when some agents entered or returned from suspension.

The experimental environment, which is shown in Fig. 1, was identical to that in [23,25], to easily clarify the effect of the proposed method. The environment $G =$

(V, E) in this figure was a two-dimensional 101×101 grid space consisting of six separate rooms that were connected with a corridor. The node $v \in V$ is located on the coordinates (x_v, y_v), where $-50 \leq x_v, y_v \leq 50$. The black lines indicate the walls. For $\forall v \in V$ in Fig. 1, their event occurrence probabilities $p(v)$ were set in advance using the colors of the nodes as follows.

$$p(v) = \begin{cases} 10^{-3} \text{ (if } v \text{ is in a red region)} \\ 10^{-4} \text{ (if } v \text{ is in an orange region)} \\ 10^{-6} \text{ (otherwise, i.e., in a while region)} \end{cases} \quad (12)$$

Therefore, events occurred more frequently at nodes with darker colors.

We set $|A| = 20$ and the charging base v_{base}^i for $\forall i \in A$ was placed at $(0, 0)$, the center of the environment, as an exceptional node at which multiple agents could stay, although we can place the charging bases at different nodes for individual agents (for this reason, we assume that agents did not communicate with each other when charging). Agent i left v_{base}^i with its battery full, patrolled the environment on the basis of its own patrolling strategy (see Sect. 3.3) and returned to v_{base}^i before its battery ran out. The agents repeated this action cycle to ensure that no events were left unprocessed to the extent possible. We set the battery capacity of each agent to 900, and the capacity is decreased by one each timestep; thus, it is exhausted in 900 timesteps. We assumed that 3 timesteps are required to regain 1 point of capacity by charging. Therefore, 2700 timesteps were necessary to complete the process. The values for the battery were set with reference to an actual cleaning robot.[1] For this reason, the data collection interval $t_e - t_s$ in our experiments to calculate $U(s)$ and $D(s)$ was set 3600 timesteps. The experimental results presented below are the means of twenty independent trials.

We set the length of one experimental trial was set to 3,500,000 timesteps and during part of this period, a number of agents stopped. We define A_1 by randomly selecting half of the agents from A and $A_2 = A \setminus A_1$ in each trial. Let us recall that a planned suspension is described as $S = (A_S, T_{sp}, T_{rs}, D_{tp})$. In our experiments, two planned suspensions, S_1 and S_2, are introduced in each trial and all agents stop alternately to undergo the inspections. In the first experiment (Exp. 1), the planned suspensions were set as

$$S_1 = (A_1, 1,000,000, 1,500,000, 500,000),$$
$$S_2 = (A_2, 2,500,000, 3,000,000, 500,000),$$

to examine the effect of the proposed method. In the second experiment (Exp. 2), we examined how the transition period length affects the performance degradation because the transition period should be as short as possible. Therefore, we set the suspensions as

$$S_1 = (A_1, 1,000,000, 1,500,000, D_{tp}),$$
$$S_2 = (A_2, 2,500,000, 3,000,000, D_{tp}),$$

and we set different values to D_{tp}.

---

[1] We assumed that a single timestep was approximately 4 s, the moving speed was approximately 0.25 m/s, while the maximum continuous operational time is 1 h. The charging time from the empty state was 3 h.

Note that half of agents were suspended in each planned suspension in our experiments, but this seems very unlikely in actual operation; we conducted experiments in extreme settings to validate the effectiveness of the proposed method.

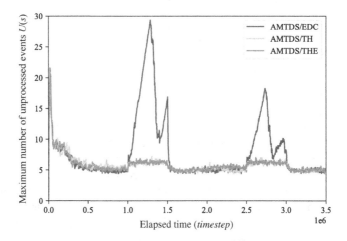

Fig. 2. Temporal changes of $U(s)$ [26].

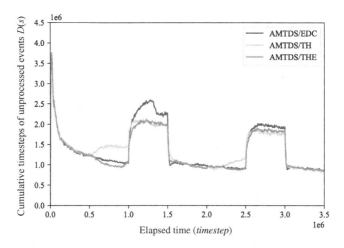

Fig. 3. Temporal changes of $D(s)$ [26].

5.2 Evaluation of Performance

We plotted the evaluation metric $U(s)$ for the security patrol and $D(s)$ for the cleaning-type application with the proposed AMTDS/THE method and the conventional methods, AMTDS/EDC and AMTDS/TH, in Figs. 2 and 3.

From these figures, the following two considerations can be observed. First, the results of the conventional AMTDS/EDC method, in which task delegation is not performed before the planned suspension, showed a large performance degradation during the planned suspension, especially a sharp and significant degradation of $U(s)$. However, the AMTDS/TH and proposed AMTDS/THE methods were able to reduce such sharp degradation. Our comparison of AMTDS/THE and AMTDS/EDC shows that $U(s)$ of AMTDS/THE were approximately 76.5% less in the first planned suspension and approximately 61.4% less in the second suspension than those of AMTDS/EDC. Similarly, for cleaning type problems, $D(s)$ was improved approximately 14.3% for the first suspension and approximately 5.68% for the second suspension. Meanwhile, we did not observe a significant difference in performance degradation during the planned suspensions between AMTDS/THE and AMTDS/TH, as shown in Figs. 3 and 2. This most likely occurred because agents scheduled to stop for inspection were able to delegate some important nodes to other agents that will not stop in the coming planned suspension, and thus, the remaining agents continued to cover the entire area, which prevented a large performance degradation. We discuss this topic in more detail in Sect. 5.4.

Second, a non-negligible performance degradation may be observed in $D(s)$ during the transition periods in AMTDS/TH, as shown in Fig. 2, and as a result, the performance gains during the suspension periods were offset by the performance losses during the transition periods. In contrast, AMTDS/THE exhibited better performance in $U(s)$ during the transition period. In contrast, AMTDS/THE not only performed better than AMTDS/TH in $U(s)$ during the transition periods, but also performed better than AMTDS/EDC, which did not delegate tasks in these periods. Our analysis indicated that AMTDS/THE reduced $D(s)$ by approximately 26.0% and approximately 9.00% for the first and second transition periods, respectively, compared to AMTDS/TH. Note that there were no significant differences in $U(s)$ during the transition periods between AMTDS/THE and AMTDS/TH.

The delegation of tasks by agents during transition periods may be expected to bias the workload and then degrade performance. However, AMTDS/THE prevented this adverse effect by gradually and evenly handing over important critical nodes that need to be covered at all times by accurately estimating the number of negotiation chances from the past experience until the start of the suspension periods. In contrast, the number of negotiation chances was not estimated in AMTDS/TH and a larger number of nodes were likely to be delegated because of the priority placed on task handover. As a result, the agents that were delegated so many nodes simultaneously could not process them well. This caused the considerable efficiency loss during the transition periods.

5.3 Analysis of Performance Characteristics

Although we found that AMTDS/THE mitigated the sudden drop in efficiency due to the planned suspension, we aimed to verify whether the resulting efficiency sufficed. As only 10 agents were operating during the planned suspension period, we compared its efficiency with the case in which the same MACPP instance was operated with 10 agents from the beginning without the planned suspension. We also examined the efficiency when all 20 agents were operated with no planned suspension. These results are plotted in Figs. 4 and 5, where the labels "Base10" and "Base20" corresponding to the cases of 10 agents and 20 agents were used from the beginning, respectively.

These figures reveal interesting results. First, $D(s)$ and $U(s)$ of AMTDS/TH(E) during the planned suspensions, especially the first suspension, were less than those

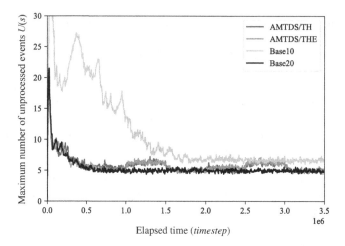

Fig. 4. Performance comparison ($U(s)$) [26].

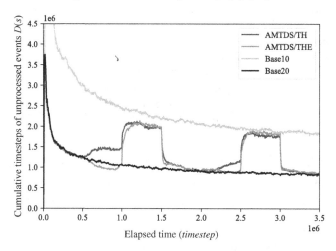

Fig. 5. Performance comparison ($D(s)$) [26].

when 10 agents worked from the beginning without suspension (labeled as "Base10" in these figures), although the number of working agents was the same. This suggests that the proposed method not only mitigated sharp performance degradation during the planned suspensions, but also prevented performance loss to a sufficient extent. Furthermore, by looking at the data during the first scheduled suspension, agents seem to have needed more time to learn their behaviors when the number of agents was less, which probably occurred because when the number of agents was 10, agents could have fewer chances to interact with each other for learning. Therefore, when 20 agents worked together, they quickly acquired coordinated behaviors and the behavior learned from more chances would have been effective even if the number of agents decreased during the suspension periods. This indicates that the proposed negotiation method can be used for other purposes. That is, a large number of agents can be trained in an early stage, and then the number of agents can be gradually reduced while appropriately delegating important tasks by the proposed method, thereby allowing the agents to learn fast and efficiently.

Furthermore, the value of $D(s)$ during the transition period before the first planned suspension between 0.5×10^6 and 1.0×10^6 (Fig. 5) shows that AMTDS/THE method was able to achieve better efficiency than the case in which 20 agents worked constantly from the beginning (i.e., "Base20"). This probably occurred because agents worked jointly at the important nodes through information-sharing by using the proposed negotiation in AMTDS/THE, albeit unilaterally.

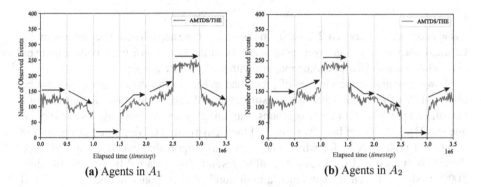

(a) Agents in A_1 (b) Agents in A_2

Fig. 6. Number of events processed by agents.

5.4 Mutual Compensation Structure to Cover the Environment

To confirm whether the nodes were actually delegated and fully covered through our proposed negotiation, we counted the numbers of events that were processed by agents in A_1 and A_2 over time and plotted them in Fig. 6), where this data was based on a randomly selected trial in Exp. 1 and arrows indicate the trends in each period whose length was 0.5 M timesteps. Of note, A_1 is the set of agents that stopped during the first suspension (Fig. 6a), and A_2 is the set of agents stopped during the second one (Fig. 6b). Figure 6 shows that during the transition period, agents that were assigned to be suspended in the next suspension period processed a considerable number of events, although their workload gradually decreased.

Let us consider the details of Fig. 6a. In the first period between 0 and 0.5×10^6 timesteps, agents in A_1 constantly processed the events found and then they hand over important nodes and thus reduce the time spent processing the events gradually, while checking whether the delegated tasks were really being processed during the transition period between 0.5×10^6 and 1.0×10^6 timesteps. After returning from the suspension 1.5×10^6 to 2.0×10^6 timesteps, they quickly covered more events to balance their workload. Then, in the second transition period, they gradually increased the number of processed events through negotiations, and maintained high performance during the second

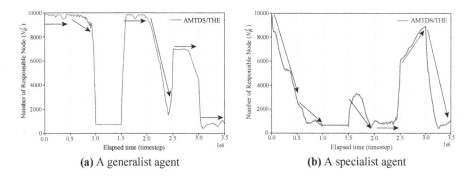

(a) A generalist agent   **(b)** A specialist agent

Fig. 7. Number of events processed by a certain agent.

suspension period between 2.5×10^6 to 3.0×10^6 timesteps. Then, after agents in A_2 returned, they also handed over tasks to maintain the fairness of workloads. Figure 6a also exhibited a similar phenomenon, but with the opposite timing.

If we investigate the number of processed events in individual agents, it may be observed that they established a sophisticated coordination structure. To see this, we classified agents in A_1 into two groups, including *generalist* and *specialist* types of agents [23], in terms of how they covered their environment. We plotted in Fig. 7a the number of nodes, $|N_R^i|$, for which one agent was responsible, where arrows indicate the trends in each period. As N_R^i was all nodes initially, it started from approximately 10000 nodes and then it maintained a high number of responsible nodes (between 0 and 0.5 M timesteps). When it entered the first transition period (between 0.5 M and 1.0 M timesteps), it tried some important nodes, but because their node importance values were relatively low and similar, the number of nodes that could actually be delegated was not high. However, it seemed that they covered relatively less important nodes, it did not cause the significant degradation during its suspension (between 1.0 M and 1.5 M timesteps). An agent that covered a relatively large number of nodes (a large area), with a correspondingly large $|N_R^i|$, is referred to as a *generalist* agent. After returning from the suspension, agents of this type still acted to cover many nodes. However, during the second transition period between 2.0 M and 2.5 M timesteps, they turned to reduce N_R^i. Although they covered a relatively large number of nodes during the second suspension period between 2.5 M and 3.0 M, between 3.0 M and 3.5 M, it reduced the number of N_R^i, meaning that it covered few but very important nodes. Here, an agent that covered a relatively small number of nodes (such that $|N_R^i|$ was small), is called a *specialist* agent.

Figure 7b indicates the different type of agent, i.e., the agent shown acted as a specialist in the first period. During the first transition period, its important nodes were delegated to other agents because a specialist agent covered only those node whose importance values were quite high. After returning from the suspension period, this agent tried to increase N_R^i, but soon it returned to operating as a specialist type. During the second suspension period, it tried to cover a large area but subsequently it returned to a specialist again.

This suggests that agents significantly change their behavioral patterns, acting as a specialist or a generalist, at the time of environmental change. Note that, the agent in Fig. 7a acted as a generalized agent first and then behaved as a specialist agent, but there were other agents that always acted as a generalist or that acted as a specialist first then acted as a generalist finally.

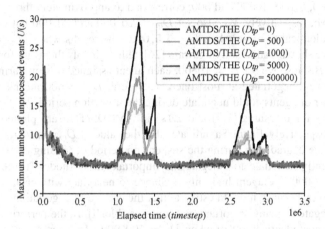

(a) Maximum number of unprocessed events $U(s)$.

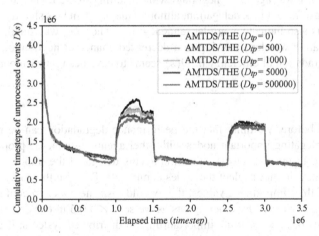

(b) Cumulative timesteps in which the events are left unprocessed $D(s)$.

Fig. 8. Effect of transition length on performance degradation.

5.5 Performance Degradation Due to Reduced Transition Periods

A planned suspension of agents is sometimes decided at the last minute. For this reason, a shorter transition period would be preferable. However, this implies a risk that the negotiated delegation of important tasks may not be enough, leading to a sudden drop in efficiency. Therefore, the purpose of Exp. 2 was to investigate the effect of the length of the transition period before the suspension, especially when it was shorter, on the overall efficiency. The results are plotted in Fig. 8 by setting $D_{tp} = 500,000$ (this is identical to the transition period in Exp. 1), 5,000, 1,000, 500, and 0. Note that when $D_{tp} = 0$, the result was identical to that of AMTDS/EDC. As mentioned earlier, 3600 timesteps is approximately four hours in our environment. Therefore, the transition periods of $D_{tp} = 500,000, 5,000, 1,000$ and 500, correspond to approximately three weeks, 6 h, 1.1 h, and 0.6 h, respectively. We also set $D_{tp} = 10,000$ and 20,000 but their results were almost identical to those when $D_{tp} = 5,000$. The results when $D_{tp} = 100,000$ and 20,000 are shown Tsuiki and Sugawara [26], although only the result for $D(s)$ was shown there. Because we set $B = 10800$, each agent assigned to stop during the next suspension period negotiated at most once. Therefore, $D_{tp} = 500$ means that only a limited number of agents could negotiate during the transition period.

The results for measures $U(s)$ and $D(s)$ in AMTDS/THE are plotted in Fig. 8a and Fig. 8a, respectively. Figure 8a indicates that the value of D_{tp} considerably affected the performance degradation during the suspension period depending on whether they could sufficiently negotiate to delegate the important tasks (nodes) to other agents. When $D_{tp} = 5000$, the agent had only a chance to negotiate with each of the other agents. However, because it could estimate that the change of negotiation was limited, it tried to delegate as many important nodes as possible. Thus, the performance degradation was almost identical to that when $D_{tp} = 500,000$. However, when $D_{tp} \leq 1000$, agents had even fewer agents to negotiate with, resulting in the temporal degradation owing to the insufficient task delegation, although the problem was slightly alleviated.

Figure 8a is also indicate a similar tendency; i.e., when D_{tp} was small, the performance degradation was larger owing to a decreased chance of negotiation. However, the rate of degradation of efficiency in $D(s)$ seems to have been rather moderate.

5.6 Remarks

As mentioned before, we think that the performance degradation can be reduced by sharing and delegating important nodes with other agents through the proposed negotiation method. In our framework, after the agents delegated the important nodes to other agents, they did not neglect the nodes completely. Because they only transferred the ratio δ_c of their importance values, they would visit the nodes to confirm that the nodes were really covered by other agents as we set $\delta_c = 0.5$ in our experiments. We believe that this behavior is quite important in real distributed systems; if an agent to which some nodes are delegated is already experiencing an overload condition, it cannot cover them sufficiently. Thus, the agents that delegated these nodes must identify such a condition and delegate the nodes to another agent.

When the length of transition period was shorter, the performance degradation was not large but was apparent. Agents may have only a few chances to negotiation for delegation. As mentioned above, the agents to which tasks are delegated may already be busy. Such situations were likely to be detected by the agents that delegated the tasks. However, if the transition period was short, they could not delegate them to other agents again, and thus a small degradation occurred.

6 Conclusion

We have proposed AMTDS/THE to alleviate the temporary but sharp performance degradation that occurs during planned suspensions in MACPP. In the proposed method, the agent being suspended delegates important parts of its tasks/nodes to other agents during the transition period to prepare for the suspension and prevent performance degradation during planned suspensions. We found that the effectiveness of this method was particularly significant in the security patrol problem. Furthermore, we found that AMTDS/THE not only prevented performance degradation during the transition period, but also allowed for more efficiency gains by reallocating tasks when there was a sufficient transition period. This performance improvement is due to the introduction of a negotiation protocol to hand over important nodes and the mechanism that allows agents to estimate the number of remaining chances for negotiations with other agents until the next planned suspension. This mechanism also allows agents to determine the number of important nodes to be delegated.

In practical applications, the agents many be heterogeneous, meaning that they have their own performance and capabilities. Therefore, we plan to introduce an additional learning method with which each agent can decide the amount of tasks to be delegated by considering the performance of their counterparts.

References

1. Ahmadi, M., Stone, P.: Continuous area sweeping: a task definition and initial approach. In: ICAR 2005. Proceedings., 12th International Conference on Advanced Robotics, pp. 316–323. IEEE (2005)
2. Ahmadi, M., Stone, P.: A multi-robot system for continuous area sweeping tasks. In: Proceedings 2006 IEEE International Conference on Robotics and Automation (ICRA 2006), pp. 1724–1729. IEEE (2006)
3. Altshuler, Y., Yanovski, V., Wagner, I.A., Bruckstein, A.M.: Multi-agent cooperative cleaning of expanding domains. Int. J. Robot. Res. **30**(8), 1037–1071 (2011). https://doi.org/10.1177/0278364910377245
4. Chen, S., Wu, F., Shen, L., Chen, J., Ramchurn, S.D.: Multi-agent patrolling under uncertainty and threats. PLoS ONE **10**(6), 1–19 (2015). https://doi.org/10.1371/journal.pone.0130154
5. Elmaliach, Y., Agmon, N., Kaminka, G.A.: Multi-robot area patrol under frequency constraints. In: Proceedings 2007 IEEE International Conference on Robotics and Automation, pp. 385–390 (2007)
6. Elor, Y., Bruckstein, A.M.: Multi-a(ge)nt graph patrolling and partitioning. In: 2009 IEEE/WIC/ACM International Joint Conference on Web Intelligence and Intelligent Agent Technology, vol. 2, pp. 52–57 (2009)
7. Gavranis, A., Kozanidis, G.: An exact solution algorithm for maximizing the fleet availability of a unit of aircraft subject to flight and maintenance requirements. Eur. J. Oper. Res. **242**(2), 631–643 (2015)
8. Ghita, B., Agnès, L., Xavier, D.: Scheduling of production and maintenance activities using multi-agent systems. In: 2018 IEEE 23rd International Conference on Emerging Technologies and Factory Automation (ETFA), vol. 1, pp. 508–515. IEEE (2018)
9. Hattori, K., Sugawara, T.: Effective area partitioning in a multi-agent patrolling domain for better efficiency. In: ICAART (1), pp. 281–288 (2021)

10. Kalra, N., Ferguson, D., Stentz, A.: Hoplites: a market-based framework for planned tight coordination in multirobot teams. In: Proceedings of the 2005 IEEE International Conference on Robotics and Automation, pp. 1170–1177 (2005)

11. Kato, C., Sugawara, T.: Decentralized area partitioning for a cooperative cleaning task. In: Boella, G., Elkind, E., Savarimuthu, B.T.R., Dignum, F., Purvis, M.K. (eds.) PRIMA 2013. LNCS (LNAI), vol. 8291, pp. 470–477. Springer, Heidelberg (2013). https://doi.org/10.1007/978-3-642-44927-7_36

12. Li, G., Chesser, G.D., Huang, Y., Zhao, Y., Purswell, J.L.: Development and optimization of a deep-learning-based egg-collecting robot. Trans. Am. Soc. Agric. Biol. Eng. **64**(5), 1659–1669 (2021)

13. Ma, H., Li, J., Kumar, T.S., Koenig, S.: Lifelong multi-agent path finding for online pickup and delivery tasks. In: Proceedings of the 16th Conference on Autonomous Agents and MultiAgent Systems, pp. 837–845. AAMAS 2017, IFAAMAS, Richland, SC (2017)

14. Moradi, H., Shadrokh, S.: A robust reliability-based scheduling for the maintenance activities during planned shutdown under uncertainty of activity duration. Comput. Chem. Eng. **130**, 106562 (2019). https://www.sciencedirect.com/science/article/pii/S0098135419307173

15. Okumura, K., Machida, M., Défago, X., Tamura, Y.: Priority inheritance with backtracking for iterative multi-agent path finding. In: Proceedings of the Twenty-Eighth International Joint Conference on Artificial Intelligence (IJCAI 2019), pp. 535–542. International Joint Conferences on Artificial Intelligence Organization (2019)

16. Othmani-Guibourg, M., El Fallah-Seghrouchni, A., Farges, J.L.: Path generation with LSTM recurrent neural networks in the context of the multi-agent patrolling. In: 2018 IEEE 30th International Conference on Tools with Artificial Intelligence (ICTAI), pp. 430–437 (2018)

17. Othmani-Guibourg, M., Fallah-Seghrouchni, A.E., Farges, J.L., Potop-Butucaru, M.: Multi-agent patrolling in dynamic environments. In: 2017 IEEE International Conference on Agents (ICA), pp. 72–77 (2017)

18. Panteleev, V., Kizim, A., Kamaev, V., Shabalina, O.: Developing a model of multi-agent system of a process of a tech inspection and equipment repair. In: Kravets, A., Shcherbakov, M., Kultsova, M., Iijima, T. (eds.) JCKBSE 2014. CCIS, vol. 466, pp. 457–465. Springer, Cham (2014). https://doi.org/10.1007/978-3-319-11854-3_39

19. Rezazadeh, N., Kia, S.S.: A sub-modular receding horizon approach to persistent monitoring for a group of mobile agents over an urban area. IFAC-PapersOnLine **52**(20), 217–222 (2019). 8th IFAC Workshop on Distributed Estimation and Control in Networked Systems NECSYS 2019

20. Sampaio, P.A., Ramalho, G., Tedesco, P.: The gravitational strategy for the timed patrolling. In: 2010 22nd IEEE International Conference on Tools with Artificial Intelligence, vol. 1, pp. 113–120 (2010)

21. Seif, J., Andrew, J.Y.: An extensive operations and maintenance planning problem with an efficient solution method. Comput. Oper. Res. **95**, 151–162 (2018)

22. Sharon, G., Stern, R., Felner, A., Sturtevant, N.R.: Conflict-based search for optimal multi-agent pathfinding. Artif. Intell. **219**, 40–66 (2015)

23. Sugiyama, A., Sea, V., Sugawara, T.: Emergence of divisional cooperation with negotiation and re-learning and evaluation of flexibility in continuous cooperative patrol problem. Knowl. Inf. Syst. **60**(3), 1587–1609 (2019)

24. Sugiyama, A., Sugawara, T.: Meta-strategy for cooperative tasks with learning of environments in multi-agent continuous tasks. In: Proceedings of the 30th Annual ACM Symposium on Applied Computing, pp. 494–500 (2015)

25. Tsuiki, S., Yoneda, K., Sugawara, T.: Reducing efficiency degradation due to scheduled agent suspensions by task handover in multi-agent cooperative patrol problems. In: The International FLAIRS Conference Proceedings, vol. 34 (2021)

26. Tsuiki, S., Yoneda, K., Sugawara, T.: Task handover negotiation protocol for planned suspension based on estimated chances of negotiations in multi-agent patrolling. In: Proceedings of the 14th International Conference on Agents and Artificial Intelligence, vol. 1, pp. 83–93. INSTICC, SciTePress (2022)
27. Vroegindeweij, B.A., van Willigenburg, G.L., Groot Koerkamp, P.W., van Henten, E.J.: Path planning for the autonomous collection of eggs on floors. Biosyst. Eng. **121**, 186–199 (2014). https://www.sciencedirect.com/science/article/pii/S1537511014000464
28. Wagner, I.A., Altshuler, Y., Yanovski, V., Bruckstein, A.M.: Cooperative cleaners: a study in ant robotics. Int. J. Robot. Res. **27**(1), 127–151 (2008). https://doi.org/10.1177/0278364907085789
29. Xie, J., et al.: Hybrid partition-based patrolling scheme for maritime area patrol with multiple cooperative unmanned surface vehicles. J. Mar. Sci. Eng. **8**(11), 936 (2020). https://www.mdpi.com/2077-1312/8/11/936
30. Yamauchi, T., Miyashita, Y., Sugawara, T.: Standby-based deadlock avoidance method for multi-agent pickup and delivery tasks. In: Proceedings of the 21st Conference on Autonomous Agents and MultiAgent Systems, pp. 1427–1535. AAMAS 2022, IFAAMAS, Richland, SC (2022)
31. Yoneda, K., Sugiyama, A., Kato, C., Sugawara, T.: Learning and relearning of target decision strategies in continuous coordinated cleaning tasks with shallow coordination1. Web Intell. **13**(4), 279–294 (2015)
32. Zhou, X., Wang, W., Wang, T., Lei, Y., Zhong, F.: Bayesian reinforcement learning for multi-robot decentralized patrolling in uncertain environments. IEEE Trans. Veh. Technol. **68**(12), 11691–11703 (2019)
33. Zhou, X., Wang, W., Wang, T., Li, M., Zhong, F.: Online planning for multiagent situational information gathering in the Markov environment. IEEE Syst. J. **14**(2), 1798–1809 (2020)

Artificial Intelligence

Comparing Beta-VAE to WGAN-GP for Time Series Augmentation to Improve Classification Performance

Domen Kavran, Borut Žalik, and Niko Lukač[✉]

Faculty of Electrical Engineering and Computer Science, University of Maribor,
Koroška cesta 46, Maribor, Slovenia
{domen.kavran1,borut.zalik,niko.lukac}@um.si

Abstract. Datasets often lack diversity to train robust classification models, capable of being used in real-life scenarios. Neural network-based generative models learn characteristics to generate synthetic (i.e. augmented) data, with the goal of increasing the diversity in datasets. A comparison is presented between Beta-VAE and WGAN-GP as ResNet-18 based generative time series models. The proposed generative models were tested on benchmark datasets to observe the effects of synthetic sets on the improvement in time series classification performance. Experiments were performed using 1-nearest neighbor algorithm and the state-of-the-art classification method MiniRocket. The choice of synthetic set size must be performed empirically to maximise the classification performance. By choosing the best synthetic set size for each dataset, the Beta-VAE generated synthetic sets led to an average increase in classification accuracy of +0,722% when used in the 1-nearest neighbor algorithm, and +1,856% when used for training the MiniRocket. The use of WGAN-GP generated synthetic sets to train classifiers led to average increases in classification accuracy of +0,654% with the 1-nearest neighbor algorithm and +1,753% with MiniRocket. The highest achieved increases in accuracy with the use of Beta-VAE and WGAN-GP generated synthetic sets were +6,84% and +10,53%, respectively.

Keywords: Time series · Augmentation · Classification · Variational autoencoder · Generative adversarial network · Beta-VAE · WGAN-GP

1 Introduction

Advanced machines and wearable smart devices, combined with the real-time capture and monitoring software, produce huge amounts of data on a daily basis. Automated analysis of structured and unstructured data is performed to assist in decision making in real-time information systems, which are used in various industries - ranging from healthcare to video games [14]. Among all forms of captured big data, time series are one of the most common. Time series are data points tracked over time. The most common time series are measurements of physical quantities, as well as financial and web activity data. Hardware sensors and monitoring applications record specific quantities. Advanced time series preprocessing methods are applied to extract information, which serve as an input to Artificial Intelligence (AI) algorithms [5]. Their goal is to learn a specific task, e.g. forecasting values and classifying time series.

A. P. Rocha et al. (Eds.): ICAART 2022, LNAI 13786, pp. 51–73, 2022.
https://doi.org/10.1007/978-3-031-22953-4_3

Time series classification plays a key part in many real-life applications, ranging from anomaly detection in industry environments to disease detection in healthcare [14]. Due to the temporal structure of time series, advanced classification methods in the fields of AI have been developed over the past decades. These state-of-the-art AI methods need large quantities of data to train robust classification models. Datasets are either labelled automatically or hand labelled manually by domain experts. Hand labelling time series samples becomes very time consuming with larger quantities of diverse data. The collected datasets are often lacking diversity to train classification models capable of being used in real-life scenarios, due to the development time and cost constraints, as well as insufficient available sources of measurements, e.g. a small set of patients in a medical research trial. A solution for increasing the diversity of datasets are data augmentations - techniques to create modified copies of original data points to be used in the training process of classification models. Time series augmentations are not trivial, because even slight changes in raw values can deteriorate the underlined properties of the original data, e.g. the frequency spectrum [18]. In the last decade, an alternative approach to augmentations emerged - the generation of synthetic data with generative models [10]. These models are capable of learning the characteristics of time series. Based on the learned properties, generative models control the characteristics of the generated time series. Generative models are trained with the collected time series, and later used to generate synthetic time series. These are then, along with the original time series, used for training the classifiers.

An augmentation method for generating synthetic time series with a ResNet-18 based Beta-Variational Autoencoder was presented in [12]. The proposed paper builds on the previous one by comparing the time series generation capabilities of the Beta-Variational Autoencoder and Wasserstein Generative Adversarial Network with Gradient Penalty [6,8]. Similar to [12], the effects of generated synthetic time series on the classification performance were observed by using the 1-nearest neighbor algorithm and the state-of-the-art classification method MiniRocket [2,4]. The results of the proposed paper were obtained on twice as many benchmark datasets as in [12].

This paper consists of six Sections. The next Section presents related work about state-of-the-art time series augmentation techniques and classification methods. The third introduces the proposed augmentation method by generating synthetic time series with a variational autoencoder and a generative adversarial network. The fourth Section presents the k-nearest neighbors algorithm and the classification method MiniRocket. The effects that synthetic time series have on classification performance are considered in the fifth Section. The conclusions are given in the sixth Section.

2   Related Work

In this Section we first present advanced methods for time series augmentations. Classification methods for time series are presented in the second subsection.

2.1   Time Series Augmentations

Tradicional time series augmentations are based on (random) transformations and the mixing of patterns. Efficient basic time series augmentations, named AddNoise, Permutation, Scaling and Warping, have been proposed, to improve the classification performance of two deep learning models, Fully Convolutional Neural Network (FCN) and Residual neural network (ResNet) [15]. These basic augmentations can be combined sequentially to form hybrid augmentations, which improve classification performance further. Certain combinations of combined augmentations made the classification performance worse, although there was always at least one augmentation method capable of improving the classification accuracy of each time series dataset [15]. The time series augmentation method based on interpolation has proven to be robust against the impairment of the trend information of the original time series, and has the advantage of low computational complexity. This augmentation method has proven to benefit the models, to improve classification performance with time series datasets from the benchmark UCR archive [18].

Authors in [10] provide an overview of an advanced approach to time series augmentations by generating new time series using generative models. These are divided into statistical models and neural network-based models. Generative models generate time series by sampling feature distributions [10].

A wide range of statistical models is used for time series generation. A statistical model of data is built typically to improve forecasting performance. The Local and Global Trend (LGT) forecasting model uses nonlinear global trends, and reduces local linear trends to model the input data [10]. GeneRAting TImeSeries (GRATIS) is a method, which utilises mixture autoregressive models to simulate time series [10]. A mixture of Gaussian trees was used to augment time series in imbalanced classes for the time series classification [10].

Neural network-based generative models are further divided into two categories: encoder-decoder networks and generative adversarial networks (GANs) [10]. Models in both categories are constructed based on four architectures: fully-connected networks, residual networks, temporal one-dimensional convolutional networks and two-dimensional convolutional networks. The latter are used to generate time-frequency spectrums. Various architectures can be combined further to form hybrid architectures [10].

Encoder-decoder networks encode the high-dimensional input into a lower-dimensional latent space vector, and then decode it back to a high-dimensional output. Data generation is performed with variational autoencoders (VAEs), which are capable of manipulating a latent space vector and decoding it to an output. Manipulation of latent space vectors by adding random noise, and also both interpolating and extrapolating the nearest latent space vectors, was performed to generate time series using an LSTM-based variational autoencoder [10]. Wasserstein autoencoders were presented as an alternative to VAEs [19].

Generative adversarial networks use adversarial training to optimise two neural networks jointly, named a generator and a discriminator. The discriminator is used only in the training process to discriminate between real and generated data from the generator. Similar to VAEs, the generator creates the output based on the latent space vector. An example of a hybrid GAN network is the Bidirectional Long Short-Term Memory Convolutional Neural Network (BLSTM-CNN) GAN. Conditional GANs (cGANs) are provided with a condition or parameter, in order to control the generated time series.

Selective GAN (sGAN) and VAE (sVAE) networks use a classification model, that was trained using the original time series dataset. Each generated time series is then classified, and only if high classification confidence was achieved, is it accepted as an augmented time series. The selective Wasserstein GAN (sWGAN) and selective VAE (sVAE) achieved better performance compared to a standard conditional WGAN (cWGAN) [10].

2.2 Time Series Classification

Researchers have developed many state-of-the-art time series classification algorithms in the recent decade, especially in the field of Deep Learning. The hierarchical Vote Collective of Transformation-based Ensembles (HIVE-COTE) is an ensemble of time series classifiers, trained in various domains [14]. Some of the classifiers are trained on time series, represented by shapelets and bag-of-words tokenization [14]. HIVE-COTE achieved the highest classification performance on benchmark datasets compared to other classification methods. The main disadvantage of this method is its very high computational complexity, which makes it impractical to use in real-world applications due to limitations in training time. InceptionTime is a deep learning ensemble of Convolutional Neural Networks (CNNs), inspired by the Inception-V4 architecture, and it has proven to be on par with HIVE-COTE [9]. Authors have proven that Inception-Time is much more scalable in terms of computational complexity and training time [9]. The classification algorithms Rocket and MiniRocket both have very low computational complexity. On larger time series datasets, MiniRocket can be up to 75 times faster and marginally more accurate than Rocket. However, MiniRocket achieved somewhat lower classification accuracies compared to HIVE-COTE [2]. The state-of-the-art is represented by the HIVE-COTE 2.0 algorithm. It introduced two novel classifiers, the Temporal Dictionary Ensemble (TDE) and Diverse Representation Canonical Interval Forest (DrCIF), to replace some of the existing ensemble members from the original algorithm. Authors have also added a new constituent to the algorithm - the Arsenal, an ensemble of Rocket classifiers [17].

3   Augmentation Method by Generating Time Series

Time series generation begins by training neural network-based generative models using the collected time series. More specifically, a single generative model is trained for each classification class. The generative model creates new time series based on the input latent space vector, also known as latent representation. It is created by sampling randomly from a distribution, or by manipulating latent variables manually, in order to change the characteristics of the generated time series [8]. All the generated time series form the so-called synthetic set. Since the generated time series will be used to improve the performance of the classification model, only time series in the train set are used to train generative models. Validation and test sets are intended for evaluation of a trained classification model, and, thus, are not used in the described time series generation workflow, which is shown in Fig. 1.

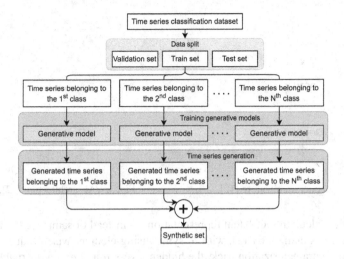

Fig. 1. Time series generation workflow.

The following subsections present the generative models used in the proposed augmentation method. The first subsection presents the Beta-Variational Autoencoder [8]. An advanced generative adversarial network, named Wasserstein GAN with Gradient Penalty, is presented in the second subsection [6].

3.1 Beta-Variational Autoencoder (Beta-VAE)

A neural network used to perform dimensionality reduction of input into efficient codings is named an autoencoder. It consists of two neural networks, namely, encoder and decoder. Dimensionality reduction of the input x is performed with the encoder. The decoding neural network, named decoder, performs the reconstruction of compressed data, also referred to as latent representation z of size z_{dim}. The described autoencoder architecture is shown in Fig. 2. Autoencoder training is done by minimising the difference between input x and the reconstruction $\hat{x}$. The difference is measured using a reconstruction loss L_r, e.g. mean squared error and categorical cross-entropy. The autoencoder learns to generate efficient codings of input data, making it suitable for anomaly detection and data compression [13].

A variational autoencoder (VAE) is a probabilistic generative model, based on a similar architecture to an autoencoder with additional hidden layers. These are mean layer μ and a Standard Deviation layer σ. Input x conditions the latent space vector through layers μ and σ. Their output values are used for sampling the Gaussian distribution $\mathcal{N}$ to obtain a latent space vector, also known as latent representation z, which consists of latent variables [13]. The variational autoencoder architecture is shown in Fig. 3.

Sampling of latent representation z is obtained by (1). A reparameterization trick is performed due to sampling of z being stochastic. It introduces a parameterless random variable ε, sampled from the standard Gaussian distribution. The reparameterization

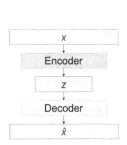

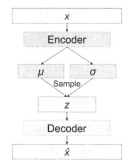

Fig. 2. Autoencoder architecture [12].   **Fig. 3.** VAE architecture [12].

trick alters the calculation of latent representation z - instead of sampling the Gaussian distribution, z is obtained by (2), with $\odot$ symbolising element-wise product [13]. By applying the reparameterization trick, the hidden layers μ and σ stay learnable during the backpropagation, and the stochasticity of latent bottleneck z is maintained.

$$z \sim \mathcal{N}(\mu, \sigma^2) \tag{1}$$

$$z = \mu + \sigma \odot \varepsilon, \varepsilon \sim \mathcal{N}(0,1) \tag{2}$$

Loss function L for training the variational autoencoder equals the sum of two different loss terms. The first one is the reconstruction term L_r, which measures the reconstruction error between x and $\hat{x}$. The second loss term is the Kullback-Leibler (KL) divergence term L_{KL}, which measures the difference between two probability distributions; one being the conditional distribution of the encoder $p(z|x)$, and the second one is the Gaussian distribution $\mathcal{N}(0,1)$. If the two distributions are equal, the Kullback-Liebler divergence equals to 0. A variational autoencoder learns a standard normal latent space distribution by introducing the divergence term L_{KL} into the loss function. A complete loss function is written by (3), where $p(z)$ is the Gaussian distribution $\mathcal{N}(0,1)$ [16].

$$L = L_r(x, \hat{x}) + L_{KL}(p(z|x), p(z)) \tag{3}$$

After the variational autoencoder model has done training, the encoder and hidden layers μ and σ are not used for data generation. To generate new data, sampling of the standard Gaussian distribution is performed to create a new latent representation z randomly, which is then passed into the decoder network. The output of the decoder is a newly generated data sample, similar to the data used for training the generative model.

Beta-VAE is a variational autoencoder intended for discovering disentangled latent variables. Latent representation z is disentangled if each latent variable is responsible for only one generative factor, while being invariant to other factors [3]. Disentangled latent representations are more efficient and interpretable, which makes data generation easier to control [8]. By training Beta-VAE for time series generation, the individual latent variable can control, e.g., abrupt changes, seasonality, short-lasting trends and noise presence in the generated time series. Beta-VAE keeps the same architecture as a variational autoencoder, with the only difference being the introduction of hyperparameter β to the loss function, written by (4) [8].

$$L = L_r(x, \hat{x}) + \beta L_{KL}(p(z|x), p(z)) \tag{4}$$

Hyperparameter β controls the weight of the Kullback-Leibler divergence term L_{KL} in the loss function. With the value of β larger than 1, the latent bottleneck z is more constrained. This results in lowering the value of L_{KL}, which indicates that the conditional probability of the encoder is becoming more like the reference Gaussian distribution. Stronger constraint of z forces latent variables to be more efficient, which results in a better disentanglement, but at the cost of higher reconstruction error L_r [8]. Only after the completion of training a Beta-VAE generative model, the generative factors can be examined and interpreted by changing the value in each latent variable manually and observing the effect it has on the generated data.

3.2   Wasserstein GAN with Gradient Penalty (WGAN-GP)

Generative Adversarial Network (GAN) is one of the most innovative deep learning advances in recent years [11]. GAN employs two neural networks: the generator G generates fake data based on noise vector z of size z_{dim}, and the discriminator D is responsible for distinguishing generated fake data from real data. These two neural networks are trained simultaneously in an adversarial manner [11]. The architecture of GAN is shown in Fig. 4.

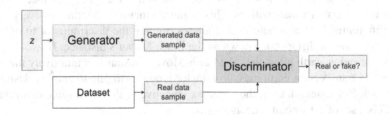

Fig. 4. Generative Adversarial Network architecture.

Through training the generator learns a distribution $p_g(x)$, which is a probability density function with a random variable x (e.g. time series values), that resembles the distribution of real data $p_{data}(x)$. The generator is trained to simulate real data based on input noise vector $z \sim p(z)$, which is sampled from a distribution $p(z)$, e.g. the uniform distribution or Gaussian distribution. The goal of the generator is to create fake data $\tilde{x} = G(z)$, so very similar to real data that the discriminator will fail to distinguish it from the real data $x \sim p_{data}$ [6]. Specifically, the generator tries to maximise the probability of detecting fake data samples as real ones. The generator learns to generate sufficient quality data through iterations of adversarial training - if the discriminator detects generated data easily as fake, the generator receives some negative feedback to help it improve the data generation process. Upon convergence, the discriminator cannot easily differentiate the real data from the generated data [11]. Adversarial training of both neural networks is performed through optimisation of the minimax objective L, given with (5), where $\mathbb{E}$ is the expected value [6]. The loss functions of the discriminator and generator, labelled $L_{discriminator}$ and $L_{generator}$, are derived from the objective L.

$$\min_{G} \max_{D} L(D,G) = \mathop{\mathbb{E}}_{x \sim p_{data}} [log(D(x))] + \mathop{\mathbb{E}}_{z \sim p_z} [log(1 - D(G(z)))]$$
$$= \mathop{\mathbb{E}}_{x \sim p_{data}} [log(D(x))] + \mathop{\mathbb{E}}_{\tilde{x} \sim p_g} [log(1 - D(\tilde{x}))] \tag{5}$$

The discriminator is a binary classifier ($D(x) \in [0,1]$), which is trained using binary cross-entropy loss [11]. Ideally, the discriminator is trained to optimality before each generator parameter update, which converts (5) into minimisation of the Jensen-Shannon (JS) divergence between p_{data} and p_g [6]. This leads to the discriminator outputting a probability of 0.5, implying that the optimally trained discriminator will be uncertain if data are real or fake [11]. The discriminator is only needed for training the generative model, and is not used for generating new data samples. To generate new data, sampling of the standard Gaussian distribution is performed to create a new noise vector z randomly, which is then passed into the generator. Its output is a newly generated data sample, similar to the data used for training the generative model. Unlike with Beta-VAE, GAN does not discover disentangled latent variables, so changing the value of a single latent variable in noise vector z affects many generative factors rather than a single one.

The divergences which GANs minimise are potentially not continuous with respect to the parameters of the generator, which leads to difficulty in training. To prevent this problem, the binary cross entropy is replaced with the first Wasserstein (1-Wasserstein) distance W or Kantorovich-Rubinstein metric, which serves as a distance function between two probability distributions. This distance function is continuous everywhere, almost differentiable everywhere, and it allows training the discriminator to optimality. The Wasserstein distance is known as the Earth-Mover's distance. If two distributions are viewed as earth piles, then the Earth-Mover's distance is intuitively the minimum cost of transporting earth mass to transform one earth pile to another. Using the Kantorovich-Rubinstein duality, the minimax objective is altered to value function (6), where $\mathcal{D}$ is a set of 1-Lipschitz functions [6].

$$\min_{G} \max_{D \in \mathcal{D}} L(D,G) = \mathop{\mathbb{E}}_{x \sim p_{data}} [D(x)] - \mathop{\mathbb{E}}_{\tilde{x} \sim p_g} [D(\tilde{x})] = W(p_{data}, p_g) \tag{6}$$

The training process of Wasserstein GAN (WGAN) will minimise the Wasserstein distance between p_{data} and p_g. The discriminator in WGAN is no longer used to classify between fake and real data, but to score the "realness" of data (WGAN's discriminator is named a critic; therefore, its loss function is labelled L_{critic}). The output of the discriminator is not bound in the range $[0,1]$, consequently, the application of sigmoid function on the output is removed. By using the WGAN value function (6), the gradient of a critic's function is better behaved compared to its GAN counterpart, which makes optimisation of the generator easier [6]. Weight clipping of the critic's neural network weights within a compact space $[-c, c]$ is performed, to enforce the Lipschitz-continuity constraint, ensuring the convergence by making the gradient of the optimal critic's function reliable [22]. The functions that satisfy the Lipschitz-continuity constraint are a subset of the k-Lipschitz functions for some k, which depends on the architecture of the critic and c. It has been observed empirically that the WGAN value function is correlated with the generated sample quality [6].

Weight clipping in WGAN can lead to optimisation difficulties. The critic D is biased towards very simple functions if the k-Lipschitz constraint is enforced with weight clipping. If the clipping threshold c is not chosen carefully, vanishing or exploding gradients can occur, due to the interaction of the weight constraint and the value function. Because the differentiable function is 1-Lipschtiz only if it has gradients with norm at most 1 everywhere, the alternative approach for enforcing the Lipschitz-continuity constraint is by constraining the gradient norm of the critic's output directly with respect to its input. This penalty on the gradient norm for random samples $\hat{x} \sim p_{\hat{x}}$ is added to the existing critic's loss, written with (7) [6].

$$L_{critic} = \underbrace{\underset{\tilde{x} \sim p_g}{\mathbb{E}} [D(\tilde{x})] - \underset{x \sim p_{data}}{\mathbb{E}} [D(x)]}_{\text{Original WGAN critic's loss}} + \underbrace{\lambda \underset{\hat{x} \sim p_{\hat{x}}}{\mathbb{E}} [(\|\nabla_{\hat{x}} D(\hat{x})\|_2 - 1)^2]}_{\text{Gradient penalty}} \qquad (7)$$

In the new critic's loss L_{critic}, the sampling of distribution $p_{\hat{x}}$ is defined along straight lines between pairs of data points from p_{data} and p_g. The definition of $p_{\hat{x}}$ is motivated from the fact that the optimal critic contains lines with gradient norm 1, which connect the coupled data points from p_{data} and p_g. A value of penalty coefficient $\lambda = 10$ has proven to work well for the gradient penalty (GP) in a variety of Wasserstein GAN with Gradient Penalty (WGAN-GP) architectures. Most architectures use batch normalisation to stabilise the training of both the generator and the discriminator. Because the gradient penalty penalises the norm of the critic's gradient with respect to each input independently, and not the entire batch, the batch normalisation layers must be omitted from the architecture of the critic in WGAN-GP. By continuing to use batch normalisation, the L_{critic} is no longer valid [6].

Both Jensen-Shannon and Kullback-Leibler divergences have the common drawback that, when two distributions are far different, the loss function becomes flat, and that results in vanishing gradients. In adversarial neural network training applications, such as GANs, the Wasserstein distance is better suited for comparing distributions, since its gradient does not vanish. Another advantage of the Wasserstein distance compared to the Kullback-Leibler divergence is that it does not contain logarithms, which makes it fairly linear, and can lead to better stability during training [21].

3.3 Proposed Beta-VAE and WGAN-GP Architectures

The proposed Beta-VAE and WGAN-GP architectures are based on 18-layer Residual neural networks (ResNets), which are adapted for time series data [20]. Residual neural networks contain sequential residual layers. Each residual layer is constructed from sequentially connected residual blocks, which are skip-connection blocks (components consisting of multiple layers) for learning residual functions with reference to the individual block input [7]. The gradient penalty does not allow the use of batch normalisation in the critic of WGAN-GP, therefore, all batch normalisation layers are replaced with instance normalisation. The ResNet-18 based block, used in the encoder of the proposed Beta-VAE architecture and the critic of the proposed WGAN-GP architecture, is shown in Fig. 5. The block in Fig. 6, where $Input_{channels}$ represents the number of channels in the $Input$, is used inside the residual layers of the Beta-VAE's decoder and WGAN-GP's generator.

Both proposed architectures generate time series of fixed length T. Each time series in a train set must have a length of at least $T = 8$, due to three residual layers in both

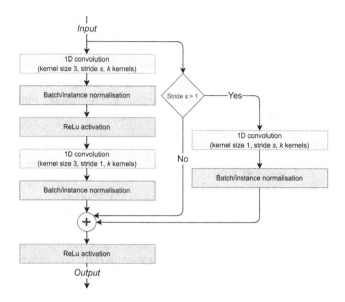

Fig. 5. ResNet-18 based block, used in the encoder of Beta-VAE and critic of WGAN-GP. The blocks in the Beta-VAE's encoder use batch normalisation, and the blocks in the WGAN-GP's critic use instance normalisation [12].

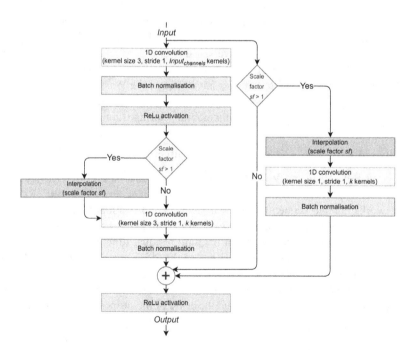

Fig. 6. ResNet-18 based block, used in the decoder of Beta-VAE and generator of WGAN-GP [12].

the Beta-VAE's encoder and WGAN-GP's critic performing convolutions with stride $s = 2$, which results in the output being eight times smaller than T before average pooling. Downsampling effects are reversed with three residual layers, which perform upscale interpolation by a scale factor $sf = 2$ in both the decoder of Beta-VAE and the generator of WGAN-GP. If the length of the time series is not divisible by 8, it should be zero padded before using it for training. Any padding should be removed from the generated time series. The proposed architectures are shown in Tables 1 and 2.

4   Time Series Classification Algorithms

The training of a time series classification model begins after the augmentations. The train set and the synthetic set, which contain the generated time series, are used for training the classification model. Numerous algorithms have many hyperparameters that need to be configured optimally to achieve the best classification performance. A combination of hyperparameters is used to configure and train a model, followed by evaluation of performance by classifying the validation set. The best performing hyperparameters are used for configuring the final classification model, which is then trained with train, synthetic and validation sets combined. The final, unbiased evaluation of the classification model is done with classification of the test set. The workflow for time series classification is shown in Fig. 7.

The following subsections present established time series classification algorithms. The first subsection presents the k-nearest neighbors algorithm. The classification method MiniRocket is described in the second subsection.

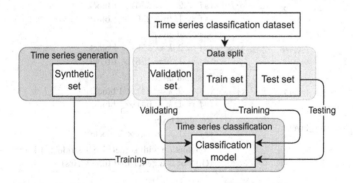

Fig. 7. Time series classification workflow.

4.1   k-Nearest Neighbors (kNN)

The idea behind the deterministic algorithm, named k-nearest neighbors, is simple; a data sample is classified as the most frequent class among the k most similar data samples in the train set. Neighbors are the closest data points to a new, yet unclassified data sample, based on a selected distance/similarity metric. Classification performance is influenced directly by the number of considered neighbors, therefore, the

Table 1. Proposed Beta-VAE architecture [12].

Stage	Layer name	Output size	Description
Encoder	conv1	$T \times 64$	**(Input is a time series)** Convolution with kernel size 3, stride 1, 64 kernels
	batch_norm	$T \times 64$	Batch normalisation
	relu	$T \times 64$	ReLu activation
	res_layer1	$T \times 64$	Residual layer $(s = 1, k = 64) \times 2$ blocks
	res_layer2	$\frac{T}{2} \times 128$	Residual layer $(s = 2, k = 128) \times 1$ block $(s = 1, k = 128) \times 1$ block
	res_layer3	$\frac{T}{4} \times 256$	Residual layer $(s = 2, k = 256) \times 1$ block $(s = 1, k = 256) \times 1$ block
	res_layer4	$\frac{T}{8} \times 512$	Residual layer $(s = 2, k = 512) \times 1$ block $(s = 1, k = 512) \times 1$ block
	avg_pool	512	Average pool
Bottleneck z	μ	z_{dim}	$512 \times z_{dim}$ fully connected layer
	σ	z_{dim}	$512 \times z_{dim}$ fully connected layer
Decoder	fully_conn	8192	**(Input is a latent space vector $z \sim \mathcal{N}(\mu, \sigma^2)$)** $z_{dim} \times 8192$ fully connected layer
	reshape	16×512	Reshape to 16×512
	interp	$\frac{T}{8} \times 512$	Interpolate to $\frac{T}{8} \times 512$
	res_layer5	$\frac{T}{4} \times 256$	Residual layer $(sf = 2, k = 256) \times 1$ block $(sf = 1, k = 256) \times 1$ block
	res_layer6	$\frac{T}{2} \times 128$	Residual layer $(sf = 2, k = 128) \times 1$ block $(sf = 1, k = 128) \times 1$ block
	res_layer7	$T \times 64$	Residual layer $(sf = 2, k = 64) \times 1$ block $(sf = 1, k = 64) \times 1$ block
	res_layer8	$T \times 64$	Residual layer $(sf = 1, k = 64) \times 2$ blocks
	conv2	T	Convolution with kernel size 3, stride 1, 1 kernel **(Output is a generated time series)**

value of parameter k must be chosen carefully. The most intuitive distance measure is the Euclidean distance, which has the advantage of fast computation. As a distance measure between two time series, however, it exhibits sensitivity to distortions and shifting of values along the time axis. The described shortcomings are solved with distance measurements based on non-linear aligning, with Dynamic Time Warping (DTW) being one of the most popular options [4].

The Euclidean distance allows one-to-one mapping of aligned data points, whereas DTW allows one-to-many alignment of data points. DTW constructs the distance matrix

Table 2. Proposed WGAN-GP architecture.

Stage	Layer name	Output size	Description
Generator	fully_conn	8192	**(Input is a noise vector z)** $z_{dim} \times 8192$ fully connected layer
	reshape	16×512	Reshape to 16×512
	interp	$\frac{T}{8} \times 512$	Interpolate to $\frac{T}{8} \times 512$
	res_layer1	$\frac{T}{4} \times 256$	Residual layer $(sf = 2, k = 256) \times 1$ block $(sf = 1, k = 256) \times 1$ block
	res_layer2	$\frac{T}{2} \times 128$	Residual layer $(sf = 2, k = 128) \times 1$ block $(sf = 1, k = 128) \times 1$ block
	res_layer3	$T \times 64$	Residual layer $(sf = 2, k = 64) \times 1$ block $(sf = 1, k = 64) \times 1$ block
	res_layer4	$T \times 64$	Residual layer $(sf = 1, k = 64) \times 2$ blocks
	conv1	T	Convolution with kernel size 3, stride 1, 1 kernel **(Output is a generated time series)**
Critic	conv2	$T \times 64$	**(Input is a time series)** Convolution with kernel size 3, stride 1, 64 kernels
	instance_norm	$T \times 64$	Instance normalisation
	relu	$T \times 64$	ReLu activation
	res_layer5	$T \times 64$	Residual layer $(s = 1, k = 64) \times 2$ blocks
	res_layer6	$\frac{T}{2} \times 128$	Residual layer $(s = 2, k = 128) \times 1$ block $(s = 1, k = 128) \times 1$ block
	res_layer7	$\frac{T}{4} \times 256$	Residual layer $(s = 2, k = 256) \times 1$ block $(s = 1, k = 256) \times 1$ block
	res_layer8	$\frac{T}{8} \times 512$	Residual layer $(s = 2, k = 512) \times 1$ block $(s = 1, k = 512) \times 1$ block
	avg_pool	512	Average pool
	score_layer	1	Convolution with kernel size 512, stride 1, 1 kernel **(Output is a 'realness' score of time series)**

between two time series, and each element (i, j) in the matrix is the Euclidean distance between the i-th data point in the first time series and the j-th data point in the second time series [4]. The value of the DTW distance measure is the minimal warping path, which is a series of adjacent cells that begins and ends at diagonally opposite corners of the distance matrix. Several other elastic distance measures have been proposed, such as Longest Common Subsequence (LCS) and Edit Distance with Real Penalty (ERP) [4].

An accepted fact among researchers is that the vanilla 1-nearest neighbor (1NN) classifier, combined with some elastic distance measure, can often be superior to more complex classification methods. It has been shown that weighted (taking the similarity degree of the nearest neighbors into account) kNN classifier with unconstrained elastic distance measure can outperform 1NN [4].

4.2 MiniRocket

The time series classification method MiniRocket achieves state-of-the-art performance on benchmark datasets compared to existing methods by using only a fraction of the computational expense [2]. MiniRocket is an almost entirely deterministic (and optionally, fully deterministic) reformulated version of the Rocket method with certain changes, making it faster on larger datasets.

The main part of the MiniRocket is feature extraction, which starts by convolving the time series with a fixed set of kernels of length 9. The kernels have weights W with values being either -1 or 2, with only three weights having the value of 2, and the sum of weights equalling to 0. 84 different kernels are formed based on the described restrictions. Each kernel is assigned the same fixed set of dilations, which are adjusted based on the length of the time series. The kernels are applied over the whole length of time series, including the dilation. A maximum of 32 dilations are set per kernel, because more dilations with higher values do not improve the classification performance. Half of the kernel/dilation combinations use zero padding, and the other half do not. For each kernel/dilation combination, the biases b are drawn from the quantiles of the convolution output for a single, randomly selected, train time series sample. Kernel biases are the only random component of the feature extraction. After the convolution $(X * W - b)$ of the input time series X, a special pooling method is applied, named 'proportion of positive values' (PPV). It is defined in (8), where n is the result size of the convolution [2].

$$PPV(X * W - b) = \frac{1}{n} \sum [X * W - b > 0] \tag{8}$$

By using a small set of fixed two-valued kernels and the smart calculation of PPV, the feature extraction achieves fast execution speed and efficiency. The optimisations of the convolution consist of computing all kernels 'almost simultaneously' for each dilation, reusing the output of convolution to compute many features, and not using multiplications inside the convolution operations. The efficiency of PPV is increased by computing the result for W and $-W$ at the same time. The described optimisations result in the feature extraction having a linear computational complexity. The feature extraction results in 10,000 features per time series. These features are then used to train a linear classifier. If a train set contains more than 10,000 time series samples, logistic regression is recommended. Otherwise, a ridge regression should be used [2].

5   Results

The effects of synthetic time series (created with Beta-VAEs and WGAN-GPs) on the classification performance of 1NN with DTW distance (1NN-DTW) and MiniRocket were observed by classifying the selected benchmark datasets from the UAE & UCR repository [1]. All the used datasets are presented in Table 3. Each dataset contains a predefined train and test set with fixed length time series. The generative models and classifiers used the recommended hyperparameter values, with the only exceptions being the size z_{dim} of latent/noise vector in the generative models and the value of β for training the Beta-VAEs.

Each dataset with N classification classes had $2N$ generative models trained. Specifically, a single generative model of the proposed Beta-VAE architecture and a single generative model of the proposed WGAN-GP architecture were trained for each classification class in the dataset. All generative models used a latent/noise vector of size $z_{dim} = 64$ for three reasons. First, the z_{dim} should be constant for all generative models in order to keep them comparable in terms of maximum possible expressiveness through information in the latent/noise vector z. Second, the latent/noise vector z must be smaller than the generated data. Third, the dataset MoteStrain has the shortest time series length of 84 among all the featured datasets. Beta-VAEs were trained with $\beta = 2$. This value was chosen empirically, based on observations during the training of the Beta-VAE models on a small subset of featured datasets - increasing $\beta > 2$ resulted in a negligible increase of disentanglement of latent variables, but it hurt the quality of the reconstructed time series significantly.

The Beta-VAEs were trained with an Adam optimizer, using the learning rate $\eta = 0.00001$ and default beta coefficients $\beta_1 = 0.9$ and $\beta_2 = 0.999$. The training was performed for 2,500 epochs, with possible early stopping if the training loss did not lower in the last 100 epochs. Each epoch consisted of 500 steps/iterations, with a batch size of 4.

GAN Networks are trained using Two Optimizers - one for training the discriminator and the other for training the generator. Following the recommendations from the authors of WGAN-GP, both optimizers in our experiments were Adam with learning rate $\eta = 0.0001$ and beta coefficients $\beta_1 = 0$ and $\beta_2 = 0.9$. The penalty coefficient λ was set to the recommended value of 10. As recommended, the critic performed 5 training iterations per single generator training iteration [6]. The training process was performed for 750 epochs, with each epoch consisting of 500 steps/iterations with a batch size of 4.

The number of synthetic time series to generate per class was calculated as a percentage of the train set size (hereinafter, the percentages of the train set size are written in decimals). This approach reduces the class imbalance. For example, dataset ECG5000 has 5 classes with 292, 177, 10, 19 and 2 time series samples. The balance of samples between classes is 0,584 : 0,354 : 0,02 : 0,038 : 0,004, which is considered imbalanced. A synthetic set of 5,000 time series is created by generating twice the size of the ECG5000 train set (500) of synthetic time series for each class. A total of 5,500 time series are then used to train a classification model. This improves the balance of samples between five classes to 0,235 : 0,214 : 0,1836 : 0,1853 : 0,1822. Examples of generated time series are shown in Figs. 8 and 9.

Table 3. Time series classification datasets, used in the experiments [12].

Dataset	Description	Time series length	Train set size	Test set size	No. of classes
ECG5000	ECG recordings of five cardiovascular diseases	140	500	4,500	5
FreezerSmallTrain	Power demand of two types of freezers	301	28	2,850	2
InsectEPGSmallTrain	EPG signals of insect interaction with plants	601	17	249	3
MoteStrain	Recordings of humidity and temperature sensors	84	20	1,252	2
SmallKitchenAppliances	Electricity consumption of three types of appliances	720	375	375	3
Haptics	Passgraph entries of five people on a touchscreen (X axis movement only)	1,092	155	308	5
MixedShapesSmallTrain	Five categories of 2D shapes converted into one-dimensional time series	1,024	100	2,425	5
ScreenType	Electricity consumption of three types of screens	720	375	375	3
UWaveGestureLibraryX	Eight simple hand gestures, measured by accelerometers (X axis movement only)	315	896	3,582	8
MedicalImages	Histograms of pixel intensity in medical images of ten different body regions	99	381	760	10

For each dataset, a single 1NN-DTW classifier and 100 MiniRocket classifiers were trained on every combination of train data (either only an original train set, or an original train set with additional class-specific synthetic time series sets of different sizes [$0,01\times$, $0,05\times$, $0,1\times$, $0,5\times$, $1,0\times$ or $2,0\times$ the size of original train set; $\times$ is the times sign]). The MiniRocket classifiers used the recommended default hyperparameters [2]. Multiple MiniRocket classifiers had to be trained, because we used the almost entirely deterministic (not the fully deterministic) version of the method. Among 100 trained MiniRocket classifiers, we selected the one which achieved the best classification performance. Performance was evaluated on the basis of the achieved classification accuracy on the test sets.

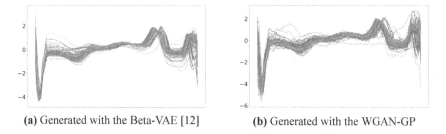

(a) Generated with the Beta-VAE [12]   (b) Generated with the WGAN-GP

Fig. 8. Synthetic time series of Class 1 in the dataset ECG5000.

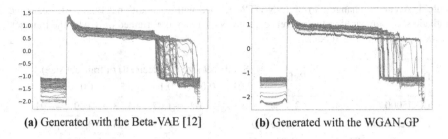

(a) Generated with the Beta-VAE [12]   **(b)** Generated with the WGAN-GP

Fig. 9. Synthetic time series of Class 1 in the dataset FreezerSmallTrain.

The effects of Beta-VAE and WGAN-GP generated synthetic sets on the performance of the 1NN-DTW are shown in Tables 4 and 5. Significant fluctuations in accuracy changes between different sizes of synthetic sets can be observed in both Tables. For 7 out of 10 datasets, the Beta-VAE generated synthetic time series samples managed to help in increasing the classification accuracy of the 1-nearest neighbor classifiers. Training the classifiers with WGAN-GP generated synthetic sets increased classification accuracy only in 5 out of 10 datasets. Beta-VAE generated synthetic sets of size 1,0× the size of the original train set led to most of the largest increases in accuracy, followed by the sizes of 2,0×, 0,5× and 0,1× the size of original train set. Three out of the five largest increases in accuracy with WGAN-GP generated synthetic sets were achieved with their sizes equalling 2,0× the size of the original train set. Beta-VAE generated synthetic sets led to the largest decrease in accuracy of -3,91% for the ECG5000 dataset, and the largest accuracy increase of +2,40% for the Screen-Type dataset. The synthetic sets that were generated by WGAN-GPs, led to the largest decrease in accuracy of −2,54% for the UWaveGestureLibraryX dataset, and the largest accuracy increase of +2,92% for the Haptics dataset. The classification accuracies of 1NN-DTW on the MedicalImages dataset improved with increasing the size of the WGAN-GP generated synthetic sets. This resulted in a starting accuracy increase of +0,13% for the synthetic set size equalling 0,01× the size of the original train set. The accuracy increase improved up to +2,37% for the synthetic set size equalling 2,0× the size of the original train set.

Tables 6 and 7 show the effects of the Beta-VAE and WGAN-GP generated synthetic sets on the performance of MiniRocket. Similar to the results for 1NN-DTW, fluctuations in accuracy changes are present in both Tables. Beta-VAE generated synthetic sets increased the performance of MiniRocket classifiers for all datasets, except UWaveGestureLibraryX. MiniRocket classifiers trained with WGAN-GP generated synthetic sets did manage to increase the accuracy on the test set of UWaveGesture-LibraryX, but that was not possible with InsectEPGSmallTrain and SmallKitchenAppliances. Beta-VAE generated synthetic sets with sizes equalling 0,5× the size of the original train set led to most of the largest accuracy increases, followed by the sizes of 0,05×, 1,0× and 2,0× the size of the train set. By using the WGAN-GP generated synthetic sets for training the MiniRocket classifiers, each tested size of synthetic sets proved to lead to the largest accuracy increase for at least one of the datasets. The MedicalImages synthetic sets, that were generated by the Beta-VAEs, led to the largest

Table 4. Accuracy change (%) of 1NN-DTW, trained with an additional Beta-VAE generated synthetic sets, compared to the reference accuracy of a classifier trained only with the train set. The best performance is in bold.

Dataset	Ref. acc.	Synth. set size (% (decimal) of train set size)					
		0,01	0,05	0,1	0,5	1,0	2,0
ECG5000	92,44%	−0,36	−1,02	−1,67	−3,33	−3,29	−3,91
FreezerSmallTrain	75,89%	0	0	−0,11	−0,25	−0,70	**+0,81**
InsectEPGSmallTrain	100%	0	0	0	0	0	0
MoteStrain	83,46%	−1,36	0	0	**+0,48**	**+0,48**	−0,48
SmallKitchenAppliances	64,26%	0	0	0	0	0	0
Haptics	37,66%	−0,33	+0,32	−0,33	−1,30	**+0,65**	−0,33
MixedShapesSmallTrain	77,97%	−0,04	+0,29	+0,50	+0,46	+0,05	**+1,37**
ScreenType	39,73%	0	+0,53	+0,80	−1,07	**+2,40**	+0,27
UWaveGestureLibraryX	72,75%	+0,11	+0,17	**+0,19**	−0,87	−0,90	−1,43
MedicalImages	73,68%	−0,26	+0,26	+0,66	**+1,32**	−0,79	+0,26

Table 5. Accuracy change (%) of 1NN-DTW, trained with an additional WGAN-GP generated synthetic sets, compared to the reference accuracy of a classifier trained only with the train set. The best performance is in bold.

Dataset	Ref. acc.	Synth. set size (% (decimal) of train set size)					
		0,01	0,05	0,1	0,5	1,0	2,0
ECG5000	92,44%	**+0,02**	−0,04	−0,31	−0,51	−0,09	−0,09
FreezerSmallTrain	75,89%	+0,07	+0,07	+0,07	−0,53	−0,32	**+0,28**
InsectEPGSmallTrain	100%	0	0	0	0	0	0
MoteStrain	83,46%	0	0	−0,64	0	−0,24	−0,48
SmallKitchenAppliances	64,26%	−0,53	−0,26	−0,26	−1,33	−1,60	−1,86
Haptics	37,66%	+0,32	+0,32	0	+2,59	+1,62	**+2,92**
MixedShapesSmallTrain	77,97%	0	**+0,95**	−1,15	+0,17	−0,41	−0,37
ScreenType	39,73%	0	0	−0,27	−0,80	−0,27	−0,27
UWaveGestureLibraryX	72,75%	−0,20	−0,50	−0,59	−0,78	−1,37	−2,54
MedicalImages	73,68%	+0,13	+0,79	+0,79	+1,58	+1,58	**+2,37**

decrease in accuracy of -7,37%, with their size equalling 0,05× the size of the original train set, and the largest increase in accuracy of +6,84%, with their size equalling 0,5× the size of the original train set. The WGAN-GP generated synthetic sets for MedicalImages also resulted in the largest decrease in accuracy of -18,29%, with their size equalling 2,0× the size of the original train set, and the largest increase in accuracy of +10,53%, with their size equalling 0,5× the size of the original train set.

Table 6. Accuracy change (%) of MiniRocket, trained with an additional Beta-VAE generated synthetic sets, compared to the reference accuracy of a classifier trained only with the train set. The best performance is in bold.

Dataset	Ref. acc.	Synth. set size (% (decimal) of train set size)					
		0,01	0,05	0,1	0,5	1,0	2,0
ECG5000	94,06%	+0,20	**+0,34**	+0,11	−0,40	−0,60	−1,13
FreezerSmallTrain	92,52%	+1,79	+0,63	+1,12	+2,56	**+2,98**	+1,37
InsectEPGSmallTrain	96,38%	0	0	0	**+0,40**	0	−0,40
MoteStrain	93,13%	−0,80	**+0,16**	−0,72	**+0,16**	−0,72	−2,00
SmallKitchenAppliances	81,13%	−1,13	−3,00	−2,20	**+1,00**	−4,60	**+1,00**
Haptics	54,22%	+0,32	**+0,65**	−0,33	−0,65	0	−2,28
MixedShapesSmallTrain	91,42%	−0,13	+0,12	−0,25	−0,29	0	**+0,86**
ScreenType	44,53%	+1,07	−0,53	+3,47	+3,73	**+5,33**	+2,40
UWaveGestureLibraryX	84,03%	0	−0,31	−0,03	−0,93	−4,44	−2,74
MedicalImages	67,23%	−2,63	−7,37	+4,08	**+6,84**	+6,58	+4,21

Table 7. Accuracy change (%) of MiniRocket, trained with an additional WGAN-GP generated synthetic sets, compared to the reference accuracy of a classifier trained only with the train set. The best performance is in bold.

Dataset	Ref. acc.	Synth. set size (% (decimal) of train set size)					
		0,01	0,05	0,1	0,5	1,0	2,0
ECG5000	94,06%	**+0,16**	−0,75	−1,91	−1,09	−1,04	−1,00
FreezerSmallTrain	92,52%	+2,95	+1,40	+1,44	+2,91	+3,30	**+3,76**
InsectEPGSmallTrain	96,38%	−0,40	−0,40	−0,40	−0,40	−0,80	−0,40
MoteStrain	93,13%	0	**+0,16**	−0,96	−0,48	**+0,16**	−0,40
SmallKitchenAppliances	81,13%	−1,13	−10,47	−7,00	−3,27	−3,00	−4,33
Haptics	54,22%	−0,33	**+0,32**	−0,98	−1,30	−2,93	−4,55
MixedShapesSmallTrain	91,42%	**+0,25**	−0,29	−0,62	−14,52	−2,27	−1,73
ScreenType	44,53%	**+2,13**	+0,80	+0,27	−0,53	−0,27	−2,93
UWaveGestureLibraryX	84,03%	−0,14	+0,05	**+0,22**	−1,15	−2,85	−5,70
MedicalImages	67,23%	+0,79	+8,82	+9,34	**+10,53**	+10,13	−18,29

Table 8 shows the largest increases in accuracy of both tested classification methods using the synthetic sets generated by the two proposed generative models. The MiniRocket classifier, which was trained using both the original train set and additional synthetic sets for each class, has proven to achieve higher accuracies in 9 out of the 10 datasets compared to 1NN-DTW. The only dataset where 1NN-DTW achieved better performance was InsectEPGSmallTrain, with 100% accuracy. Using the 1NN-DTW, the Beta-VAE generated synthetic sets led to achieving the largest accuracy increase in five datasets, compared to the WGAN-GP generated synthetic sets, which helped in

Table 8. Largest increases in accuracy with the use of synthetic sets in the training process. The results are derived from Tables 4, 5, 6 and 7. The accuracy is in parentheses. The value '0%' indicates no increase in accuracy. A generative model won, if the generated data led to the largest increase in the accuracy of a classifier for an individual dataset. The best performance is in bold.

Dataset	1NN-DTW		MiniRocket	
	Beta-VAE	WGAN-GP	Beta-VAE	WGAN-GP
ECG5000	0%	**+0,02%**	**+0,34%**	+0,16%
	(92,44%)	**(92,46%)**	**(94,40%)**	(94,22%)
FreezerSmallTrain	**+0,81%**	+0,28%	+2,98%	**+3,76%**
	(76,70%)	(76,17%)	(95,50%)	**(96,28%)**
InsectEPGSmallTrain	0%	0%	**+0,40%**	0%
	(100%)	(100%)	**(96,78%)**	(96,38%)
MoteStrain	**+0,48%**	0%	**+0,16%**	**+0,16%**
	(83,94%)	(83,46%)	**(93,29%)**	**(93,29%)**
SmallKitchenAppliances	0%	0%	**+1,00%**	0%
	(64,26%)	(64,26%)	**(82,13%)**	(81,13%)
Haptics	+0,65%	**+2,92%**	**+0,65%**	+0,32%
	(38,31%)	**(40,58%)**	**(54,87%)**	(54,54%)
MixedShapesSmallTrain	**+1,37%**	+0,95%	**+0,86%**	+0,25%
	(79,34%)	(78,92%)	**(92,28%)**	(91,67%)
ScreenType	**+2,40%**	0%	**+5,33%**	+2,13%
	(42,13%)	(39,73%)	**(49,86%)**	(46,66%)
UWaveGestureLibraryX	**+0,19%**	0%	0%	**+0,22%**
	(72,94%)	(72,75%)	(84,03%)	**(84,25%)**
MedicalImages	+1,32%	**+2,37%**	+6,84%	**+10,53%**
	(75,00%)	**(76,05%)**	(74,07%)	**(77,76%)**
Average	**+0,722%**	+0,654%	**+1,856%**	+1,753%
Number of wins	**5/10**	3/10	**7/10**	4/10

achieving the largest increase in accuracy in three datasets. In two datasets, no increase in accuracy was achieved by using the generated synthetic sets. Using the MiniRocket, the Beta-VAE generated synthetic sets helped in achieving the largest accuracy increase in seven datasets, compared to the WGAN-GP generated synthetic sets, which led to achieving the largest increase in accuracy in four datasets. Using Beta-VAE generated synthetic sets in 1NN-DTW resulted in the average largest increase in accuracy of +0,722%, compared to +0,654% with WGAN-GP generated synthetic sets. Similar to 1NN-DTW, training the MiniRocket with additional Beta-VAE generated synthetic sets led to the average largest increase in accuracy of +1,856%, compared to +1,753% with the WGAN-GP generated synthetic sets.

According to the results in Table 8, the Beta-VAEs produce synthetic time series of higher quality than WGAN-GPs, which leads to better results of both classification methods for most of the datasets. Besides that, the Beta-VAEs should also be preferred, due to their capability of discovering disentangled latent variables and often faster train process compared to WGAN-GPs. Significant fluctuations in accuracy changes between sizes of synthetic sets for both of the proposed generative models can be seen in Tables 4, 5, 6 and 7. These fluctuations in accuracy changes occur because generated time series contain new unique characteristics; the classifier's performance can deteriorate if it utilizes misleading characteristics or learns incorrect features from the time series in a synthetic set. Variation in characteristics/features also depends on the size of a synthetic set. Based on these facts, different sizes of synthetic sets should be considered and tested. The MiniRocket classifiers, which were trained only with original train sets, achieved an average accuracy of 79,87%, compared to the average classification accuracy of 71,78% achieved by the 1NN-DTW classifiers (the percentages are calculated as averages of the reference accuracies in Tables 4, 5, 6 and 7). By training the classification models with additional synthetic time series, the average classification accuracy increased to 82,19% for the MiniRocket classifiers, and to 72,84% for the 1NN-DTW classifiers (the percentages are calculated as averages of the highest (bold) accuracies in Table 8). The results in Table 8 reveal that the classification method MiniRocket almost always outperforms the 1NN-DTW.

6   Conclusions

This paper presented a comparison of the Beta-Variational Autoencoder (Beta-VAE) and Wasserstein Generative Adversarial Network with Gradient Penalty (WGAN-GP) as ResNet-18 based generative time series models. The effects of the generated synthetic time series on the classification performance were observed using the 1-nearest neighbor algorithm with Dynamic Time Warping distance (1NN-DTW) and state-of-the-art classifier MiniRocket.

The results show that MiniRocket outperformed the 1-nearest neighbor classifier in almost every time series classification dataset. Without the use of additional synthetic sets, the MiniRocket classifiers achieved an average accuracy of 79,87%, compared to 1NN-DTW's average accuracy of 71,78%. With the use of synthetic sets, generated by Beta-VAEs or WGAN-GPs, in the training process, the average accuracy of MiniRocket classifiers rose to 82,19%, and to 72,84% for the 1NN-DTW. The size of a synthetic set should be chosen empirically, because of the potential performance deterioration of a classifier. By choosing the best size of synthetic set for individual datasets empirically, the WGAN-GP generated synthetic sets were capable of increasing accuracy up to +10,53% compared to +6,84% with Beta-VAE generated synthetic sets. However, the Beta-VAE generated synthetic sets resulted in higher average accuracy increases compared to WGAN-GP generated synthetic sets. Beta-VAE generated synthetic sets led to an average increase in accuracy of +0,722% when used in 1NN-DTW, and +1,856% when used for training the MiniRocket. The use of WGAN-GP generated synthetic sets in 1NN-DTW resulted in an average increase in accuracy of +0,654%, and +1,753% when used in the training process of MiniRocket. These results prove that synthetic sets generated by Beta-VAEs are of higher quality, and lead to overall better results than WGAN-GP generated synthetic sets.

In the future, the proposed Beta-VAE and WGAN-GP architectures will be modified with additional input conditions, to support time series generation for various classes within a single model. The modified architectures will also support the generation of multivariate time series.

Acknowledgements. The authors acknowledge joint financial support from the Slovenian Research Agency and Slovenian Ministry of the Interior (target research programme No. V2-2117). The authors acknowledge the financial support from the Slovenian Research Agency (Research Core Funding No. P2-0041).

References

1. Bagnall, A., Lines, J., Vickers, W., Keogh, E.: The UEA and UCR Time Series Classification Repository (2021). www.timeseriesclassification.com
2. Dempster, A., Schmidt, D.F., Webb, G.I.: MiniRocket: a very fast (almost) deterministic transform for time series classification. In: Proceedings of the 27th ACM SIGKDD Conference on Knowledge Discovery and Data Mining, KDD 2021, pp. 248–257. Association for Computing Machinery, New York (2021). https://doi.org/10.1145/3447548.3467231
3. Esmaeili, B., et al.: Structured disentangled representations. In: Chaudhuri, K., Sugiyama, M. (eds.) Proceedings of the Twenty-Second International Conference on Artificial Intelligence and Statistics. Proceedings of Machine Learning Research, vol. 89, pp. 2525–2534. PMLR (2019). https://proceedings.mlr.press/v89/esmaeili19a.html
4. Geler, Z., Kurbalija, V., Ivanović, M., Radovanović, M.: Weighted kNN and constrained elastic distances for time-series classification. Expert Syst. Appl. **162**, 113829 (2020). https://doi.org/10.1016/j.eswa.2020.113829. https://www.sciencedirect.com/science/article/pii/S0957417420306412
5. Gian Antonio, S., Angelo, C., Matteo, T.: Chapter 9 - Time-series classification methods: review and applications to power systems data, pp. 179–220 (2018). https://doi.org/10.1016/B978-0-12-811968-6.00009-7
6. Gulrajani, I., Ahmed, F., Arjovsky, M., Dumoulin, V., Courville, A.: Improved training of Wasserstein GANs. In: Proceedings of the 31st International Conference on Neural Information Processing Systems, NIPS 2017, pp. 5769–5779. Curran Associates Inc., Red Hook (2017)
7. He, K., Zhang, X., Ren, S., Sun, J.: Deep residual learning for image recognition. In: 2016 IEEE Conference on Computer Vision and Pattern Recognition (CVPR), pp. 770–778 (2016). https://doi.org/10.1109/CVPR.2016.90
8. Higgins, I., et al.: Beta-VAE: learning basic visual concepts with a constrained variational framework. In: ICLR (2017)
9. Ismail Fawaz, H., et al.: InceptionTime: finding AlexNet for time series classification. Data Min. Knowl. Disc. **34**(6), 1936–1962 (2020). https://doi.org/10.1007/s10618-020-00710-y
10. Iwana, B.K., Uchida, S.: An empirical survey of data augmentation for time series classification with neural networks. PLoS ONE **16**(7), e0254841 (2021). https://doi.org/10.1371/journal.pone.0254841
11. Jozdani, S., Chen, D., Pouliot, D., Alan Johnson, B.: A review and meta-analysis of Generative Adversarial Networks and their applications in remote sensing. Int. J. Appl. Earth Obs. Geoinf. **108**, 102734 (2022). https://doi.org/10.1016/j.jag.2022.102734. https://www.sciencedirect.com/science/article/pii/S0303243422000605

12. Kavran, D., Žalik, B., Lukač, N.: Time series augmentation based on beta-VAE to improve classification performance. In: Proceedings of the 14th International Conference on Agents and Artificial Intelligence, ICAART, vol. 2, pp. 15–23. INSTICC, SciTePress (2022). https://doi.org/10.5220/0010749200003116

13. Kingma, D., Welling, M.: Auto-encoding variational bayes. In: Proceedings of the 2nd International Conference on Learning Representations (ICLR) (2014)

14. Lines, J., Taylor, S., Bagnall, A.: HIVE-COTE: the hierarchical vote collective of transformation-based ensembles for time series classification. In: 2016 IEEE 16th International Conference on Data Mining (ICDM), pp. 1041–1046 (2017). https://doi.org/10.1109/ICDM.2016.0133

15. Liu, B., Zhang, Z., Cui, R.: Efficient time series augmentation methods. In: 2020 13th International Congress on Image and Signal Processing, BioMedical Engineering and Informatics (CISP-BMEI), pp. 1004–1009 (2020). https://doi.org/10.1109/CISP-BMEI51763.2020.9263602

16. Liu, W., et al.: Towards visually explaining variational autoencoders. In: Proceedings of the IEEE/CVF Conference on Computer Vision and Pattern Recognition (CVPR) (2020)

17. Middlehurst, M., Large, J., Flynn, M., Lines, J., Bostrom, A., Bagnall, A.: HIVE-COTE 2.0: a new meta ensemble for time series classification. Mach. Learn. **110** (2021). https://doi.org/10.1007/s10994-021-06057-9

18. Oh, C., Han, S., Jeong, J.: Time-series data augmentation based on interpolation. Procedia Comput. Sci. **175**, 64–71 (2020). https://doi.org/10.1016/j.procs.2020.07.012

19. Tolstikhin, I., Bousquet, O., Gelly, S., Schoelkopf, B.: Wasserstein auto-encoders. In: International Conference on Learning Representations (2018). https://openreview.net/forum?id=HkL7n1-0b

20. Wang, Z., Yan, W., Oates, T.: Time series classification from scratch with deep neural networks: a strong baseline. In: 2017 International Joint Conference on Neural Networks (IJCNN), pp. 1578–1585 (2017). https://doi.org/10.1109/IJCNN.2017.7966039

21. Yoo, J., Park, J., Wang, A., Mohaisen, D., Kim, J.: On the performance of generative adversarial network (GAN) variants: a clinical data study. In: 2020 International Conference on Information and Communication Technology Convergence (ICTC), pp. 100–104 (2020). https://doi.org/10.1109/ICTC49870.2020.9289248

22. Zhou, Z., Song, Y., Yu, L., Yu, Y.: Understanding the effectiveness of Lipschitz constraint in training of GANs via gradient analysis. CoRR abs/1807.00751 (2018). http://arxiv.org/abs/1807.00751

Safe Policy Improvement Approaches and Their Limitations

Philipp Scholl[1]($\boxtimes$), Felix Dietrich[2], Clemens Otte[3], and Steffen Udluft[3]

[1] Ludwig-Maximilians University, Munich, Germany
scholl@math.lmu.de
[2] Technical University of Munich, Munich, Germany
felix.dietrich@tum.de
[3] Siemens Technology, Munich, Germany
{clemens.otte,steffen.udluft}@siemens.com

Abstract. Safe Policy Improvement (SPI) is an important technique for offline reinforcement learning in safety critical applications as it improves the behavior policy with a high probability. We classify various SPI approaches from the literature into two groups, based on how they utilize the uncertainty of state-action pairs. Focusing on the Soft-SPIBB (Safe Policy Improvement with Soft Baseline Bootstrapping) algorithms, we show that their claim of being provably safe does not hold. Based on this finding, we develop adaptations, the Adv-Soft-SPIBB algorithms, and show that they are provably safe. A heuristic adaptation, Lower-Approx-Soft-SPIBB, yields the best performance among all SPIBB algorithms in extensive experiments on two benchmarks. We also check the safety guarantees of the provably safe algorithms and show that huge amounts of data are necessary such that the safety bounds become useful in practice.

Keywords: Risk-sensitive reinforcement learning · Safe policy improvement · Markov decision processes

1 Introduction

Reinforcement learning (RL) in industrial control applications such as gas turbine control [17] often requires learning solely from pre-recorded observational data (called offline or batch RL [4,9,12]) to avoid a potentially unsafe online exploration. This is especially necessary when simulations of the system are not available. Since it is difficult to assess the actual quality of the learned policy in this situation [6,24], Safe Policy Improvement (SPI) [14,23] is an attractive option. SPI aims to ensure that the learned policy is, with high probability, at least approximately as good as the behavioral policy given, for example, by a conventional controller.

In this paper, we review and benchmark current SPI algorithms and divide them into two classes. Among them, we focus on the class of Soft-SPIBB algorithms [14] and show that they are, contrary to the authors' claim, not provably safe. Therefore, we introduce the adaptation Adv-Approx-Soft-SPIBB. We also develop the heuristic Lower-Approx-Soft-SPIBB, following an idea presented in Laroche et al. [10]. Additionally, we conduct experiments to test these refined algorithms against their predecessors and other promising SPI algorithms. Here, our taxonomy of the SPI algorithms

© The Author(s), under exclusive license to Springer Nature Switzerland AG 2022
A. P. Rocha et al. (Eds.): ICAART 2022, LNAI 13786, pp. 74–98, 2022.
https://doi.org/10.1007/978-3-031-22953-4_4

is helpful, as the two classes of algorithms show different behavior. In summary, we extend observations from Scholl et al. [20] in several ways:

- We include a detailed presentation of the competitor SPI algorithms to equip the reader with an in-depth understanding of various SPI mechanisms and our taxonomy.
- We present the complete proof of the safety of Adv-Soft-SPIBB with further adaptations from the one from Nadjahi et al. [14] and discuss the usage of a tighter error bound (Maurer and Pontil [13]) to strengthen the safety theorem.
- We test empirically the error bounds of all provably safe algorithms to check their applicability and identify some limitations, as some algorithms need huge amounts of data to produce good policies while maintaining a meaningful error bound at the same time.

The code for the algorithms and experiments can be found in the accompanying repository.[1] The next section introduces the mathematical framework necessary for the later sections. Section 3 introduces other SPI algorithms, divides them into two classes and explains the most promising ones in more detail. In Sect. 4, we present the work done by Nadjahi et al. [14] and show that their algorithms are not provably safe. In Sect. 5, we refine the algorithms of Nadjahi et al. [14] and prove the safety of one of them. Tests against various competitors on two benchmarks are described in Sect. 6. The test for the usefulness of the safety guarantees is discussed in Sect. 7.

2 Mathematical Framework

The control problem we want to tackle with reinforcement learning consists of an agent and an environment, modeled as a finite Markov Decision Process (MDP). A finite MDP M^* is represented by the tuple $M^* = (\mathcal{S}, \mathcal{A}, P^*, R^*, \gamma)$, where $\mathcal{S}$ is the finite state space, $\mathcal{A}$ the finite action space, P^* the unknown transition probabilities, R^* the unknown stochastic reward function, the absolute value of which is assumed to be bounded by R_{max}, and $0 \leq \gamma < 1$ is the discount factor.

The agent chooses action $a \in \mathcal{A}$ with probability $\pi(a|s)$ in state $s \in \mathcal{S}$, where π is the policy controlling the agent. The return at time t is defined as the discounted sum of rewards $G_t = \sum_{i=t}^{T} \gamma^{i-t} R^*(s_i, a_i)$, with T the time of termination of the MDP. As the reward function is bounded the return is bounded as well, since $|G_t| \leq \frac{R_{max}}{1-\gamma}$. So, let G_{max} be a bound on the absolute value of the return. The goal is to find a policy π which optimizes the expected return, i.e., the state-value function $V_{M^*}^{\pi}(s) = E_{\pi}[G_t|S_t = s]$ for the initial state $s \in \mathcal{S}$. Similarly, the action-value function is defined as $Q_{M^*}^{\pi}(s, a) = E_{\pi}[G_t|S_t = s, A_t = a]$.

Given data $\mathcal{D} = (s_j, a_j, r_j, s_j')_{j=1,...,n}$ collected by the baseline policy π_b, let $N_{\mathcal{D}}(s, a)$ denote the number of visits of the state-action pair (s, a) in $\mathcal{D}$ and $\hat{M} = (\mathcal{S}, \mathcal{A}, \hat{P}, \hat{R}, \gamma)$ the Maximum Likelihood Estimator (MLE) of M^* where

$$\hat{P}(s'|s, a) = \frac{\sum_{(s_j=s,a_j=a,r_j,s_j'=s') \in \mathcal{D}} 1}{N_{\mathcal{D}}(s, a)} \text{ and } \hat{R}(s, a) = \frac{\sum_{(s_j=s,a_j=a,r_j,s_j') \in \mathcal{D}} r_j}{N_{\mathcal{D}}(s, a)}.$$

$$(1)$$

---

[1] https://github.com/Philipp238/Safe-Policy-Improvement-Approaches-on-Discrete-Markov-Decision-Processes.

3   Related Work

Safety is an overloaded term in Reinforcement Learning, because it can refer to the inherent uncertainty, safe exploration techniques, or parameter uncertainty [5]. In this paper we focus on the latter. In the following subsection we will introduce a taxonomy of SPI algorithms defined by us, and then go into detail for the most promising methods in the other subsections.

3.1   Taxonomy

Many existing Safe Policy Improvement (SPI) algorithms utilize the uncertainty of state-action pairs in one of the two following ways (see also Fig. 1):

1. The uncertainty is applied to the action-value function to decrease the value of uncertain actions. Therefore, these algorithms usually adapt the Policy Evaluation (PE) step.
2. The uncertainty is used to restrict the set of policies that can be learned. Therefore, these algorithms usually adapt the Policy Iteration (PI) step.

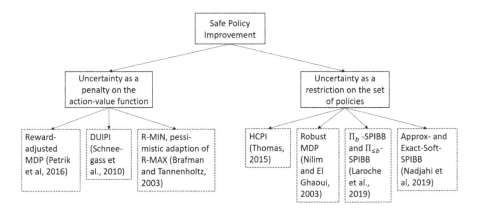

Fig. 1. Taxonomy of SPI algorithms [20].

In the remainder of this section we introduce all algorithms shown in Fig. 1, except for High Confidence Policy Improvement (HCPI) [23] and Robust MDP [15], as they have been shown in Laroche et al. [10] and Nadjahi et al. [14] to be not competitive in practice against many of the other SPI algorithms. We also do not introduce the Soft-SPIBB algorithms, as they are investigated in more detail in Sect. 4.

3.2 RaMDP

Petrik et al. [16] showed that maximizing the difference between the new policy and a baseline policy on a rectangular uncertainty set of the transition probabilities is NP-hard and, thus, derived the approximation Reward-adjusted MDP (RaMDP). RaMDP applies the uncertainty to penalize the reward and, therefore, the action-value function. Laroche et al. [10] extended this algorithm by a hyper-parameter which controls the influence of the uncertainty and modifies the reward matrix to incorporate the uncertainty in the following way:

$$\tilde{R}(s,a) = \hat{R}(s,a) - \frac{\kappa}{\sqrt{N_D(s,a)}}, \tag{2}$$

where $\kappa > 0$ is some hyper-parameter.

3.3 DUIPI

While RaMDP computes the uncertainty simply as a function of the number of visits to a state-action pair, Schneegass et al. [18] try a more sophisticated approach to estimate the uncertainty for Diagonal Approximation of Uncertainty Incorporating Policy Iteration (DUIPI) by approximating the variance of the action-value function.

Contrary to most other papers which reduce the reward function to $R : \mathcal{S} \times \mathcal{A} \rightarrow \mathbb{R}$, they consider

$$\hat{R}_3 : \mathcal{S} \times \mathcal{A} \times \mathcal{S} \rightarrow \mathbb{R}, \quad \hat{R}_3(s,a,s') = \frac{\sum_{(s_j=s,a_j=a,r_j,s'_j=s') \in \mathcal{D}} r_j}{N_D(s,a,s')}. \tag{3}$$

The calculation of the action-value function for some policy π in the MDP with the estimates $\hat{P}$ and $\hat{R}_3$ is classically done by Iterative Policy Evaluation, i.e., by inserting the estimate of the action-value function iteratively into the action Bellman equation [22]:

$$Q_{k+1}(s,a) = \sum_{s'} \hat{P}(s'|s,a)(\hat{R}_3(s,a,s') + \gamma \sum_{a'} \pi(a'|s')Q_k(s',a')). \tag{4}$$

The variance of Q is then also calculated iteratively by using uncertainty propagation, i.e., the fact that

$$\mathrm{Var}(f(X)) \approx D \, \mathrm{Var}(X) D^T \tag{5}$$

holds for a function $f : \mathbb{R}^m \rightarrow \mathbb{R}^n$ with Jacobian $D_{i,j} = \frac{\partial f_i}{\partial x_j}$. Schneegass et al. [18] present two different approaches in their paper, the first makes use of the complete covariance matrix, while the second neglects the correlations between state-action pairs. The authors show that the second approach is significantly faster and that the correlation is less important for MDPs with bigger state and action spaces. In the benchmark where it made a difference, there were 6 states with 2 actions and in the one where it did not matter anymore there were 18 states and 4 actions. As all benchmarks considered in this paper use MDPs which are greater than those two, we concentrate on the second approach called DUIPI (Diagonal Approximation of Uncertainty Incorporating Policy Iteration). By neglecting the covariances, Eq. 5 becomes

$$\text{Var}(f(X)) \approx \sum_i \left(\frac{\partial f}{\partial X_i} \right)^2 \text{Var}(X_i), \tag{6}$$

which should be read component-wise. Applying Eq. 6 to the action-value update in Eq. 4 yields

$$\text{Var}(Q^m(s,a)) \approx \sum_{s'} (D_{Q,Q}^m)^2 \left(\sum_{a'} \pi(a'|s')^2 \text{Var}(Q^{m-1}(s',a')) \right) \\ + \sum_{s'} D_{Q,\hat{P}}^m \text{Var}(\hat{P}(s'|s,a)) + \sum_{s'} D_{Q,\hat{R}_3}^m \text{Var}(\hat{R}_3(s,a,s'))) \tag{7}$$

with the derivatives

$$D_{Q,Q}^m = \gamma \hat{P}(s'|s,a), \; D_{Q,\hat{P}}^m = \hat{R}_3(s,a,s') + \gamma \sum_{a'} \pi(a'|s')^2 Q^{m-1}(s',a') \\ \text{and } D_{Q,\hat{R}_3}^m = \hat{P}(s'|s,a). \tag{8}$$

Equation 7 shows that the variance of the action-value function at the current step depends on the variance of the action-value function at the previous step and on the variance of the estimators $\hat{P}$ and $\hat{R}_3$.

To make use of the variance of the action-value function, which is simultaneously computed in the PE step, the authors propose to define

$$Q_u(s,a) = Q_{\hat{M}}^{\pi}(s,a) - \xi \sqrt{\text{Var}(Q_{\hat{M}}^{\pi}(s,a))} \tag{9}$$

and use the uncertainty incorporating action-value function Q_u instead of $Q_{\hat{M}}^{\pi}$ in the PI step. The policy is then chosen in a non greedy way, for details see Schneegass et al. [18]. By choosing $\xi > 0$, the uncertainty of one state-action pair has a negative influence on Q_u and the new policy prefers state-action pairs with a low variance.

Assuming that the variance is well approximated, even though uncertainty propagation is used and covariances between the state-action pairs are neglected, and a normal distribution as the prior for the action-value function is close to reality, yields a confidence interval on the real action-value function Q, as

$$\mathbb{P}(Q(s,a) > Q_u(s,a)) = 1 - F(\xi) \tag{10}$$

holds, with Q_u as defined in Eq. 9 and F as the CDF of a standard normal distribution [18].

One question that remains is how to determine the covariances of the estimators $\hat{P}$ and $\hat{R}_3$. The authors present a Bayesian approach applying the Dirichlet distribution as a prior for this, which will be used in this paper.

In the experiments in Sect. 6 we observed that DUIPI's estimation of the transition probabilities results in the possibility that unobserved state-action pairs are chosen, which is highly dangerous for safe reinforcement learning. For this reason we implemented a mechanism which checks if a state-action pair has been visited at least once in the training data and if it has not been visited, the probability of the new policy to choose this state-action pair will be set to 0 if possible. In our experiments this adjustment turned out to yield a strong performance improvement and, thus, we use only this new implementation of DUIPI for the experiments in the Sects. 6 and 7.

3.4 R-MIN

Brafman and Tannenholtz [1] introduce the R-MAX algorithm as a simple online algorithm for exploration. Its basic idea is to set the value of a state-action pair to the highest possible value, if it has not been visited more than $N_\wedge$ times yet, to encourage the algorithm to try these state-action pairs for an efficient exploration.

The problem considered in this paper is quite opposite to that. First of all, we are confronted with a batch offline learning problem. Furthermore, we are not interested in exploration but in safety. Consequently, we invert their technique and instead of setting the value of uncertain state-action pairs to the best possible value, we set it to the worst possible value, which is why we renamed the algorithm to R-MIN. The action-value function, thus, computes as

$$Q_{k+1}(s,a) = \begin{cases} \sum_{s',r} p(s',r|s,a)(r + \gamma \sum_{a'} \pi(a'|s')Q_k(s',a')), & \text{if } N_{\mathcal{D}}(s,a) > N_\wedge \\ \dfrac{R_{min}}{1-\gamma}, & \text{if } N_{\mathcal{D}}(s,a) \leq N_\wedge, \end{cases} \tag{11}$$

as $\frac{R_{min}}{1-\gamma}$ is the sharpest lower bound on the value function which works for any MDP, without any additional knowledge about its structure. Note that it is important to apply Eq. 11 in every iteration of the PE step and not only at the end, as the uncertainty of one state-action pair should also influence the value of state-action pairs leading to the uncertain one with a high probability.

3.5 SPIBB

Regarding algorithms restricting the policy set, Laroche et al. [10] only allow deviations from the baseline policy at a state-action pair if the uncertainty is low enough, otherwise it remains the same. To decide whether the uncertainty of a state-action pair is high, they only regard the times a state-action pair has been visited and use the bootstrapped set $\mathcal{B}$ as the set of uncertain state-action pairs, which has been visited less than some hyperparameter $N_\wedge$:

$$\mathcal{B} = \{(s,a) \in \mathcal{S} \times \mathcal{A} : N_{\mathcal{D}}(s,a) \leq N_\wedge\}. \tag{12}$$

Laroche et al. [10] propose two algorithms: Π_b-SPIBB, which is provably safe, and $\Pi_{\leq b}$-SPIBB, which is a heuristic relaxation. Π_b-SPIBB approximately solves the following optimization problem in its Policy Improvement step:

$$\pi' = \arg\max_\pi \sum_{a \in \mathcal{A}} Q^\pi_{\hat{M}}(s,a)\pi(a|s), \text{ subject to:} \tag{13a}$$

$$\pi'(\cdot|s) \text{ being a probability density over } \mathcal{A} \text{ and} \tag{13b}$$

$$\pi'(a|s) = \pi_b(a|s), \ \forall (s,a) \in \mathcal{B}. \tag{13c}$$

The fact that a policy computed by Π_b-SPIBB equals the behavior policy π_b for any state-action pair in the bootstrapped set, enables the authors to prove that Π_b-SPIBB produces policies π for which

$$V^\pi_{M^*}(s) - V^{\pi_b}_{M^*}(s) \geq -\frac{4V_{max}}{1-\gamma}\sqrt{\frac{2}{N_\wedge}\log\frac{2|\mathcal{S}||\mathcal{A}|2^{|\mathcal{S}|}}{\delta}} \tag{14}$$

holds with probability $1 - \delta$ for any state $s \in \mathcal{S}$.

Its heuristic variation $\Pi_{\leq b}$-SPIBB does not exhibit any theoretical safety. However, it performed even better than Π_b-SPIBB in their benchmarks. Its most concise description is probably via its optimization problem,

$$\pi' = \arg\max_\pi \sum_{a \in \mathcal{A}} Q^\pi_{\hat{M}}(s,a)\pi(a|s), \text{ subject to:} \tag{15a}$$

$$\pi'(\cdot|s) \text{ being a probability density over } \mathcal{A} \text{ and} \tag{15b}$$

$$\pi'(a|s) \leq \pi_b(a|s), \ \forall (s,a) \in \mathcal{B}. \tag{15c}$$

This problem only differs in its second constraint to the optimization problem corresponding to Π_b-SPIBB. While Π_b-SPIBB prohibits the change of the behavior policy for uncertain state-action pairs, $\Pi_{\leq b}$-SPIBB just does not allow to add more weight to them but allows to reduce it.

4   Safe Policy Improvement with Soft Baseline Bootstrapping

Nadjahi et al. [14] continue the line of work on the SPIBB algorithms and relax the hard bootstrapping to a softer version, where the baseline policy can be changed at any state-action pair, but the amount of possible change is limited by the uncertainty at this state-action pair. They claim that these new algorithms, called Safe Policy Improvement with Soft Baseline Bootstrapping (Soft-SPIBB), are also provably safe, a claim that is repeated in Simao et al. [21] and Leurent [11]. Furthermore, they extend the experiments from Laroche et al. [10] to include the Soft-SPIBB algorithms, where the empirical advantage of these algorithms becomes clear. However, after introducing the algorithms and the theory backing up their safety, we will show in Sect. 4.4 that they are in fact not provably safe, which motivates our adaptations in Sect. 5.

4.1   Preliminaries

To bound the performance of the new policy, it is necessary to bound the estimate of the transition probabilities $\hat{P}$. By applying Hoelder's inequality, Nadjahi et al. [14] show that

$$||P(\cdot|s,a) - \hat{P}(\cdot|s,a)||_1 \leq e_P(s,a), \tag{16}$$

holds with probability $1 - \delta$, where

$$e_P(s, a) = \sqrt{\frac{2}{N_{\mathcal{D}}(s, a)} \log \frac{2|\mathcal{S}||\mathcal{A}|2^{|\mathcal{A}|}}{\delta}}. \tag{17}$$

The error function is used to quantify the uncertainty of each state-action pair.

Definition 1. *A policy π is (π_b, ϵ, e)-constrained w.r.t. a baseline policy π_b, an error function e and a hyper-parameter $\epsilon > 0$, if*

$$\sum_{a \in \mathcal{A}} e(s, a)|\pi(a|s) - \pi_b(a|s)| \leq \epsilon \tag{18}$$

holds for all states $s \in \mathcal{S}$.

Therefore, if a policy π is (π_b, ϵ, e)-constrained, it means that the l^1-distance between π and π', weighted by some error function e, is at most ϵ.

4.2 Algorithms

The new class of algorithms Nadjahi et al. [14] introduce aims at solving the following constrained optimization problem during the Policy Improvement step:

$$\pi' = \arg\max_{\pi} \sum_{a \in \mathcal{A}} Q_{\hat{M}}^{\pi}(s, a)\pi(a|s), \text{ subject to:} \tag{19a}$$

$$\pi'(\cdot|s) \text{ being a probability density over } \mathcal{A} \text{ and} \tag{19b}$$

$$\pi^{(i+1)} \text{ being } (\pi_b, \epsilon, e)\text{-constrained.} \tag{19c}$$

This computation leads to the optimal—w.r.t. the action-value function of the previous policy—(π_b, ϵ, e)-constrained policy. The two algorithms introduced in Nadjahi et al. [14], which numerically solve this optimization problem, are Exact-Soft-SPIBB and Approx-Soft-SPIBB. The former solves the linear formulation of the constrained problem by a linear program [3] and the latter uses a budget calculation for the second constraint to compute an approximate solution. In experiments, it is shown that both algorithms achieve similar performance, but Exact-Soft-SPIBB takes considerably more time [14].

4.3 The Safety Guarantee

Nadjahi et al. [14] derive the theoretical safety of their algorithms from two theorems. The first theorem, however, needs an additional property their algorithms do not fulfill. For that reason we will move its discussion to Sect. 5, where we will also introduce refined algorithms which fulfill said property. To make up for this property, Nadjahi et al. [14] use Assumption 1 to prove Theorem 1.

Assumption 1. *There exists a constant $\kappa < \frac{1}{\gamma}$ such that, for all state-action pairs $(s, a) \in \mathcal{S} \times \mathcal{A}$, the following holds:*

$$\sum_{s',a'} e_P(s', a')\pi_b(a'|s')P^*(s'|s, a) \leq \kappa e_P(s, a) \tag{20}$$

Interpreting $\pi_b(a'|s')P^*(s'|s, a)$ as the probability of observing the state-action pair (s', a') after observing (s, a) we can rewrite Eq. 20 to

$$E_{P,\pi_b}[e_P(S_{t+1}, A_{t+1})|S_t = s, A_t = a] \leq \kappa e_P(s, a), \tag{21}$$

which shows that Assumption 1 assumes an upper bound on the uncertainty of the next state-action pair dependent on the uncertainty of the current one. Intuitively this makes sense, but we show in the next section that the bound does not hold in general. However, using this assumption Nadjahi et al. [14] prove Theorem 1 which omits the advantageous assumption of the new policy.

Theorem 1. *Under Assumption 1, any (π_b, ϵ, e_P)-constrained policy π satisfies the following inequality in every state s with probability at least $1 - \delta$:*

$$V_{M^*}^\pi(s) - V_{M^*}^{\pi_b}(s) \geq V_{\hat{M}}^\pi(s) - V_{\hat{M}}^{\pi_b}(s)+$$

$$2||d_M^\pi(\cdot|s) - d_M^{\pi_b}(\cdot|s)||_1 V_{max} - \frac{1+\gamma}{(1-\gamma)^2(1-\kappa\gamma)}\epsilon V_{max} \tag{22}$$

Here, $d_M^\pi(s'|s) = \sum_{t=0}^{\infty} \gamma^t \mathbb{P}(S_t = s'|S_t \sim P\pi S_{t-1}, S_0 = s)$ denotes the expected discounted sum of visits to s' when starting in s.

4.4   Shortcomings of the Theory

As explained above, the theoretical guarantees, Nadjahi et al. [14] claim for the Soft-SPIBB algorithms, stem from Theorem 1. However, we now show that Assumption 1 does not hold for any $0 < \gamma < 1$.

Theorem 2. *Let the discount factor $0 < \gamma < 1$ be arbitrary. Then there exists an MDP M with transition probabilities P such that for any behavior policy π_b and any data set $\mathcal{D}$, which contains every state-action pair at least once, it holds that, for all $0 < \delta < 1$,*

$$\sum_{s',a'} e_P(s', a')\pi_b(a'|s')P(s'|s, a) > \frac{1}{\gamma}e_P(s, a). \tag{23}$$

This means that Assumption 1 can, independent of the discount factor, not be true for all MDPs.

Proof. Let $0 < \gamma < 1$ be arbitrary and $n \in \mathbb{N}$ be such that $\sqrt{n} > \frac{1}{\gamma}$. Let M be the MDP displayed in Fig. 2. It has $n + 1$ states, from which n states are terminal states, labeled 1, 2, ..., n. In the only non-terminal state 0, there is only one action available and choosing it results in any of the terminal states with probability $\frac{1}{n}$. As there is only

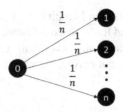

Fig. 2. MDP with $n + 1$ states, n of them are final states and in the non-final state, there is only 1 action, leading to one of the others with equal probability [20].

one action, one can omit the action in the notation of e_P and there is only one possible behavior policy. So, Eq. 23 can be reduced to

$$\sum_{i=1}^{n} \frac{e_P(i)}{n} > \frac{e_P(0)}{\gamma}. \tag{24}$$

Now, we show that

$$\sum_{i=1}^{n} \frac{e_P(i)}{n} \geq \sqrt{n} e_P(0), \tag{25}$$

which implies Eq. 24 as $\sqrt{n} > \frac{1}{\gamma}$. Let $\mathcal{D}$ denote the data collected on this MDP such that every state has been visited at least once. Thus, $N_{\mathcal{D}}(i) > 0$—the number of visits to state i—holds for every i. Equation 25 is equivalent to

$$\frac{1}{n} \sum_{i=1}^{n} \frac{1}{\sqrt{N_{\mathcal{D}}(i)}} \geq \frac{\sqrt{n}}{\sqrt{N}} \tag{26}$$

where $N = N_{\mathcal{D}}(0) = \sum_{i=1}^{n} N_{\mathcal{D}}(i)$. Equation 26 follows by applying Jensen's inequality once for the convex function $x \mapsto \frac{1}{x}$, restricted to $x > 0$, and once for the concave function $x \mapsto \sqrt{x}$, also restricted to $x > 0$:

$$\frac{1}{n} \sum_{i=1}^{n} \frac{1}{\sqrt{N_{\mathcal{D}}(i)}} \geq \frac{1}{\frac{1}{n} \sum_{i=1}^{n} \sqrt{N_{\mathcal{D}}(i)}} \geq \frac{1}{\sqrt{\frac{1}{n} \sum_{i=1}^{n} N_{\mathcal{D}}(i)}} = \frac{1}{\sqrt{\frac{N}{n}}} = \frac{\sqrt{n}}{\sqrt{N}}.$$

This concludes the proof.

The class of MDPs used in the proof and depicted in Fig. 2 gives a good impression what kind of constellations are critical for Assumption 1. An MDP does not have to exhibit exactly the same structure to have similar effects, it might already be enough if there is a state-action pair from which a lot of different state-action pairs are exclusively accessible.

Although Assumption 1 is invalid in its generality shown at some specific class of MDPs, it might still hold on simple MDPs which are not built in order to disprove Assumption 1. One consideration here is that n does not need to be especially big as the proof only required $\sqrt{n} > \frac{1}{\gamma}$. So, for any $\gamma > \frac{1}{\sqrt{2}} \approx 0.707$ it suffices to choose $n = 2$.

Furthermore, we tested Assumption 1 empirically on the Random MDPs benchmark considered in [14] where we found for no discount factor greater than 0.6 a baseline policy and data set such that the assumption holds for all state-action pairs.[2] Consequently, we conclude that Assumption 1 is not reasonable and, thus, Theorem 1 cannot be relied upon.

5   Advantageous Soft-SPIBB

In the last section we have shown that there is no safety guarantee for the Soft-SPIBB algorithms. However, Nadjahi et al. [14] proved another theorem which we present in its corrected form together with adapted algorithms to which it is applicable.

5.1   Preliminaries

We follow Nadjahi et al. [14] and define the error function e_Q as

$$e_Q(s,a) = \sqrt{\frac{2}{N_{\mathcal{D}}(s,a)} \log \frac{2|\mathcal{S}||\mathcal{A}|}{\delta}}, \tag{27}$$

since that way we can bound the difference between the true action-value function and its estimate. Contrary to them, we use a different estimate as the bound again relies on Hoeffding's inequality [8] which can only be applied to a sum of random variables and, to the best of our knowledge, we do not know how it can be applied to $Q_M^{\pi_b}(s,a)$.

For our proof it is necessary to use the Monte-Carlo estimate for $Q_M^{\pi_b}(s,a)$ from data $\mathcal{D}$

$$\hat{Q}_{\mathcal{D}}^{\pi_b}(s,a) = \frac{1}{n} \sum_{i=1}^{n} G_{t_i} \tag{28}$$

where $t_1, ..., t_n$ are times such that $(S_{t_i}, A_{t_i}) = (s, a)$, for all $i = 1, ..., n$. As $E[G_{t_i}] = Q_M^{\pi_b}(s,a)$ it is possible to apply the Hoeffding's inequality for $\hat{Q}_{\mathcal{D}}^{\pi_b}$, similar to how it is done in Nadjahi et al. [14].

Lemma 1. *For e_Q as defined in Eq. 27, it holds for an arbitrary MDP M with G_{max} as an upper bound on the absolute value of the return in any state-action pair of any policy and behavior policy π_b, that*

$$\mathbb{P}_{\mathcal{D}}\left(\forall (s,a) \in \mathcal{S} \times \mathcal{A} : |Q_M^{\pi_b}(s,a) - \hat{Q}_{\mathcal{D}}^{\pi_b}(s,a)| \le e_Q(s,a)G_{max}\right) \ge 1 - \delta, \tag{29}$$

if the G_{t_i} used to estimate $\hat{Q}_{\mathcal{D}}^{\pi_b}(s,a)$ are independent. Here, the subscript $\mathcal{D}$ of $\mathbb{P}$ emphasizes that the dataset generated by π_b is the random quantity.

---

[2] https://github.com/Philipp238/Safe-Policy-Improvement-Approaches-on-Discrete-Markov-Decision-Processes/blob/master/auxiliary_tests/assumption_test.py.

Proof. First, note that Hoeffding's inequality implies that

$$\mathbb{P}(|\sum_{i=1}^{n} X_i - E[\sum_{i=1}^{n} X_i]| \geq t) \leq 2\exp(-2nt^2), \tag{30}$$

for $X_i \in [0,1]$ independent. Fix the state-action pair $(s,a) \in \mathcal{S} \times \mathcal{A}$. Then,

$$\mathbb{P}_{\mathcal{D}}\left(\left|Q_M^{\pi_b}(s,a) - \hat{Q}_{\mathcal{D}}^{\pi_b}(s,a)\right| > e_Q(s,a)G_{max}\right)$$

$$= \mathbb{P}_{\mathcal{D}}\left(\left|\frac{(Q_M^{\pi_b}(s,a) + G_{max}) - (\hat{Q}_{\mathcal{D}}^{\pi_b}(s,a) + G_{max})}{2G_{max}}\right| > \sqrt{\frac{1}{2N_{\mathcal{D}}(s,a)}\log\frac{2|\mathcal{S}||\mathcal{A}|}{\delta}}\right)$$

$$\leq 2\exp\left(-2N_{\mathcal{D}}(s,a)\frac{1}{2N_{\mathcal{D}}(s,a)}\log\frac{2|\mathcal{S}||\mathcal{A}|}{\delta}\right) = \frac{\delta}{|\mathcal{S}||\mathcal{A}|}, \tag{31}$$

where it is possible to apply Hoeffding's inequality in the second step since

$$\frac{\hat{Q}_{\mathcal{D}}^{\pi_b}(s,a) + G_{max}}{2G_{max}} = \frac{1}{n}\sum_{i=1}^{n}\frac{G_{t_i} + G_{max}}{2G_{max}} \tag{32}$$

is the empirical mean of independent variables which are bounded in $[0,1]$ as G_{t_i} are independent and bounded in $[-G_{max}, G_{max}]$ and

$$E[\hat{Q}_{\mathcal{D}}^{\pi_b}(s,a)] = E[G_{t_i}] = Q_M^{\pi_b}(s,a). \tag{33}$$

Another change in this inequality compared to Nadjahi et al. [14] is, that we get G_{max} instead of V_{max}, since G_t does in general not lie in the interval $[-V_{max}, V_{max}]$.

The first theorem from Nadjahi et al. [14] relies on the algorithms to produce *advantageous* policies. This property has to be slightly generalized to make it applicable to the Monte Carlo estimate of the action value function.

Definition 2. *A policy π is π_b-advantageous w.r.t. the function $Q : \mathcal{S} \times \mathcal{A} \to \mathbb{R}$, if*

$$\sum_a Q(s,a)\pi(a|s) \geq \sum_a Q(s,a)\pi_b(a|s) \tag{34}$$

holds for all states $s \in \mathcal{S}$.

Interpreting Q as an action-value function, Definition 2 yields that the policy π chooses higher-valued actions than policy π' for every state.

5.2 Algorithms

In this subsection we introduce the adaptation Adv-Approx-Soft-SPIBB which produces (π_b, e_Q, ϵ)-constrained and π_b-advantageous w.r.t. $\hat{Q}_{\mathcal{D}}^{\pi_b}$ policies and is, thus, provably safe by Theorem 3 in Sect. 4.3. Additionally, we present the heuristic adaptation Lower-Approx-Soft-SPIBB. As both algorithms function similarly to their predecessors by constraining the policy set, they also belong to the category "Uncertainty as a restriction on the set of policies" in the taxonomy in Fig. 1.

Adv-Approx-Soft-SPIBB. The advantageous version of the Soft-SPIBB algorithms solves the following problem in the Policy Improvement (PI) step:

$$\pi' = \arg\max_{\pi} \sum_{a \in \mathcal{A}} Q_{\hat{M}}^{\pi}(s, a)\pi(a|s), \text{ subject to:} \tag{35a}$$

$$\pi'(\cdot|s) \text{ being a probability density over } \mathcal{A}, \tag{35b}$$

$$\pi^{(i+1)} \text{ being } (\pi_b, \epsilon, e)\text{-constrained and} \tag{35c}$$

$$\pi^{(i+1)} \text{ being } \pi_b\text{-advantageous w.r.t. } \hat{Q}_{\mathcal{D}}^{\pi_b}. \tag{35d}$$

The original Soft-SPIBB algorithms solve this optimization problem without the constraint in Eq. 35d as shown in Sect. 4.2. Adv-Approx-Soft-SPIBB works exactly as its predecessor Approx-Soft-SPIBB except that it keeps an additional budgeting variable ensuring that the new policy is π_b-advantageous w.r.t. $\hat{Q}_{\mathcal{D}}^{\pi_b}$. The derivation of a successor algorithm of Exact-Soft-SPIBB is straightforward since the constraint in Eq. 35d is linear, however, we observed for Exact-Soft-SPIBB and its successor numerical issues, so, we omit them in the experiments in Sect. 6.

Lower-Approx-Soft-SPIBB. To introduce the heuristic adaptation of Approx-Soft-SPIBB we need a relaxed version of the constrainedness property.

Definition 3. *A policy π is (π_b, ϵ, e)-lower-constrained w.r.t. a baseline policy π_b, an error function e, and a hyper-parameter ϵ, if*

$$\sum_{a \in \mathcal{A}} e(s, a) \max\{0, \pi(a|s) - \pi_b(a|s)\} \le \epsilon \tag{36}$$

holds for all states $s \in \mathcal{S}$.

This definition does not punish a change in uncertain state-action pairs if the probability of choosing it is decreased, which follows the same logic as the empirically very successful adaptation $\Pi_{\le b}$-SPIBB [10]. The optimization problem solved by Lower-Approx-Soft-SPIBB is the following:

$$\pi' = \arg\max_{\pi} \sum_{a \in \mathcal{A}} Q_{\hat{M}}^{\pi}(s, a)\pi(a|s), \text{ subject to:} \tag{37a}$$

$$\pi'(\cdot|s) \text{ being a probability density over } \mathcal{A} \text{ and} \tag{37b}$$

$$\pi^{(i+1)} \text{ being } (\pi_b, \epsilon, e)\text{-lower-constrained.} \tag{37c}$$

Even though Lower-Approx-Soft-SPIBB is—just as its predecessor Approx-Soft-SPIBB—not provably safe, the experiments in Sect. 6 show that it performs empirically the best out of the whole SPIBB family.

5.3   Safety Guarantee

In this subsection, we prove Theorem 3 which states that algorithms that pro-
duce (π_b, ϵ, e_Q)-constrained policies which are π_b-advantageous w.r.t. $\hat{Q}_{\mathcal{D}}^{\pi_b}$—as Adv-
Approx-Soft-SPIBB does—are safe. Before that, it is necessary to introduce some nota-
tion from the predecessor paper [10]. To enable the use of matrix operations all the
quantities introduced so far are denoted as vectors and matrices in the following. The
value functions become

$$Q^\pi = (Q^\pi(1,1), ..., Q^\pi(1,|\mathcal{A}|), Q^\pi(2,1), ..., Q^\pi(|\mathcal{S}|,|\mathcal{A}|)) \in \mathbb{R}^{|\mathcal{S}||\mathcal{A}|} \qquad (38)$$

and

$$V^\pi = (V^\pi(1), ..., V^\pi(|\mathcal{S}|)) \in \mathbb{R}^{|\mathcal{S}|}. \qquad (39)$$

Similarly, the reward vector is

$$R = (R(1,1), ..., R(1,|\mathcal{A}|), R(2,1), ..., R(|\mathcal{S}|,|\mathcal{A}|)) \in \mathbb{R}^{|\mathcal{S}||\mathcal{A}|}. \qquad (40)$$

The policy is denoted by

$$\pi = (\pi_{\cdot 1} ... \pi_{\cdot |\mathcal{S}|}) \in \mathbb{R}^{|\mathcal{S}||\mathcal{A}| \times |\mathcal{S}|}, \qquad (41)$$

with columns $\pi_{kj} = \pi(k|j)$ for $(j-1)|\mathcal{A}| + 1 \le k \le j|\mathcal{A}|$ and $\pi_{kj} = 0$ otherwise.
Lastly, the transition probabilities are

$$P = \begin{pmatrix} P(1|1,1) & \cdots & P(1|1,|\mathcal{A}|) & \cdots & P(1||\mathcal{S}|,|\mathcal{A}|) \\ \vdots & & \vdots & & \vdots \\ P(|\mathcal{S}||1,1) & \cdots & P(|\mathcal{S}||1,|\mathcal{A}|) & \cdots & P(|\mathcal{S}|||\mathcal{S}|,|\mathcal{A}|) \end{pmatrix} \in \mathbb{R}^{|\mathcal{S}| \times |\mathcal{S}||\mathcal{A}|}. \quad (42)$$

Note that we omit the current MDP M in all these notations, as we always do, if it is
clear or not relevant which MDP is currently used. Using this notation, we can present
Proposition 1 without its proof from Nadjahi et al. [14].

Proposition 1. *Let π_1 and π_2 be two policies on an MDP M. Then*

$$V_M^{\pi_1} - V_M^{\pi_2} = Q_M^{\pi_2}(\pi_1 - \pi_2)d_M^{\pi_1} \qquad (43)$$

holds.

Proposition 1 yields a decomposition of the difference of the state value function for
two different policies on the same MDP which is utilized to prove the corrected version
of Theorem 1 from Nadjahi et al. [14].

Theorem 3. *For any (π_b, ϵ, e_Q)-constrained policy that is π_b-advantageous w.r.t. $\hat{Q}_{\mathcal{D}}^{\pi_b}$,
which is estimated with independent returns for each state-action pair, the following
inequality holds:*

$$\mathbb{P}_{\mathcal{D}}\left(\forall s \in \mathcal{S} : V_{M^*}^\pi(s) - V_{M^*}^{\pi_b}(s) \ge -\frac{\epsilon G_{max}}{1-\gamma}\right) \ge 1 - \delta,$$

*where M^* is the true MDP on which the data $\mathcal{D}$ gets sampled by the baseline policy π_b,
$0 \le \gamma < 1$ is the discount factor, and $\delta > 0$ is the safety parameter for e_Q.*

Proof. We start by applying Proposition 1:

$$V_M^\pi - V_M^{\pi_b} = Q_M^{\pi_b}(\pi - \pi_b)d_M^\pi = (Q_M^{\pi_b} - \hat{Q}_D^{\pi_b} + \hat{Q}_D^{\pi_b})(\pi - \pi_b)d_M^\pi$$
$$= (Q_M^{\pi_b} - \hat{Q}_D^{\pi_b})(\pi - \pi_b)d_M^\pi + \hat{Q}_D^{\pi_b}(\pi - \pi_b)d_M^\pi. \tag{44}$$

The goal of this proof is to lower bound these two summands. For the first summand, notice that it is a row vector and, so, a bound on the ℓ^1 norm gives a simultaneous bound for all states. Thus, applying a vector-matrix version of Hoelder's inequality, which is proven in Lemma 2 later on, yields

$$||(Q_M^{\pi_b} - \hat{Q}_D^{\pi_b})(\pi - \pi_b)d_M^\pi||_1 \le ||((Q_M^{\pi_b} - \hat{Q}_D^{\pi_b})(\pi - \pi_b))^T||_\infty ||d_M^\pi||_1, \tag{45}$$

where all the norms refer to matrix norms. Using Lemma 1 and that π is (π_b, e_Q, ϵ)-constrained yields that

$$|| \left((Q_M^{\pi_b} - \hat{Q}_D^{\pi_b})(\pi - \pi_b)\right)^T ||_\infty \le \max_s \sum_a |Q_M^{\pi_b}(s,a) - \hat{Q}_D^{\pi_b}(s,a)||\pi(a|s) - \pi_b(a|s)|$$

$$\le \max_s \sum_a e_Q(s,a)G_{max}|\pi(a|s) - \pi_b(a|s)| \le \epsilon G_{max} \tag{46}$$

holds with probability $1 - \delta$. The next step is to compute

$$||d_M^\pi||_1 = \max_s \sum_{s'} \sum_{t=0}^\infty \gamma^t \mathbb{P}(S_t = s'|X_t \sim P\pi S_t, S_0 = s)$$

$$= \max_s \sum_{t=0}^\infty \gamma^t \sum_{s'} \mathbb{P}(S_t = s'|X_t \sim P\pi S_t, S_0 = s) = \max_s \sum_{t=0}^\infty \gamma^t = \frac{1}{1-\gamma}. \tag{47}$$

Thus, the first summand can be lower bounded by $-\frac{\epsilon G_{max}}{1-\gamma}$ with probability $1 - \delta$. To lower bound the second summand, note that all entries of d_M^π are non-negative, so Theorem 3 follows if $\hat{Q}_D^{\pi_b}(\pi - \pi_b)(s) \ge 0$ for every state $s \in \mathcal{S}$. So, let $s \in \mathcal{S}$ be arbitrary. Then,

$$\hat{Q}_D^{\pi_b}(\pi - \pi_b)(s) = \sum_a \hat{Q}_D^{\pi_b}(s,a)(\pi(a|s) - \pi_b(a|s)) \ge 0 \tag{48}$$

holds, since π is π_b-advantageous w.r.t. $\hat{Q}_D^{\pi_b}$.

As mentioned in the proof, it remains to show that the inequality in Eq. 45 holds.

Lemma 2. *Let $n \in \mathbb{N}$, $v \in \mathbb{R}^n$ and $A \in \mathbb{R}^{n\times n}$ be arbitrary. Then,*

$$||v^T A||_1 \le ||v||_\infty ||A||_1 \tag{49}$$

holds, where all norms refer to matrix norms.

Proof. Denote the columns of A by $a^1, ..., a^n$. Then,

$$||v^T A||_1 = ||(v^T a^1, ..., v^T a^n)||_1 = \max_{i=1,...,n} \{|v^T a^i|\}$$
$$\leq \max_{i=1,...,n} \{||v||_\infty ||a^i||_1\} = ||v||_\infty \max_{i=1,...,n} \{||a^i||_1\} = ||v||_\infty ||A||_1 \tag{50}$$

where we used the definition of the ℓ^1 norm for matrices as the maximum absolute column sum in the second and the last step and Hoeffding's inequality in the third step.

One possibility to improve Theorem 3 is to increase the sharpness of the error function. For this, note that for Theorem 3 it is sufficient that the error function fulfills the inequality from Lemma 1. One disadvantage of using Hoeffding's inequality to define the error function e_Q as in Eq. 27 is that it only incorporates the number of observations to estimate the uncertainty, while it neglects additional knowledge of the data, e.g., its variance. It should be clear that less observations of a quantity are necessary to estimate it with high confidence, if the quantity has a low variance. This is incorporated in the bound derived by Maurer and Pontil [13].

Lemma 3 (*Maurer and Pontil*). *Let $X_1, ..., X_n$ be i.i.d. variables with values in $[0, 1]$ and denote with X the random vector $X = (X_1, ..., X_n)$. Then,*

$$\mathbb{P}\left(\bar{X} - E[\bar{X}] \leq \sqrt{\frac{2\widehat{\mathrm{Var}}(X) \log \frac{2}{\delta}}{n}} + \frac{7 \log \frac{2}{\delta}}{3(n-1)}\right) \geq 1 - \delta \tag{51}$$

for any $\delta > 0$. Here, $\widehat{\mathrm{Var}}(X) = \frac{1}{n(n-1)} \sum_{1 \leq i < j \leq n}(Z_i - Z_j)^2$ denotes the sample variance.

Following Lemma 3 we define

$$e_Q^B(s, a) = 2\left(\sqrt{\frac{2\widehat{\mathrm{Var}}(\frac{G}{2G_{max}}) \log(\frac{4|\mathcal{S}||\mathcal{A}|}{\delta})}{N_{\mathcal{D}}(s, a)}} + \frac{7 \log(\frac{4|\mathcal{S}||\mathcal{A}|}{\delta})}{3(N_{\mathcal{D}}(s, a) - 1)}\right) \tag{52}$$

with $G = (G_{t_1}, ..., G_{t_n})$. With exactly the same proof as for Lemma 1 for e_Q, it is possible to show the same inequality for e_Q^B, if one applies the empirical version of Bennett's inequality instead of Hoeffding's inequality:

Lemma 4. *For e_Q^B as defined in Eq. 52, it holds for an arbitrary MDP M with G_{max} as an upper bound on the absolute value of the return in any state-action pair of any policy and behavior policy π_b, that*

$$\mathbb{P}_{\mathcal{D}}\left(\forall (s, a) \in \mathcal{S} \times \mathcal{A} : |Q_M^{\pi_b}(s, a) - \hat{Q}_{\mathcal{D}}^{\pi_b}(s, a)| \leq e_Q^B(s, a)G_{max}\right) \geq 1 - \delta, \tag{53}$$

if the G_{t_i} used to estimate $\hat{Q}_{\mathcal{D}}^{\pi_b}$ are independent.

The advantage of this new error function is the improved asymptotic bound, especially for low variance returns. There are also two disadvantages. The first is that if only a few observations are available, the bound is worse than the bound achieved by the Hoeffding's bound. The second is that the value G_{max} is used in the definition of e_Q^B. However, the maximal return is not necessarily known. There are various possible approaches to solve this issue. Either by estimating it from the observations G_t, lower bounding it by $\frac{1}{2}(\max_t G_t - \min_t G_t)$ or approximating it using $\frac{R_{max}}{1-\gamma}$. The first approach might be very accurate in practice when enough data is available, the second approach might be less powerful, however, Lemma 3 is certain to hold for any lower bound on G_{max} and $\frac{R_{max}}{1-\gamma}$ might be a good a priori known approximation for some MDPs and it would also work to substitute G_{max} in this whole theory by $\frac{R_{max}}{1-\gamma}$, which makes also Theorem 3 more interpretable but less powerful.

In Sect. 7 we empirically investigate how the error function relying on the Maurer and Pontil bound compare to the one relying on Hoeffding's bound.

6 Experiments

We test the adapted Soft-SPIBB algorithms against Basic RL (classical Dynamic Programming [22] on the MLE MDP $\hat{M}$), Approx-Soft-SPIBB [14], its predecessors Π_b- and $\Pi_{\leq b}$-SPIBB [10], DUIPI [18], RaMDP [16] and R-MIN, the pessimistic adaptation of R-MAX [1].

Since the adaptation of DUIPI to avoid unknown state-action pairs, as described in Sect. 3.3, proved in these experiments to be an important and consistent improvement, we display only the results of this adaptation of DUIPI in Sect. 6.2. We also checked if the error function relying on the bound by Maurer and Pontil [13] improved the performance of the Soft-SPIBB algorithms. However, it did not provide a significant improvement and, thus, we also only show the results for the algorithms applying the error function based on Hoeffding's inequality.

6.1 Experimental Settings

We use two different benchmarks for our comparison. The first one is the Random MDPs benchmark already used in Laroche et al. [10] and Nadjahi et al. [14]. As the second benchmark we use the Wet Chicken benchmark [7] which depicts a more realistic scenario.

We perform a grid-search to choose the optimal hyper-parameter for each algorithm for both benchmarks. Our choices can be found in the table below. The hyper-parameter selection is the main difference to the experiments we conduct in Sect. 7 as the hyper-parameters here are solely optimized for performance without considerations of the safety guarantees, while we choose the hyper-parameter in Sect. 7 such that the bounds are meaningful.

In both experiments we conduct $10,000$ iterations for each algorithm. As we are interested in Safe Policy Improvement, we follow Chow et al. [2], Laroche et al. [10], and Nadjahi et al. [14] and consider besides the mean performance also the 1%-CVaR (Critical Value at Risk) performance, which is the mean performance over the worst 1% of the runs.

Table 1. Chosen hyper-parameters for both benchmarks [20].

Algorithms	Random MDPs	Wet Chicken
Basic RL	–	–
RaMDP	$\kappa = 0.05$	$\kappa = 2$
R-MIN	$N_\wedge = 3$	$N_\wedge = 3$
DUIPI	$\xi = 0.1$	$\xi = 0.5$
Π_b-SPIBB	$N_\wedge = 10$	$N_\wedge = 7$
$\Pi_{\leq b}$-SPIBB	$N_\wedge = 10$	$N_\wedge = 7$
Approx-Soft-SPIBB	$\delta = 1, \epsilon = 2$	$\delta = 1, \epsilon = 1$
Adv-Approx-Soft-SPIBB (ours)	$\delta = 1, \epsilon = 2$	$\delta = 1, \epsilon = 1$
Lower-Approx-Soft-SPIBB (ours)	$\delta = 1, \epsilon = 1$	$\delta = 1, \epsilon = 0.5$

Random MDP Benchmark. First we consider the grid-world like Random MDPs benchmark introduced in Nadjahi et al. [14] which generates a new MDP in each iteration. The generated MDPs consist of 50 states, including an initial state (denoted by 0) and a final state. In every non-terminal state there are four actions available and choosing one leads to four possible next states. All transitions yield zero reward except upon entering the terminal state, which gives a reward of 1. As the discount factor is chosen as $\gamma = 0.95$, maximizing the return is equivalent to finding the shortest route to the terminal state.

The baseline policy on each MDP is computed such that its performance is approximately $\rho_{\pi_b} = V_{M^*}^{\pi_b}(0) = \eta V_{M^*}^{\pi_*}(0) + (1 - \eta)V_{M^*}^{\pi_u}(0)$, where $0 \leq \eta \leq 1$ is the baseline performance target ratio interpolating between the performance of the optimal policy π_* and the uniform policy π_u. The generation of the baseline policy starts with a softmax on the optimal action-value function and continues with adding random noise to it, until the desired performance is achieved [14]. To counter the effects from incorporating knowledge about the optimal policy, the MDP is altered after the generation of the baseline policy by transforming one regular state to a terminal one which also yields a reward of 1.

The performances are normalized to make them more comparable between different runs by calculating $\bar{\rho}_\pi = \frac{\rho_\pi - \rho_{\pi_b}}{\rho_{\pi_*} - \rho_{\pi_b}}$. Thus, $\bar{\rho}_\pi < 0$ means a worse performance than the baseline policy, $\bar{\rho}_\pi > 0$ means an improvement w.r.t. the baseline policy and $\bar{\rho}_\pi = 1$ means the optimal performance was reached.

Wet Chicken Benchmark. The second experiment uses the more realistic Wet Chicken benchmark [7] because of its heterogeneous stochasticity. Figure 3 visualizes the setting of the Wet Chicken benchmark. The basic idea behind it is that a person floats in a small boat on a river. The river has a waterfall at one end and the goal of the person is to stay as close to the waterfall as possible without falling down. Thus, the closer the person gets to the waterfall the higher the reward gets, but upon falling down they start again at the starting place, which is as far away from the waterfall as possible. It is modeled as a non-episodic MDP.

The whole river has a length and width of 5, so, there are 25 states. The starting point is $(x, y) = (0, 0)$ and the waterfall is at $x = 5$. The position of the person at time

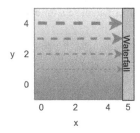

Fig. 3. The setting of the Wet Chicken benchmark used for reinforcement learning. The boat starts at $(x, y) = (0, 0)$ and starts there again upon falling down the waterfall at $x = 5$. The arrows show the direction and strength of the stream towards the waterfall. Additionally, turbulence is stronger for small y. The goal for the boat is to stay as close as possible to the waterfall without falling down [20].

t is denoted by the pair (x_t, y_t). The river itself has a turbulence ($b_t = 3.5 - v_t$) which is stronger for small y and a stream ($v_t = y_t \frac{3}{5}$) towards the waterfall which is stronger for larger y. The effect of the turbulence is stochastic; so, let $\tau_t \sim U(-1, 1)$ be the parameter describing the stochasticity of the turbulence at time t.

The person can choose from five actions listed below with a_x and a_y describing the influence of an action on x_t and y_t, respectively:

- Drift: The person does nothing, $(a_x, a_y) = (0, 0)$.
- Hold: The person paddles back with half their power $(a_x, a_y) = (-1, 0)$.
- Paddle back: The person wholeheartedly paddles back, $(a_x, a_y) = (-2, 0)$.
- Right: The person goes to the right parallel to the waterfall, $(a_x, a_y) = (0, 1)$.
- Left: The person goes to the left parallel to the waterfall, $(a_x, a_y) = (0, -1)$.

The new position of the person assuming no river constraints is then calculated by

$$(\hat{x}, \hat{y}) = (\text{round}(x_t + a_x + v_t + \tau_t b_t), \text{round}(x_t + a_y)), \tag{54}$$

where the $round$ function is the usual one, i.e., a number is getting rounded down if the first decimal is 4 or less and rounded up otherwise. Incorporating the boundaries of the river yields the new position as

$$x_{t+1} = \begin{cases} \hat{x}, & \text{if } 0 \leq \hat{x} \leq 4 \\ 0, & \text{otherwise} \end{cases} \quad \text{and} \quad y_{t+1} = \begin{cases} 0, & \text{if } \hat{x} > 4 \\ 4, & \text{if } \hat{y} > 4 \\ 0, & \text{if } \hat{y} > 0 \\ \hat{y}, & \text{otherwise} \end{cases}. \tag{55}$$

As the aim of this experiment is to have a realistic setting for Batch RL, we use a realistic behavior policy. Thus, we do not incorporate any knowledge about the transition probabilities or the optimal policy as it has been done for the Random MDPs benchmark. Instead we devise heuristically a policy, considering the overall structure of the MDP.

Our behavior policy follows the idea that the most beneficial state might lie in the middle of the river at $(x, y) = (2, 2)$. This idea stems from two trade-offs. The first

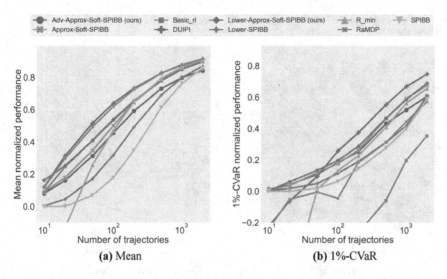

Fig. 4. Mean (a) and 1%-CVaR (b) normalized performance over 10,000 trials on the Random MDPs benchmark for $\rho_{\pi_b} = 0.9$. In the context of SPI the focus lies on the 1%-CVaR. The mean performance is dominated by the algorithms applying a penalty on the action-value function, while the restricting algorithms are winning for few data points in the risk-sensitive 1%-CVaR measure and only lose to DUIPI in the long run. Among the SPIBB class, Lower-Approx-Soft-SPIBB shows the best performance in both runs [20].

trade-off is between low rewards for a small x and a high risk of falling down for a big x and the second trade-off is between a high turbulence and low velocity for a low y and the opposite for big y. To be able to ensure the boat stays at the same place turbulence and velocity should both be limited.

This idea is enforced through the following procedure. If the boat is not in the state $(2, 2)$, the person tries to get there and if they are already there, they use the action *paddle back*. Denote this policy with π'_b. We cannot use this exact policy, as it is deterministic, i.e., in every state there is only one action which is chosen with probability 1. This means that for each state there is at most 1 action for which data is available when observing this policy. This is countered by making π'_b ϵ-greedy, i.e., define the behavior policy π_b as the mixture

$$\pi_b = (1 - \epsilon)\pi'_b + \epsilon\pi_u \tag{56}$$

where π_u is the uniform policy which chooses every action in every state with the same probability. ϵ was chosen to be 0.1 in the following experiments. By calculating the transition matrix of the Wet Chicken benchmark, it is possible to determine the performances of our polices exactly and compute the optimal policy. This helps to get a better grasp on the policies' performances: The baseline policy with $\epsilon = 0.1$ has a performance of 29.8, the uniform policy π_u of 20.7 and the optimal policy of 43.1.

6.2 Results

The results with optimized hyper-parameters as shown in Table 1 can be seen in Fig. 4 and 5 for the Random MDPs and Wet Chicken benchmark, respectively. The perfor-

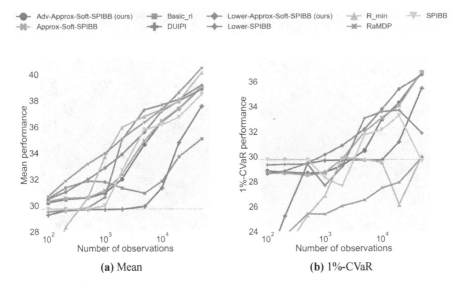

Fig. 5. Mean (a) and 1%-CVaR (b) performance over 10,000 trials on the Wet Chicken benchmark for $\epsilon = 0.1$ for the baseline policy. The mean performance is dominated by RaMDP, while the restricting algorithms are winning in the risk-sensitive 1%-CVaR measure. Among the SPIBB class, Lower-Approx-Soft-SPIBB shows the best mean and 1%-CVaR performance [20].

mances for both benchmarks are very similar, except for DUIPI which apparently has strong problems to estimate the variance in the complex environment of the Wet Chicken benchmark. In general, the algorithms penalizing the action-value function dominate the mean performance, especially when large amounts of data are available, but they lose against the class of restricting algorithms when it comes to the 1%-CVaR performance, which is the more interesting metric when talking about safety. The strongest performing algorithm among the class of restricting algorithm with respect to both metrics—thus, also the safest among both classes—and in both benchmarks is Lower-Approx-Soft-SPIBB. It is followed by Approx-Soft-SPIBB which is slightly better than its theoretical adaptation Adv-Approx-Soft-SPIBB. The worst algorithms from this class are the original SPIBB algorithms: Π_b-SPIBB (SPIBB) and $\Pi_{\leq b}$-SPIBB (Lower-SPIBB).

Interestingly, Basic RL is outperformed by various algorithms in the mean performance, which might be surprising as the others are intended for safe RL instead of an optimization of their mean performance. The reason for this might be that considering the uncertainty of the action-value function is even beneficial for the mean performance. Also, considering its 1%-CVaR performance—not even visible in Fig. 5b due to its inferior performance—the safety advantage of the SPI algorithms becomes very clear.

These two experiments demonstrate that restricting the set of policies instead of adjusting the action-value function can be very beneficial for the safety aspect of RL, especially in complex environments and for a low number of observations. On the contrary, from a pure mean performance point of view it is favorable to rather adjust the action-value function.

7 Critical Discussion of the Safety Bounds

In this section we want to check the strength of the safety bounds in the experiments. The only theoretically safe algorithms among those in the last section are Adv-Approx-Soft-SPIBB, Π_b-SPIBB and DUIPI. However, DUIPI only uses an approximation of the variance and additionally assumes that the action-value function is normally distributed. This has to be kept in mind when comparing the different bounds. To test these bounds we repeat the experiments on the Wet Chicken benchmark and this time choose the hyper-parameters such that the bound is a useful one.

Adv-Approx-Soft-SPIBB. For Adv-Approx-Soft-SPIBB the safety guarantee is Theorem 3 and, thus, we set $\delta > 0$ close to 0 and also $\epsilon > 0$ small enough to make Eq. 44 meaningful. All the parameters are known a priori so one can choose ϵ and directly know the value of the bound. As we use $\gamma = 0.95$, all the returns are between 0 and 80 ($80 = \frac{4}{1-\gamma}$) and, therefore, $G_{max} = 40$, as there is an MDP equivalent to the usual Wet Chicken benchmark but with centered returns and G_{max} only needs to be an upper bound on these centered ones. We choose ϵ to be at most 0.01, as this yields a lower bound of -8 below the baseline policy's performance.

As mentioned before, G_{max} is known exactly in this setting, which enables the use of the error function relying on the Maurer and Pontil bound for Adv-Approx-Soft-SPIBB. In Sect. 5 we propose this new error function specifically for its improved asymptotic tightness and consequently we will test it out in this experiment as well.

Π_b-SPIBB. In Sect. 3.5 we mentioned that Π_b-SPIBB produces policies which are ξ-approximate $(1 - \delta)$-safe policy improvements w.r.t. the behavior policy π_b, where

$$\xi = \frac{4V_{max}}{1-\gamma} \sqrt{\frac{2}{N_\wedge} \log \frac{2|\mathcal{S}||\mathcal{A}|2^{|\mathcal{S}|}}{\delta}}. \tag{57}$$

So, one has to choose the hyper-parameter $N_\wedge$, which is the number of visits a state-action pair needs for the behavior policy to be changed at this state-action pair, such that this lower bound becomes meaningful. In the Wet Chicken benchmark, $|\mathcal{S}| = 25$, $|\mathcal{A}| = 5$ and $V_{max} \approx 20$ (referring to an MDP with centered performances). We use $\gamma = 0.95$ and want $\delta \leq 0.05$. To choose $N_\wedge$, Eq. 57 is transformed to

$$N_\wedge = \frac{32V_{max} \log \left(\frac{2|\mathcal{S}||\mathcal{A}|2^{|\mathcal{S}|}}{\delta} \right)}{\xi^2(1-\gamma)^2}. \tag{58}$$

To gain again a lower bound of at least -8, one has to set $\xi = 8$ and inserting all the values into Eq. 58 yields $N_\wedge = 1,832,114$ for $\delta = 0.05$. For a smaller δ this is even bigger. It is obvious that Π_b-SPIBB does not work for a $N_\wedge$ that high, as the output policy would always be the behavior policy unless there are far more than $10,000,000$ observations available, which seems unreasonable for such a small MDP. For this reason, we exclude Π_b-SPIBB from this experiment.

DUIPI. Lastly, DUIPI's safety stems from the calculation of the variance of the action-value function by assuming a distribution on the action-value function and then applying the bound through Eq. 10. For example, for a lower bound which applies to 99% one has to choose $\xi > 2.33$. Contrary to Adv-Approx-Soft-SPIBB it is unknown in advance what the lower bound is, as this depends on the variance which depends on the policy itself.

Table 2. Performance and bounds of the provably safe algorithms.

Algorithms	Adv-Approx-Soft-SPIBB (Hoeffding)		Adv-Approx-Soft-SPIBB (Maurer and Pontil)		DUIPI	
Length trajectory	1%-CVaR performance	Bound	1%-CVaR performance	Bound	1%-CVaR performance	Bound
5,000	29.6	21.5	29.6	21.5	29.7	25.2
10,000	29.7	21.5	29.7	21.5	29.7	26.5
50,000	30.1	21.5	30.3	21.5	29.7	28.2
100,000	30.4	21.5	30.9	21.5	30.1	29.5
500,000	31.4	21.5	33.7	21.5	37.7	37.2
1,000,000	32.1	21.5	35.4	21.5	38.0	37.6

Table 2 shows the algorithms with their respective 1%-CVaR performances over 10,000 runs and the safety bounds. The hyper parameters were chosen for each of the algorithms such that the bound holds at least for 99% of the runs, however, in these experiments they actually held all of the time, indicating that the bounds might be too loose. The baseline policy is as described in the previous section, however, it is 0.2-greedy this time and has a performance of 29.5.

These experiments show that for all algorithms a huge amount of data is necessary to get a sharp bound and produce a good policy at the same time. Adv-Approx-Soft-SPIBB applying the error function relying on Hoeffding's inequality performs arguably the worst. While still achieving the same security, the performance of the computed policies is significantly higher by using the error function relying on the Maurer and Pontil bound. DUIPI simply reproduces the greedy version of the baseline policy until a trajectory length of 50,000. As soon as 500,000 steps are in the data set, however, DUIPI strongly outperforms its competitors and also yields meaningful lower bounds on its performance. However, one has to keep in mind that DUIPI uses a first order Taylor approximation for the uncertainty propagation, approximates the full covariance matrix only by the diagonal and assumes a prior distribution on the action-value function.

Adv-Approx-Soft-SPIBB is very sensitive to changes in ϵ. E.g., for $\epsilon = 0.005$, which yields a safety bound of 25.5, Adv-Approx-Soft-SPIBB using Hoeffding's inequality achieves only a 1%-CVaR performance of 30.9 for a trajectory length of 1,000,000 and of 33.2 if it uses the inequality of Maurer and Pontil. Contrary to that, changes in δ have a weaker effect on its performance, as setting $\delta = 0.001$ results in a 1%-CVaR performance of 31.9 and 34.9 for Adv-Approx-Soft-SPIBB relying on the inequalities by Hoeffding and by Maurer and Pontil, respectively. DUIPI only has one parameter to control the likelihood of the bound being correct and choosing it such that the bound holds with 99.9% (corresponding to a $\delta = 0.001$), leaves the 1%-CVaR performance for a trajectory with 1,000,000 steps unchanged but deteriorates the 1%-CVaR performance for smaller data sets, i.e., for less than 500,000 observations the new policy will simply be the greedy baseline policy and for 500,000 the 1%-CVaR performance becomes 35.4.

8 Conclusion

In this paper, we reviewed and classified multiple SPI algorithms. We showed that the algorithms in Nadjahi et al. [14] are not provably safe and have proposed a new version that is provably safe. Adapting their ideas, we also derived a heuristic algorithm which shows, among the entire SPIBB class on two different benchmarks, both the best mean performance and the best 1%-CVaR performance, which is important for safety-critical applications. Furthermore, it proves to be competitive in the mean performance against other state of the art uncertainty incorporating algorithms and especially to outperform them in the 1%-CVaR performance. Additionally, it has been shown that the theoretically supported Adv-Approx-Soft-SPIBB performs almost as well as its predecessor Approx-Soft-SPIBB, only falling slightly behind in the mean performance.

The experiments also demonstrate different properties of the two classes of SPI algorithms in Fig. 1: algorithms penalizing the action-value functions tend to perform better in the mean, but lack in the 1%-CVaR, especially if the available data is scarce.

In our experiments in Sect. 7, we demonstrate that the safety guarantees only become helpful when huge amounts of data are available, which restricts their use cases for now. However, we also show that there are still possible improvements, for example, relying on tighter error functions. To explore this idea further or to look for improvements of the bound in Theorem 3, as already started in Scholl [19], would be important next steps to make SPI more applicable in practice.

Perhaps the most relevant direction of future work is to apply this framework to continuous MDPs, which has so far been explored by Nadjahi et al. [14] and Scholl [19] without theoretical safety guarantees. Apart from the theory, we hope that our observations of the two classes of SPI algorithms can contribute to the choice of algorithms for the continuous case.

Acknowledgements. FD was partly funded by Deutsche Forschungsgemeinschaft (DFG, German Research Foundation), project 468830823. PS, CO and SU were partly funded by German Federal Ministry of Education and Research, project 01IS18049A (ALICE III).

References

1. Brafman, R.I., Tennenholtz, M.: R-MAX - a general polynomial time algorithm for near-optimal reinforcement learning. J. Mach. Learn. Res. **3** (2003)
2. Chow, Y., Tamar, A., Mannor, S., Pavone, M.: Risk-sensitive and robust decision-making: a CVaR optimization approach. In: Proceedings of the 28th International Conference on Neural Information Processing Systems (2015)
3. Dantzig, G.B.: Linear Programming and Extensions. RAND Corporation, Santa Monica (1963)
4. Fujimoto, S., Meger, D., Precup, D.: Off-policy deep reinforcement learning without exploration. In: Proceedings of the 36th International Conference on Machine Learning (2019)

5. García, J., Fernandez, F.: A comprehensive survey on safe reinforcement learning. J. Mach. Learn. Res. **16** (2015)
6. Hans, A., Duell, S., Udluft, S.: Agent self-assessment: determining policy quality without execution. In: IEEE Symposium on Adaptive Dynamic Programming and Reinforcement Learning (2011)
7. Hans, A., Udluft, S.: Efficient uncertainty propagation for reinforcement learning with limited data. In: Artificial Neural Networks - ICANN, vol. 5768 (2009)
8. Hoeffding, W.: Probability inequalities for sums of bounded random variables. J. Am. Stat. Assoc. **58**(301), 13–30 (1963)
9. Lange, S., Gabel, T., Riedmiller, M.: Batch reinforcement learning. In: Wiering, M., van Otterlo, M. (eds.) Reinforcement Learning. ALO, vol. 12, pp. 45–73. Springer, Heidelberg (2012). https://doi.org/10.1007/978-3-642-27645-3_2
10. Laroche, R., Trichelair, P., Tachet des Combes, R.: Safe policy improvement with baseline bootstrapping. In: Proceedings of the 36th International Conference on Machine Learning (2019)
11. Leurent, E.: Safe and efficient reinforcement learning for behavioural planning in autonomous driving. Theses, Université de Lille (2020)
12. Levine, S., Kumar, A., Tucker, G., Fu, J.: Offline reinforcement learning: tutorial, review, and perspectives on open problems. CoRR abs/2005.01643 (2020)
13. Maurer, A., Pontil, M.: Empirical Bernstein bounds and sample-variance penalization. In: COLT (2009)
14. Nadjahi, K., Laroche, R., Tachet des Combes, R.: Safe policy improvement with soft baseline bootstrapping. In: Brefeld, U., Fromont, E., Hotho, A., Knobbe, A., Maathuis, M., Robardet, C. (eds.) ECML PKDD 2019. LNCS (LNAI), vol. 11908, pp. 53–68. Springer, Cham (2020). https://doi.org/10.1007/978-3-030-46133-1_4
15. Nilim, A., El Ghaoui, L.: Robustness in Markov decision problems with uncertain transition matrices. In: Proceedings of the 16th International Conference on Neural Information Processing Systems (2003)
16. Petrik, M., Ghavamzadeh, M., Chow, Y.: Safe policy improvement by minimizing robust baseline regret. In: Proceedings of the 30th International Conference on Neural Information Processing Systems, NIPS 2016, Curran Associates Inc., Red Hook (2016)
17. Schaefer, A.M., Schneegass, D., Sterzing, V., Udluft, S.: A neural reinforcement learning approach to gas turbine control. In: International Joint Conference on Neural Networks (2007)
18. Schneegass, D., Hans, A., Udluft, S.: Uncertainty in reinforcement learning - awareness, quantisation, and control. In: Robot Learning. Sciyo (2010)
19. Scholl, P.: Evaluation of safe policy improvement with soft baseline bootstrapping. Master's thesis, Technical University of Munich (2021)
20. Scholl, P., Dietrich, F., Otte, C., Udluft, S.: Safe policy improvement approaches on discrete Markov decision processes. In: Proceedings of the 14th International Conference on Agents and Artificial Intelligence, ICAART, vol. 2, pp. 142–151. INSTICC, SciTePress (2022). https://doi.org/10.5220/0010786600003116
21. Simão, T.D., Laroche, R., Tachet des Combes, R.: Safe policy improvement with an estimated baseline policy. In: Proceedings of the 19th International Conference on Autonomous Agents and MultiAgent Systems (2020)
22. Sutton, R.S., Barto, A.G.: Reinforcement Learning: An Introduction. MIT Press, Cambridge (2018)
23. Thomas, P.S.: Safe reinforcement learning. Doctoral dissertations. University of Massachusetts (2015)
24. Wang, R., Foster, D., Kakade, S.M.: What are the statistical limits of offline RL with linear function approximation? In: International Conference on Learning Representations (2021)

Integrative System of Deep Classifiers Certification: Case of Convolutional Attacks

Imen Smati[1], Rania Khalsi[1], Mallek Mziou-Sallami[2]([✉]), Faouzi Adjed[3], and Faouzi Ghorbel[1]

[1] CRISTAL Laboratory, GRIFT Research Group, Ecole Nationale des Sciences de l'Informatique (ENSI), La Manouba University, 2010 La Manouba, Tunisia
{imen.smati,rania.oueslati,faouzi.ghorbel}@ensi-uma.tn
[2] CEA, The French Alternative Energies and Atomic Energy Commission, 91000 Île-de-France, France
Mallek.mziou@cea.fr
[3] IRT SystemX, Palaiseau, France
faouzi.adjed@irt-systemx.fr

Abstract. Deep learning models robustness have been first studied under simple image attacks (2D rotation, brightness), and then, subsequently, under other perturbations such as filtering. These systems often evoke a single learning model on a single type of data.

Here, we intend to introduce an integrative method to certify deep classifiers against convolutional attacks. We study the impact of combining several data sources on the strengthen of the verification process. Using the abstract interpretation theory, we propose a new verification routine dealing with curves as well as images. We formulate the lower and upper bounds with abstract intervals to support other classes of advanced attacks including image and 2D contours filtering. Experimentation are conducted on MNIST, CIFAR10 and MPEG7 databases. The obtained results prove the utility of combining different entries in the certification system.

Keywords: DNN robustness · Shape classification · Abstract interpretation · Convolutional attacks · Uncertainty in AI

1 Introduction

Recent advances in deep learning (DL) have enabled Deep Neural Networks (DNNs) to penetrate in safety critical areas and systems. Examples include autonomous driving [1], robotics [2], collision avoidance systems [3] and medical image analysis [4]. However, experiments have proved that DNNs are overly sensitive to small disturbances within their input data. Adversarial examples could be generated by applying geometrical transformation [5,6] for instance. Moreover, the non-transparent nature of DNNs makes robustness verification of DNNs a major challenge facing the many different possibilities of disturbances.

I. Smati, R. Khalsi and M. M. Sallami—These authors contributed equally to this work.

© The Author(s), under exclusive license to Springer Nature Switzerland AG 2022
A. P. Rocha et al. (Eds.): ICAART 2022, LNAI 13786, pp. 99–121, 2022.
https://doi.org/10.1007/978-3-031-22953-4_5

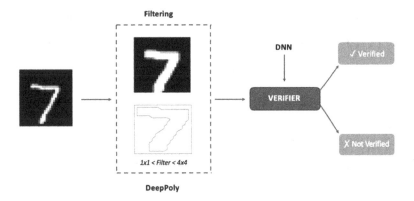

Fig. 1. Integrative system of deep classifiers certification against convolutional attacks

To overcome this challenge and come up with a solution, many DNN robustness verification frameworks have been proposed such as DeepSymbol [7], ERAN [8], DeepG [9], Reluplex [10], PLANET [11] and PRODeep [12]. The common idea behind all these verification tools is the prediction of disturbed input model using an approximate neural network behavior. Table 1 summarizes some research dealing with different datasets.

In another approach, researchers focus on robustness study during the design phase to build more accurate models [13,14]. It should be noted that robustness verification is a different approach from the empirical evaluation of neural networks [15–19]. Typically, static analysis with abstract interpretation or SAT solvers approaches are applied to neural networks and leverages the important progress of formal methods over the last decades. Such approaches estimate bounds on the perturbation of the inputs and formally guarantee the same DNN prediction within these bounds. However, formal methods over DNN for image perception system have often been applied to simple image attacks [20]. Existing robustness verification tools consider norm based robustness or brightness robustness. For example, authors, in [8,21,22], have introduced a neural network certification method based on the abstract interpretation. Experimental results on MNIST and CIFAR databases have proven the capability of a such system to certify the robustness against attacks including simple contrast, FGSM (Fast Gradient Signed Method) noise and L_∞ attacks. Other works have explored certification against geometrical transformation such as 2D rotation [23], scaling [9], 3D rotations [24] [16] and finally [25] they have certified robustness against Real-World distribution shifts. In recent work, we proposed a system to certify image deep classifiers against filtering [26]. Such a system complements existing methods that focus on geometrical attacks applied on images (see Table 2).

Most DNNs deal with images as input data to be classified [40]. Therefore, most robustness methods are associated with image classifiers. However, contour information is mandatory and recently several deep models was developed for shape classification. We cite ContourCNN [41] a convolutional neural network

Table 1. State of the art to DNNs verification dealing with different dataset formats

Verifier	Dataset	Dataset type	References
Verifier with constraints	MNIST, CIFAR10	Image	[27]
Planet	MNIST	Image	[28]
Reluplex	MNIST	image	[10]
	Drebin	Multidimensional vector	
MIPVerify	MNIST, CIFAR10	Image	[29]
Neurify	MNIST	Image	[30],[31]
	Drebin	Multidimensional vector	
DeepZono	MNIST, CIFAR10	Image	[8]
RefineZono	MNIST, CIFAR10	Image	[32]
RefinePoly	MNIST, CIFAR10	Image	[33]
DeepPoly	MNIST, CIFAR10	Image	[23],[31]
VeriNet	CIFAR10	Image	[31]
POPQORN	MNIST	sequence dataset	[34]
RnnVerif	VCTK	speech data	[35]
DNN Robustness Guarantees on videos	UCF101	Video dataset	[36]
Prover	FSDD	Audio/Speech dataset	[37]
	GSC v2	Audio/speech dataset	
	MNIST	Flatten each Image	
BppAttack	MNIST,CIFAR-10	Image	[38]
	GTSRB	Image	
	CelebA	image	
ContourVerifier	Contour extracted (MNIST) MPEG7	Contour	[39]

for contour data classification and Deep Signatures [42] a CNN architecture to learn invariants of planar curves [43] and [44] a deep contour classifier based on multi-scale feature extraction. In most cases, accuracy is used as measure to evaluate deep classifiers models. But, reasoning only about DNN system's accuracy is unsubstantial, stability and robustness assessment are no less important to evaluate performance. Recently in [45], we proposed a system to evaluate the robustness of contour classifiers against convolutional attacks. And since, the existing information in pixel regions is different from that in the contours, certification on the images do not replace that carried out on the contours. But rather, these two methods are complementary. Hence the idea of creating a system that certifies classifiers against both image and contours at the same time. We believe it is very important to combine two inputs of different formats to strengthen evaluation of the robustness. To the best of our knowledge, there is **no** previous work done to study the robustness of deep classifiers simultaneously on different types of inputs.

Here, we present a new system called the "Integrative Certification System" see Fig. 1 in which the robustness metric is calculated using the regions as well as curves.

The remainder of this work is organized as follows: in the next Sect. 2, we recall the state of the art containing the theory of abstract interpretation. In Sect. 3, we present the integrative system of DNNs certification against convolutional attacks. Our experimentation settings will be given in Sect. 4. Section 5 is devoted to the experimental results.

Table 2. Summary of research work related to DNNs verification based on Abstract Interpretations under different attacks.

DNNs Certification					
DeepG			DeepPoly		
Attacks	Data type	References	Attacks	Data type	References
Translation	image	[9]	Translation	contour	[39]
Rotation 2D	image	[9]	FGSM	image	[8, 21–23]
Scaling	image	[9]	Rotation 2D	image	[23]
				contour	[39]
Sheering	image	[9]	Rotation 3D	image	[24]
Vector Fields	image	[46]	Convolution	image	[24] [26]
				Contour	[45]
			Brightness,L_∞	image	[8, 21–23]

2   Background

Several techniques allowing the verification of neural networks have been developed in the literature. Abstract interpretation is one of the most used theories. First, it was proposed to infer semantic properties from programs and demonstrate their soundness [47]. It is used for automatic debugging, compilers optimizing, code execution and the certification of programs against some classes of bugs. One of the first application of static analysis with abstract interpretation for neural networks is implemented by Pulina and Tacchella [48] in 2010. However, their work was focused on shallow NN (MLP). Recently, several scientific contributions adapted this method for verifying the robustness property of larger neural networks by proposing abstract transformers[1] for each type of activation function [8, 21–23]. In what follows, we recall in a synthetic way some concepts.

Let $\bar{X}$ be a given input. $\bar{X}$ may undergo a deformation or even an attack. In such a case, $\bar{x} \in \bar{X}$ will be transformed into $\bar{x}_\epsilon$. The original inputs perturbed

---

[1] Abstract transformer is a step of abstract interpretation construction which is a abstract set that includes all concrete outputs corresponding to the real data.

by ϵ are denoted by $R_{\bar{X},\epsilon}$. Verifying the robustness property for $R_{\bar{X},\epsilon}$ consists of checking the property over the whole possible perturbation of $\bar{X}$.

Let C_L be the output sets with the same label L. We denote $\bar{Y}$ as the set of each prediction for each element in $R_{\bar{X},\epsilon}$.

$$C_L = \{\bar{y} \in \bar{Y} | \arg\max \bar{y}_i = L\} \tag{1}$$

The $(R_{\bar{X},\epsilon}, C_L)$ robustness property is verified only if the outputs O_R of $R_{\bar{X},\epsilon}$ are included in C_L. However, in reality, we are not able to control the behavior of hidden layers. Accordingly, we have no knowledge about O_R. The abstract interpretation is an alternative to face this defect. In fact, it allows to determine an abstract domain thought transformers and verifies the inclusion condition in new abstract domains α_R, which is an abstraction of $\bar{X}$. We denote the output abstract domain α_R^O. The $(R_{\bar{X},\epsilon}, C_L)$ property is checked:

- If the outputs O_R of $R_{\bar{X},\epsilon}$ are included in C_L.
- If the outputs α_R^O of the abstraction of $R_{\bar{X},\epsilon}$ (α_R) are included in C_L.

It seems necessary to define abstract transformers that are precise for the different existing activation functions. However, the scalability is one of the major shortcoming in the implementation of this approach. That is why, Singh et al. [21] proposed an alternative solution, called DeepPoly. It is characterized by its high precision arithmetic in floating point and it manages several activation functions, including **ReLU** (*Rectified Linear Unit*), **TanH**, and **Sigmoid**. Based on several studies, DeepPoly is the most precise analyzer as compared to AI^2 [21] and DeepZ [8] since it is scalable and supports deep convolutional neural networks.

In DeepPoly, the lower and upper bounds are the limits of accepted disturbance. In the case of luminosity disturbance, the lower bound (LB) and the upper bound (UB) are respectively the minimum and maximum brightness values. We can approximate it to a brightness shift. Indeed, these two values allow us to define the abstract intervals that we need. In the case of plane rotation, the contribution of the neighboring pixels to the intensity of the disturbed pixel is proportional to its distance from the initial pixel. This approximation lets us estimate the possible LB and UB, which give us the polyhedron in which each rotated pixel is going to end. Combined with abstract intervals, they allow us to compute the needed abstract domain. It is recommended to add a tracing algorithm which split the rotation interval into sub-intervals. Such procedure validate whether the neural network is able to recognize the object when it changes orientation in the image.

3   Proposed Method

In our previous works, we have introduced two different and separate systems for the certification of deep learning models against convolutional attacks. The first one is designed for deep image classifiers and the second one deals with deep contour classifiers. However, mapping the relationship between what happens within image pixels after an ε-perturbation and the deformation resulting in the contours presenting the object within this image leads us to not only integrate both certification methods in the same system, but also to proceed a double verification approach for verifying the robustness based on two structures within an image (pixels and contours). Our proposed system integrates two verifiers: one for images and the second for contours. Indeed, after the estimation of the LB and UB (see Algorithm 2), we extract the contours of the latter then we integrate them into the Deepoly verifier which supports the data contours, and in parallel the deepoly verifier supporting the image. An image is verified if it is simultaneously verified with the two verifiers cited above. The robustness value is estimated as a percentage value on the robustness of the image classifiers according to an interval of filtering attacks. Figure 2 illustrates all this in more detail.

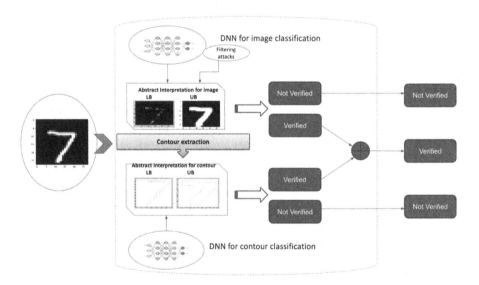

Fig. 2. End-to-end DNN double verification against filtering attacks for image and contours

In the following, we present in detail how certification against convolutional attacks is handled in the case of images and contours.

3.1 Certification Against Filtering Attack for Images

Filtering is among the most common image attacks in signal processing [49]. It depends upon the structural variability of the neighborhood of each pixel. This practice for enhancing images consists mathematically in the result of the convolution of a function (image) with a kernel. Let denote by h a filter with size $d \times d$ applied to the input image I. Every pixel in the filtered image $I \otimes h$ will have the following value:

$$(I \otimes h)(i,j) = \sum_{n=-\frac{d-1}{2}}^{n=\frac{d-1}{2}} \sum_{m=-\frac{d-1}{2}}^{m=\frac{d-1}{2}} I(i-n, j-m)h(n,m) \qquad (2)$$

In the image processing field, the resulting image depends on the choice of the kernel which could be used for different purposes such as blurring, enhancement, smoothing or filtering, etc. The Gaussian filter for instance is used for noising and denoising an image depending on the variance of the kernel. Particularly, a Gaussian distribution is approximated by a convolution kernel in order to build a convolution matrix [50]. This is approximated by the randomly applied noise in the case of the real world (fog or snow for example). Although the perturbation being applied to the input image, it is mandatory that the neural network recognizes the object. Hence, for a convolutional filter with different kernel sizes, our proposed method may certify all the possible values of the filter as illustrated in Fig. 2. When the image is captured and some pixels are masked, recognizing an object in the image depends strongly on the size of the mask applied. With the convolution, locally (pixel by pixel), we can adjust the weights of the kernel to reproduce the same noise. Nevertheless, it will not be possible to create a kernel for each pixel, therefore we suggest building an interval for every pixel and to verify it formally using the abstract interpretation theory. It can be seen as a 3D image with variable voxels.

The determination of the lower bound (LB) and the upper bound (UB) of a convolved input image is a first step for our approach. These bounds are calculated independently of the filter coefficients applied. While, the estimate of the filtered image depends on the size of the filter. In fact, the LB and the UB of each pixel are computed using the pixel's neighborhood. Indeed, the value of pixel after the convolution will have the minimum value of its neighborhood for the LB and the maximum for the UB. i.e.,

$$I_{LB(i,j)} = \sum_{n=-\frac{d-1}{2}}^{n=\frac{d-1}{2}} \sum_{m=-\frac{d-1}{2}}^{m=\frac{d-1}{2}} I(i-n, j-m)\mathbb{1}_{\min \mathcal{N}((I \otimes h)(i,j))} \qquad (3)$$

$$I_{UB(i,j)} = \sum_{n=-\frac{d-1}{2}}^{n=\frac{d-1}{2}} \sum_{m=-\frac{d-1}{2}}^{m=\frac{d-1}{2}} I(i-n, j-m)\mathbb{1}_{\max \mathcal{N}((I \otimes h)(i,j))} \qquad (4)$$

where $\mathcal{N}(I \otimes h(i,j))$ defines the neighborhood of the pixel (i,j), I defines the original image and h is the filter The Fig. 3 illustrates the principle to calculate neighborhood $(\mathbb{1}_{\min \mathcal{N}((I \otimes h)(i,j))})$ and maximum neighborhood $(\mathbb{1}_{\max \mathcal{N}((I \otimes h)(i,j))})$.

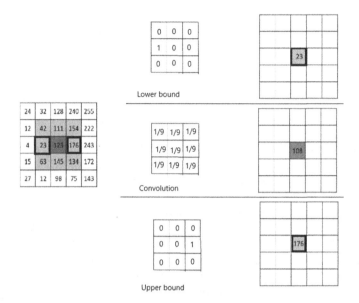

Fig. 3. Lower and upper bound for convolution. The first line convolution illustrates the lower bound kernel, the second line convolution represents an example of convolution (Box blur), whereas the third line illustrates the upper bound kernel. [26]

Algorithms 1 and 2 describe how we calculate the final LB and UB with more details in the different steps, where p_h and p_v are the horizontal and vertical position of the pixel in the image, w and h are the filters and dim defines its size. In Algorithm 1, depending on the filter size, we extract for each pixel its neighborhood, whereas Algorithm 2 computes the lower and upper bounds of the selected neighborhood. Figures 4 and 5 show the application of these algorithms.

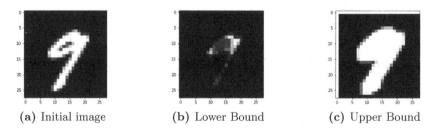

(a) Initial image   (b) Lower Bound   (c) Upper Bound

Fig. 4. MNIST Database: Lower and Upper bounds in Convolutional attacks (for dim1 = 0 and dim2 = 1) [26]

Algorithm 1. Neighbors

1: **procedure** PROCEDURE NEIGHBORS
   Require: Image $\in [0, 255]^{m \times n}$, dim $\in [1, N]$
   Require:$p_h \in [1, m]$, $p_v \in [1, n]$
2:    $Neighbors \leftarrow []$
3:    **for** $t_1 \in \{-\dim, \ldots, \dim\}$; $t_2 \in \{-\dim, \ldots, \dim\}$ **do**
4:      **if** $\Big((0 < p_h - t_1 < m) \ \& \ (0 < p_v - t_2 < n) \Big)$ **then**
5:        $Neighbors \leftarrow Neighbors \cup \mathrm{Image}[p_h - t_1 : p_h + t_1; \ p_v - t_2 : p_v + t_2]$
6:      **end if**
7:    **end for**
8:    **Return** $Neighbors$
9: **end procedure**

Algorithm 2. Lower and Upper Bound image for convolution

1: **procedure** PROCEDURE CONVOLUTION_LOWER_UPPER_BOUND
    Input $I \in [0, 255]^{m \times n}$; $h, w \in [\![1, T]\!]$, T size of the filter
2:    $I_{LB}, I_{UB} \leftarrow I$
3:    **for** $p_h \in \{1, \ldots, m\}$; $p_v \in \{1, \ldots, n\}$ **do**
4:      $L_1[p_h, p_v] \leftarrow \min(Neighbors(I, h, p_h, p_v))$
5:      $U_1[p_h, p_v] \leftarrow \max(Neighbors(I, h, p_h, p_v))$
6:      $L_2[p_h, p_v] \leftarrow \min(Neighbors(I, w, p_h, p_v))$
7:      $U_2[p_h, p_v] \leftarrow \max(Neighbors(I, w, p_h, p_v))$
8:      $I_{LB}[p_h, p_v] \leftarrow \min(L_1[p_h, p_v], L_2[p_h, p_v])$
9:      $I_{UB}[p_h, p_v] \leftarrow \max(U_1[p_h, p_v], U_2[p_h, p_v])$
10:   **end for**
11:   **Return** I_{LB}, I_{UB}
12: **end procedure**

 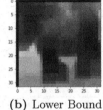 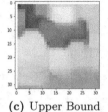

   (a) Real image   **(b)** Lower Bound   **(c)** Upper Bound

Fig. 5. CIFAR10 Database: Lower and Upper bounds in Convolutional attacks (for dim1 = 0 and dim2 = 2) [26]

3.2   Certification Against Filtering Attack for Contours

Let Γ be a 2D contours presented by its x and y Cartesian coordinates. Its parameterization $\Gamma(t)$ is a function of a parametric variable t such as in the following expression:

$$\Gamma : [0,1] \mapsto \mathbb{R}^2 \qquad t \mapsto [x(t), y(t)]^T \tag{5}$$

Since the parameterization of the curve is not unique, contour coordinates are expressed in terms of arc-length parametrization [51] as follow:

$$\Gamma^*(s) = [x(\phi^{-1}(s)), y(\phi^{-1}(s))]^T \tag{6}$$

where $\phi^{-1}(s)$ represents the inverse of the arc length function defined as:

$$\phi(t) = s(t) - s(0) = \int_0^t \|\Gamma'(u)\| du \tag{7}$$

When image is filtered, 2D contour are convolved with a two-dimensional kernel h (see Fig. 6). A new one $(\Gamma \otimes h)$ is generated. For every x and y coordinates having i_x and i_y positions of the filtered contour, we have:

$$(\Gamma \otimes h)(i_x, i_y) = \sum_{t=-\frac{d-1}{2}}^{t=\frac{d-1}{2}} \sum_{t_1=-\frac{d-1}{2}}^{t_1=\frac{d-1}{2}} \Gamma(i_x - t, i_y - t_1) h(t, t_1) \tag{8}$$

So, the abstract domain of a the disturbed point receives the minimum and the maximum values of its neighborhood respectively for the LB and the UB such as in following expressions:

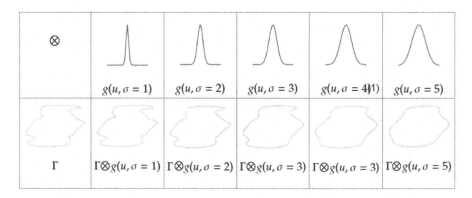

$\otimes$	$g(u, \sigma = 1)$	$g(u, \sigma = 2)$	$g(u, \sigma = 3)$	$g(u, \sigma = 4)1)$	$g(u, \sigma = 5)$
Γ	$\Gamma \otimes g(u, \sigma = 1)$	$\Gamma \otimes g(u, \sigma = 2)$	$\Gamma \otimes g(u, \sigma = 3)$	$\Gamma \otimes g(u, \sigma = 3)$	$\Gamma \otimes g(u, \sigma = 5)$

Fig. 6. Convolution attack with Gaussian kernels for a given contour from MPEG7 dataset. On the top: Gaussian kernels with sigma varies from 1 to 5 (step = 1). On the bottom: the results of convolving the initial contour Γ with the different Gaussian kernels.

$$\Gamma_{UB(i_x,i_y)} = \mathbb{1}_{\max \mathcal{N}(\Gamma(i_x,i_y))}, \text{if } \left\{ 0 < i_x - t, i_y - t_1 < d_\Gamma, \text{and }, t, t_1 \in \{-\tfrac{d-1}{2}, \dots, \tfrac{d-1}{2}\} \right. \quad (9)$$

$$\Gamma_{LB(i_x,i_y)} = \mathbb{1}_{\min \mathcal{N}(\Gamma(i_x,i_y))}, \text{if } \left\{ 0 < i_x - t, i_y - t_1 < d_\Gamma, \text{and }, t, t_1 \in \{-\tfrac{d-1}{2}, \dots, \tfrac{d-1}{2}\} \right. \quad (10)$$

where $\mathcal{N}(\Gamma(i_x, i_y))$ are the neighborhood of the point (x, y) and d is the filter's size. Algorithm 3 details the different steps to estimate the abstract domain: $\Gamma_{LB(x,y)}$ and $\Gamma_{UB(x,y)}$.

Algorithm 3. LB and UB contour under convolutional attack

1: **procedure** CONVOLUTION LOWER UPPER BOUND
   Input: $\Gamma \in 1 \times d_\Gamma$, $d1 \in [1, N], d2 \in [1, N]$
2:     $\Gamma_{LB}, \Gamma_{UB} \leftarrow \Gamma$
   Require: $len(x) = len(y) = d_\Gamma$ and $i_x, i_y \in 1, \dots, dim_\Gamma$,
3:     **for** $i_x, i_y \in \{1, \dots, d_\Gamma\}$ **do**
4:         $N1 \leftarrow []$
5:         **for** $t, t_1 \in \{-d1, \dots, d1\}$ **do**
6:             **if** $\Big((0 < i_x - t < d_\Gamma) \ \& \ (0 < i_y - t < d_\Gamma) \Big)$ **then**
7:                 $N1 \leftarrow N1 \cup \Gamma\big[i_x - t{:}i_x + t; \, i_y - t_1{:} i_y + t_1\big]$
8:             **end if**
9:         **end for**
10:         $N2 \leftarrow []$
11:         **for** $t, t_1 \in \{-d2, \dots, d2\}$ **do**
12:             **if** $\Big((0 < i_x - t < d_\Gamma) \ \& \ (0 < i_y - t < d_\Gamma) \Big)$ **then**
13:                 $N2 \leftarrow N2 \cup \Gamma\big[i_x - t{:}i_x + t; \, i_y - t_1{:} i_y + t_1\big]$
14:             **end if**
15:         **end for**
16:         $x_{low}[i_x] \leftarrow \min(N1[i_x], N2[i_x])$
17:         $x_{up}[i_x] \leftarrow \max(N1[i_x], N2[i_x])$
18:         $y_{low}[i_y] \leftarrow \min(N1[i_y], N2[i_x])$
19:         $y_{up}[i_y] \leftarrow \max(N1[i_y], N2[i_x])$
20:         $\Gamma_{LB}[i_x, i_y] \leftarrow (x_{low}, y_{low})$
21:         $\Gamma_{UB}[i_x, i_y] \leftarrow (x_{up}, y_{up})$
22:     **end for**
23:     **Return** Γ_{LB}, Γ_{UB}
24: **end procedure**

---

4   Experimental Settings

In this section we highlight our experimental settings that enable us to evaluate the effectiveness of our proposed system. We first present the used image and contour datasets for the verification of the robustness properties against convolutional attacks. Second, we provide an overview about our implementation environment.

4.1   Datasets

In the following, we present the used datasets.

- Image Dataset: In this work, we use the well known MNIST and CIFAR datasets to evaluate the impact of filter's size on the robustness of deep neural network image classification models.

1. MNIST image dataset [52,53] contains gray scale images of size 28×28 pixels. Each one is normalized and centered in a fixed-size image representing a handwritten digit. For the evaluation, we select 100 images.
2. CIFAR 10 dataset [54] contains color images of size 32×32 pixels. It is composed of 10 different and exclusive classes where 100 images are selected for the evaluation.

- Contour Dataset: We use both MPEG7 existing contour dataset and our contour dataset extracted from MNIST using a mathematical morphology based algorithm.

1. MPEG-7 shape dataset is composed of 70 classes, each presented by 20 contours (some samples are illustrated in Fig. 7). The database is challenging because it contains examples that are visually dissimilar from other members of their class and other examples that are highly similar to members of other classes. 100 images are selected for the evaluation.

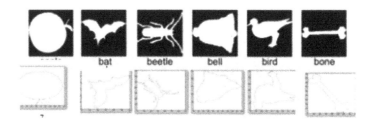

Fig. 7. MPEG7: On the top, some samples from MPEG-7 image dataset; On the bottom, the corresponding extracted contours for each sample.

2. MNIST contours dataset (Fig. 8) is generated using our proposed algorithm 4 and 100 contours are used for the evaluation.

Algorithm 4. Generating 2D contour dataset

1: **Input:**Image dataset (images)
2: **Input:** Contour dataset (contours)
3: **Initialize** height ← image height   ▷ 28 in case of MNIST
4: **Initialize** width ← image width   ▷ 28 in case of MNIST
5: N ← Number of contour points
6: **for** $i = 1 :$ size(Image dataset) **do**
7:     $j \leftarrow 1$
8:     image$\{i, 1\}$ ← reshape(image($i, :$) ,height,width)$;$
9:     colormap gray;
10:    imagesc (imgage $\{i, 1\}$) ;
11:    BW$\{i, 1\}$ = im2bw(image$\{i, 1\}$))   ▷ Convert image to binary image
12:    boundary$\{i, 1\}$ = bwboundaries(BW$\{i, 1\}$)   ▷ Trace region boundaries in
       binary image
13:    x_1 ← boundary$\{i, 1\}\{1, 1\}(:, 1)$
14:    y_1 ← boundary$\{i, 1\}\{1, 1\}(, 2)$
15:    $[x', y', N]$ ← $arc\_length\_parameterization(x_1, y_1, N)$;
16:    contours$\{i, 1\}(j, :)$ ← x'
17:    contours$\{i, 1\}(j + 1, :)$ ← y'
18:    $j \leftarrow j + 1$
19: **end for**

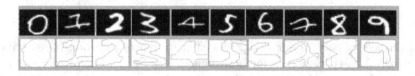

Fig. 8. MNIST Dataset: On the top some samples from the MNIST image datest; On the bottom corresponding MNIST contour dataset

4.2   Implementation

In this work, we use Python for the implementation of the abstract domain in the case of convolutional attacks and we use the DeepPoly solution as an abstract interpretation analyzer. This last is mainly based on ERAN and ELINA libraries respectively coded in Python and C programming languages. In order to evaluate the impact of filter's size on the robustness of the selected neural network models, we present in Table 3 the evaluated models for image datasets (MNIST and CIFAR-10). In addition, in Table 4 we summarize our pre-trained fully-connected and convolutional models evaluated using MNIST and MPEG7 contour datasets.

The robustness criterion is estimated as the fraction between the number of Verified samples (the number of well classified images (or contours) after the attack) and the number of Well classified samples (the correctly classified images (or contours) before any disturbance). It is expressed as follows:

$$Robustness = \frac{\# \text{ Verified images (or contours)}}{\# \text{ Well classified images (or contours)}} \qquad (11)$$

Values resulting from Eq. 11 vary between 0 and 1.

Table 3. Deep Neural Network models for **image** classification

Dataset	Model	Type	#units	#Layers	Activation function
MNIST	3×50	Fully connected	110	3	ReLU
	3×100	Fully connected	210	3	ReLU
	6×100	Fully connected	510	6	ReLU
	9×200	Fully connected	$1,610$	9	ReLU
	convMaxPool	Convolutional	$13,798$	9	ReLU
CIFAR10	4×100	Fully connected	140	4	ReLU
	6×100	Fully connected	610	6	ReLU
	9×200	Fully connected	$1,810$	9	ReLU
	convMaxPool	Convolutional	$53,938$	9	ReLU

5   Results

As described in Sect. 3, our designed system supports the robustness evaluation of DNN-based classifiers for both images (see Sect. 3.1) and contours (see Sect. 3.2). Hence, in this section, we will follow the same order for presenting the obtained results for each component.

5.1   Case of Images

In the case of the certification of deep image classifiers against convolutional attacks, we have evaluated the robustness for different sizes of filters given MNIST and CIFAR10 datasets. Figure 9 (resp Fig. 10) shows an example of robustness function for $dim_1 \in [0,9]$, $dim_2 \in [0,9]$ on 100 images from MNIST dataset (resp CIFAR dataset).

We present in Fig. 9 the robustness results obtained based on the Eq. (11) for MNIST dataset. The graph shows the square filter (i.e 1 in the x-axis is equivalent to the filter 3×3, in other words $dim1 = 1$ and $dim2 = 1$). The y-axis represents the robustness metric. In this figure, we see that the robustness of *convMaxPool* model is equal to 30% when MNIST images are filtered using a 3×3 filter. Hence, we can conclude that convolutional models are more robust than fully connected models especially for filters with size not exceeding 13×13. This could be due to the feature extraction block in convolutional models. Beyond this size (13×13), model robustness decreases, same for fully connected models with the exception of the *mnist_relu_3_50* model. In fact, filtering images with a large filter greatly modifies the initial information within these images. *mnist_relu_3_50* model did

Table 4. Deep Neural Network architectures for MPEG7 and MNIST **contours** classification

Dataset	Model	Type	#Units	#Layers	Activation function
MPEG7	1Conv	Convolutional	51,502	4	ReLU
	1Conv_MaxPool	Convolutional	51,502	5	ReLU
	2Conv	Convolutional	51,533	5	ReLU
	2Conv_MaxPool	Convolutional	51,533	6	ReLU
	3 × 100	Fully connected	51,471	3	ReLU
	3 × 150	Fully connected	92,171	3	ReLU
	6 × 100	Fully connected	81,771	6	ReLU
MNIST	1Conv	Convolutional	35,213	4	ReLU
	1Conv_MaxPool	Convolutional	35,213	5	ReLU
	2Conv	Convolutional	35,244	5	ReLU
	2Conv_MaxPool	Convolutional	35,244	6	ReLU
	3 × 100	Fully connected	45,310	3	ReLU
	3 × 150	Fully connected	45,310	3	ReLU
	6 × 100	Fully connected	75,610	6	ReLU

not capture images details during the training stage. Therefore, it is invariant with respect to the filtering operation.

Figure 10 illustrates the robustness results obtained using CIFAR10 dataset. Also in this figure, convolutional models are more robust under filtering attacks with dimensions larger than 2. This confirms that multilayer perceptron models are more sensitive to filtering regardless of the dataset.

Comparing the two graphs of Figs. 9 and 10, we clearly visualize that the robustness on CIFAR10 dataset is overall more important. This is due to multiple factors. First, images from the CIFAR dataset have a larger size. This changes the proportion between the filter size and the image size. Second, in presence of a convolution-type perturbation, part of the information will be deleted from the initial image. CIFAR models may persist since their images contain more information and more texture. Figure 11 presents the comparison between the two evaluation metrics: accuracy and robustness on the MNIST images. It highlights the importance of robustness metric and results prove that even though the high accuracy of some models, they have a very low robustness. Hence the accuracy measure is not necessarily correlated with the model's robustness. Taking the example of the convolutional model, it has an accuracy of 94% which is smaller than the other models but it is the most robust model against filtering attacks. Consequently, it is important to join the robustness and the accuracy metrics. Nevertheless, all models for image dataset are sensitive to convolution attacks with a maximum of 30% of robustness. This could be interpreted as the model

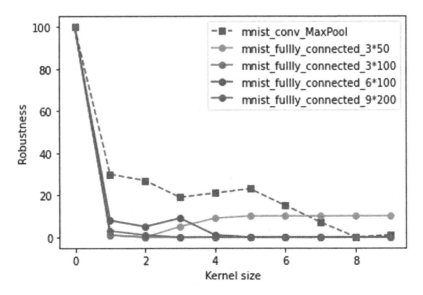

Fig. 9. MNIST robustness variation according to the filer's size for deep image classifier

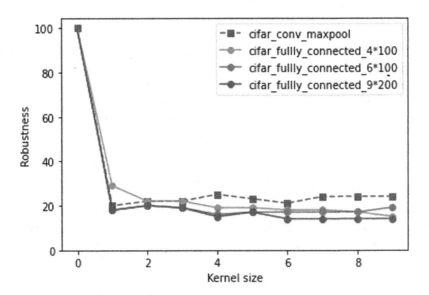

Fig. 10. CIFAR robustness variation according to the filer's size for deep image classifier

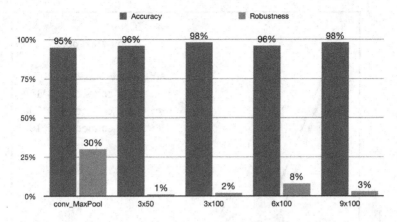

Fig. 11. Accuracy & Robustness variation (%) tested with different models for MNIST image under convolution attacks (for dim1 = 0 and dim2 = 1)

learns more on the object texture than on the object structure, this causes its loss (dramatically) on robustness even with a small disturbance of the structure.

5.2   Case of Contours

In order to study the efficiency of our proposed method, we must first evaluate the robustness of contour classifiers against different filter sizes. Indeed, we present in the Figs. 12 (resp Fig. 13) the variation of robustness according to the size of the kernel in the case of 100 contours resulting from the datasets MNIST contour and MPEG7. In this work, we use an interval of filters for presenting the different possibilities of attacks. Let consider a bi-dimensional filter with a size between $d_1 \in [0,5]$, and $d_2 \in [0,5]$ for MNIST dataset (resp MPEG7 dataset). Results show the square filter i.e. 3 in the x-axis of the graph is equivalent to the filter 3×1 applied on the x and y Cartesian coordinates of the contour. The robustness metric here is also computed using the Eq. 11 and given by the y-axis. MNIST results show that the "$1Conv$" model which contains one convolutional layer is the most robust (Fig. 14). In the case of the MPEG7 dataset, the robust model is "$2conv$". Therefore, convolutional models are often more robust than $fully\_connected$ due to their feature extraction block that gradually extracts invariants. The fact that the models are more robust to filtering attacks in the case of MNIST contours could be explained by the nature of objects described in each set as well as the number of classes. Consequently, filtering has a low impact on robustness although it modifies the contour content.

5.3   Double Verification Results

After evaluating the robustness of image and contour classifiers separately, we devote this section to present the results of our proposed integrative system for

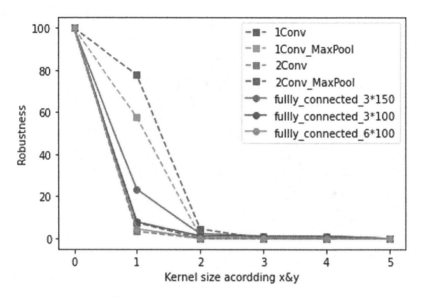

Fig. 12. MNIST contour robustness variation according to the filter's size for contour classifier

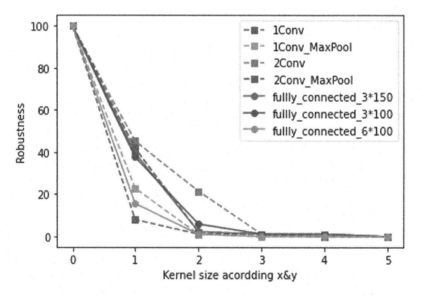

Fig. 13. MPEG7 robustness variation according to the filter's size for contour classifier

the verification of image classifiers based on both image and contour information within an image. In Fig. 15, the green bars show the robustness of images perturbed with a filtering attack of dim1=0 and dim2=1. At this level, we extract the contours of the generated upper and lower bounds of the images, and we

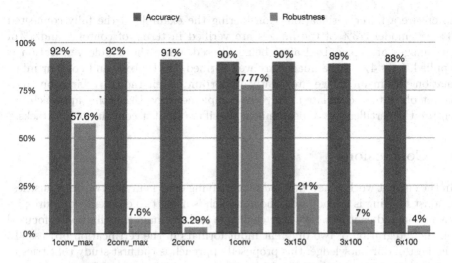

Fig. 14. Accuracy & Robustness variation (%) tested with different models for MNIST contour under convolution attacks (for $dim1 = 0$ and $dim2 = 1$)

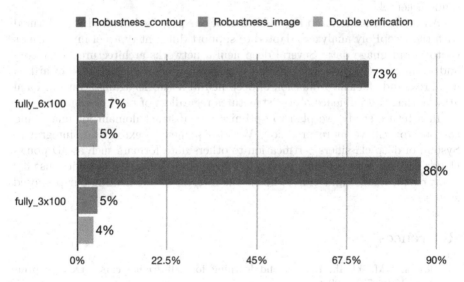

Fig. 15. Robustness variation for double verification approach tested with different models (for $dim1 = 0$ and $dim2 = 1$)

define the abstract domain of the contours within the original input images. This allows us to plot the blue bars representing the robustness based on contours. Once the image is verified based on both its generated abstract domain (image) and abstract domain encompassing its contours (contour), the double verification results are presented by the yellow bars. In fact, it shows that the input perturbed image must be jointly verified in the cases of image and contours, to ensure a fairer verification. Considering the example of the fully-connected 6×100 model, 73% of the images are verified in terms of contour, and 7% of the images are recognized after being filtered. Once the double verification is applied, only 4% of the images are well verified. Both pixels and contour information within an image are jointly important. Even though their robustness is not obligatory correlated, they are complementary. Using this approach, we ensure the certification of deep image classifiers against convolutional attacks.

6   Conclusions

In the current work, a new method for certifying deep neural networks robustness against filtering is introduced. The approach is using two different structure pixels region and contours. The core challenge and the main contribution is focused on the integration of two different input formats in the certification process. To the best of our knowledge, this proposed approach is the first study that tries to prove the robustness of a neural network by combining two different structures of image (pixels region and contours) when the input image is convoluted by a random kernel.

An implementation and an evaluation of our proposed method is performed with the DeepPoly analyzer adapted to support different types of input such as contour and image data. Several deep neural networks architectures are tested and evaluated. The obtained results are showing a promising step towards a more real and efficient evaluation of deep neural networks against convolutional attacks that can influence object structures regardless of pixel or contour.

In a future study, we plan to optimize our abstract domain for image and contour to achieve more precision. We also planed to extend our integrative System of deep classifiers certification to others data formats such as 3D points clouds or time series. Today, perception systems in autonomous vehicle use 3D point cloud, images and videos, hence the interest of augmenting our proposed system.

References

1. Bojarski, M., et al.: End to end learning for self-driving cars. arXiv preprint arXiv:1604.07316 (2016)
2. Khedher, M.I., Mziou-Sallami, M., Hadji, M.: Improving decision-making-process for robot navigation under uncertainty. In: ICAART (2), pp. 1105–1113 (2021)
3. Julian, K.D., Lopez, J., Brush, J.S., Owen, M.P., Kochenderfer, M.J.: Policy compression for aircraft collision avoidance systems. In: 2016 IEEE/AIAA 35th Digital Avionics Systems Conference (DASC), pp. 1–10. IEEE (2016)
4. Shen, D., Wu, G., Suk, H.-I.: Deep learning in medical image analysis. Annu. Rev. Biomed. Eng. **19**, 221–248 (2017)
5. Biggio, B., et al.: Evasion attacks against machine learning at test time. In: Blockeel, H., Kersting, K., Nijssen, S., Železný, F. (eds.) ECML PKDD 2013. LNCS (LNAI), vol. 8190, pp. 387–402. Springer, Heidelberg (2013). https://doi.org/10.1007/978-3-642-40994-3_25

6. Szegedy, C., et al.: Intriguing properties of neural networks. arXiv preprint arXiv:1312.6199 (2013)
7. Li, J., Liu, J., Yang, P., Chen, L., Huang, X., Zhang, L.: Analyzing deep neural networks with symbolic propagation: towards higher precision and faster verification. In: Chang, B.-Y.E. (ed.) SAS 2019. LNCS, vol. 11822, pp. 296–319. Springer, Cham (2019). https://doi.org/10.1007/978-3-030-32304-2_15
8. Singh, G., Gehr, T., Mirman, M., Püschel, M., Vechev, M.: Fast and effective robustness certification. In: Advances in Neural Information Processing Systems, pp. 10825–10836 (2018)
9. Balunovic, M., Baader, M., Singh, G., Gehr, T., Vechev, M.: Certifying geometric robustness of neural networks. In: Advances in Neural Information Processing Systems, pp. 15313–15323 (2019)
10. Katz, G., Barrett, C., Dill, D.L., Julian, K., Kochenderfer, M.J.: Reluplex: an efficient SMT solver for verifying deep neural networks. In: Majumdar, R., Kunčak, V. (eds.) CAV 2017. LNCS, vol. 10426, pp. 97–117. Springer, Cham (2017). https://doi.org/10.1007/978-3-319-63387-9_5
11. Bunel, R.R., Turkaslan, I., Torr, P., Kohli, P., Mudigonda, P.K.: A unified view of piecewise linear neural network verification. In: Advances in Neural Information Processing Systems, pp. 4790–4799 (2018)
12. Li, R., et al.: Prodeep: a platform for robustness verification of deep neural networks. In: Proceedings of the 28th ACM Joint Meeting on European Software Engineering Conference and Symposium on the Foundations of Software Engineering, pp. 1630–1634 (2020)
13. Xiao, C., Zhu, J.-Y., Li, B., He, W., Liu, M., Song, D.: Spatially transformed adversarial examples. arXiv preprint arXiv:1801.02612 (2018)
14. Jaderberg, M., Simonyan, K., Zisserman, A., et al.: Spatial transformer networks. In: Advances in Neural Information Processing Systems, vol. 28, pp. 2017–2025 (2015)
15. Engstrom, L., Tran, B., Tsipras, D., Schmidt, L., Madry, A.: Exploring the landscape of spatial robustness. In: International Conference on Machine Learning, pp. 1802–1811. PMLR (2019)
16. Adjed, F., Mziou Sallami, M., Taima, A.: Abstract interpretation limitations for deep neural network robustness evaluation. In: Traitement & Analyse de l'information Methodes et applications, pp. 68–76 (2022)
17. Goodfellow, I., Lee, H., Le, Q., Saxe, A., Ng, A.: Measuring invariances in deep networks. In: Advances in Neural Information Processing Systems, vol. 22, pp. 646–654 (2009)
18. Fawzi, A., Moosavi-Dezfooli, S.-M., Frossard, P.: The robustness of deep networks: a geometrical perspective. IEEE Signal Process. Mag. 34(6), 50–62 (2017)
19. Alaifari, R., Alberti, G.S., Gauksson, T.: ADef: an iterative algorithm to construct adversarial deformations. arXiv preprint arXiv:1804.07729 (2018)
20. Kerboua-Benlarbi, S., Mziou-Sallami, M., Doufene, A.: A novel GAN-based system for time series generation: application to autonomous vehicles scenarios generation. In: Boulouard, Z., Ouaissa, M., Ouaissa, M., El Himer, S. (eds.) AI and IoT for Sustainable Development in Emerging Countries. LNDECT, vol. 105, pp. 325–352. Springer, Cham (2022). https://doi.org/10.1007/978-3-030-90618-4_16
21. Gehr, T., Mirman, M., Drachsler-Cohen, D., Tsankov, P., Chaudhuri, S., Vechev, M.: AI2: safety and robustness certification of neural networks with abstract interpretation. In: 2018 IEEE Symposium on Security and Privacy (SP), pp. 3–18. IEEE (2018)

22. Singh, G., Gehr, T., Püschel, M., Vechev, M.T.: Boosting robustness certification of neural networks. In: ICLR (Poster) (2019)
23. Singh, G., Gehr, T., Püschel, M., Vechev, M.: An abstract domain for certifying neural networks. In: Proceedings of the ACM on Programming Languages, vol. 3, no. POPL, pp. 1–30 (2019)
24. Mziou Sallami, M., Ibn Khedher, M., Trabelsi, A., Kerboua-Benlarbi, S., Bettebghor, D.: Safety and robustness of deep neural networks object recognition under generic attacks. In: Gedeon, T., Wong, K.W., Lee, M. (eds.) ICONIP 2019. CCIS, vol. 1142, pp. 274–286. Springer, Cham (2019). https://doi.org/10.1007/978-3-030-36808-1_30
25. Wu, H., et al.: Toward certified robustness against real-world distribution shifts. arXiv preprint arXiv:2206.03669 (2022)
26. Mziou-Sallami, M., Adjed, F.: Towards a certification of deep image classifiers against convolutional attacks. In: Proceedings of the 14th International Conference on Agents and Artificial Intelligence, vol. 2, pp. 419–428 (2022)
27. Bastani, O., Ioannou, Y., Lampropoulos, L., Vytiniotis, D., Nori, A., Criminisi, A.: Measuring neural net robustness with constraints. In: Advances in Neural Information Processing Systems, pp. 2613–2621 (2016)
28. Ehlers, R.: Formal verification of piece-wise linear feed-forward neural networks. In: D'Souza, D., Narayan Kumar, K. (eds.) ATVA 2017. LNCS, vol. 10482, pp. 269–286. Springer, Cham (2017). https://doi.org/10.1007/978-3-319-68167-2_19
29. Tjeng, V., Xiao, K., Tedrake, R.: Evaluating robustness of neural networks with mixed integer programming. arXiv preprint arXiv:1711.07356 (2017)
30. Wang, S., Pei, K., Whitehouse, J., Yang, J., Jana, S.: Efficient formal safety analysis of neural networks. arXiv preprint arXiv:1809.08098 (2018)
31. Henriksen, P., Lomuscio, A.: Efficient neural network verification via adaptive refinement and adversarial search. In: ECAI 2020, pp. 2513–2520. IOS Press (2020)
32. Singh, G., Gehr, T., Püschel, M., Vechev, M.: Boosting robustness certification of neural networks. In: International Conference on Learning Representations (2018)
33. Singh, G., Ganvir, R., Püschel, M., Vechev, M.: Beyond the single neuron convex barrier for neural network certification. In: Advances in Neural Information Processing Systems, vol. 32 (2019)
34. Ko, C.-Y., Lyu, Z., Weng, L., Daniel, L., Wong, N., Lin, D.: POPQORN: quantifying robustness of recurrent neural networks. In: International Conference on Machine Learning, pp. 3468–3477. PMLR (2019)
35. Jacoby, Y., Barrett, C., Katz, G.: Verifying recurrent neural networks using invariant inference. In: Hung, D.V., Sokolsky, O. (eds.) ATVA 2020. LNCS, vol. 12302, pp. 57–74. Springer, Cham (2020). https://doi.org/10.1007/978-3-030-59152-6_3
36. Wu, M., Kwiatkowska, M.: Robustness guarantees for deep neural networks on videos. In: Proceedings of the IEEE/CVF Conference on Computer Vision and Pattern Recognition, pp. 311–320 (2020)
37. Ryou, W., Chen, J., Balunovic, M., Singh, G., Dan, A., Vechev, M.: Scalable polyhedral verification of recurrent neural networks. In: Silva, A., Leino, K.R.M. (eds.) CAV 2021. LNCS, vol. 12759, pp. 225–248. Springer, Cham (2021). https://doi.org/10.1007/978-3-030-81685-8_10
38. Wang, Z., Zhai, J., Ma, S.: BppAttack: stealthy and efficient trojan attacks against deep neural networks via image quantization and contrastive adversarial learning. In: Proceedings of the IEEE/CVF Conference on Computer Vision and Pattern Recognition, pp. 15074–15084 (2022)

39. Khalsi, R., Sallami, M., Smati, I., Ghorbel, F.: ContourVerifier: a novel system for the robustness evaluation of deep contour classifiers. In: Proceedings of the 14th International Conference on Agents and Artificial Intelligence, vol. 3, pp. 1003–1010 (2022)

40. Adjed, F., et al.: Coupling algebraic topology theory, formal methods and safety requirements toward a new coverage metric for artificial intelligence models. Neural Comput. Appl. **34**, 1–16 (2022). https://doi.org/10.1007/s00521-022-07363-6

41. Droby, A., El-Sana, J.: ContourCNN: convolutional neural network for contour data classification. arXiv preprint arXiv:2009.09412 (2020)

42. Velich, R., Kimmel, R.: Deep signatures-learning invariants of planar curves. arXiv preprint arXiv:2202.05922 (2022)

43. Ghorbel, F.: Invariants de formes et de mouvement 11 cas du 1d au 4d et de l'euclidien aux projectifs. La Manouba: ARTS-PI edition (2013)

44. Lu, P., et al.: Few-shot pulse wave contour classification based on multi-scale feature extraction. Sci. Rep. **11**(1), 1–11 (2021)

45. Khalsi, R., Smati, I., Sallami, M.M., Ghorbel, F.: A novel system for deep contour classifiers certification under filtering attacks. In: Image, vol. 15, no. 12 (2022)

46. Ruoss, A., Baader, M., Balunović, M., Vechev, M.: Efficient certification of spatial robustness. arXiv preprint arXiv:2009.09318 (2020)

47. Cousot, P., Cousot, R.: Abstract interpretation and application to logic programs. J. Logic Program. **13**(2–3), 103–179 (1992)

48. Pulina, L., Tacchella, A.: An abstraction-refinement approach to verification of artificial neural networks. In: Touili, T., Cook, B., Jackson, P. (eds.) CAV 2010. LNCS, vol. 6174, pp. 243–257. Springer, Heidelberg (2010). https://doi.org/10.1007/978-3-642-14295-6_24

49. Vassaux, B., Nguyen, P., Baudry, S., Bas, P., Chassery, J.-M.: Survey on attacks in image and video watermarking. In: Applications of Digital Image Processing XXV, vol. 4790, pp. 169–179. SPIE (2002)

50. Gedraite, E.S., Hadad, M.: Investigation on the effect of a gaussian blur in image filtering and segmentation. In: Proceedings ELMAR-2011, pp. 393–396. IEEE (2011)

51. Ghorbel, F., de la Tocnaye, J.D.B.: Automatic control of lamellibranch larva growth using contour invariant feature extraction. Pattern Recogn. **23**(3–4), 319–323 (1990)

52. LeCun, Y.: The MNIST database of handwritten digits (1998). http://yann.lecun.com/exdb/mnist/

53. LeCun, Y., Bottou, L., Bengio, Y., Haffner, P., et al.: Gradient-based learning applied to document recognition. Proc. IEEE **86**(11), 2278–2324 (1998)

54. Krizhevsky, A., Hinton, G., et al.: Learning Multiple Layers of Features from Tiny Images. Toronto, ON, Canada (2009)

Co-operative Multi-agent Twin Delayed DDPG for Robust Phase Duration Optimization of Large Road Networks

Priya Shanmugasundaram[1]([envelope])[ORCID] and Shalabh Bhatnagar[2][ORCID]

[1] Shiv Nadar University, Greater Noida, Uttar Pradesh, India
ps602@snu.edu.in
[2] Indian Institute of Science, Bangalore, Karnataka, India
shalabh@iisc.ac.in

Abstract. Large road networks overflowing with vehicles have called for increased traffic congestion, the impact of which is felt on an everyday basis and across different dimensions like decreased traveller satisfaction, increased fuel usage and increased air pollution among many other troubles. Improved traffic control strategies that can self-learn to adapt their decisioning in response to dynamic changes in the traffic flows and are capable of mitigating overall network congestion as opposed to localized congestion at intersections, are of great importance in mitigating traffic congestion. Traffic control strategies which were rule-based or historical-demand based were over-simplified and could not scale to large real-world road networks. To effectively control traffic congestion at scale, the need for co-operation and communication between the different intersections of a large road network is crucial. Multi-agent reinforcement learning methods are an apt choice for traffic signal control of large scale road networks as they can learn to perform predictive control actions that will reduce overall network congestion dynamically at scale. In this paper, we extend the work done in [24] to traffic signal timing (green phase duration) control using Multi-agent Twin Delayed Deep Deterministic Policy Gradients (MATD3) on large scale real-world road networks. The solution strategy was exposed to simulations of different road networks and time-varying traffic flows. The experimental results showed that our strategy is robust to the different kinds of road networks and vehicular traffic flows, and consistently outperformed its adaptive and rule-based counterparts by significantly reducing the average vehicular delay and queue length.

Keywords: Traffic signal timing control · Multi-agent reinforcement learning · Deep reinforcement learning · Adaptive congestion control

1 Introduction

As population and urbanization increased over the years, it has caused a steady increase in the volume of vehicles on the road. This has given rise to increased traffic congestion across urban traffic networks. Traffic congestion is the root cause of various social and economic problems like increased pollution, increased fuel or energy consumption

© The Author(s), under exclusive license to Springer Nature Switzerland AG 2022
A. P. Rocha et al. (Eds.): ICAART 2022, LNAI 13786, pp. 122–142, 2022.
https://doi.org/10.1007/978-3-031-22953-4_6

and increased travel times. It is of crucial importance to develop improvements over existing traffic signal control technology and infrastructure to deal with this growing traffic demand and to efficiently mitigate traffic congestion and its ill effects. We aim to use data-driven methods, which sample sensor data from traffic networks to perceive the current state of the traffic and use it to dynamically learn an optimal strategy for controlling the traffic flow by taking appropriate actions.

Traffic signal control is a complex problem that requires solutions that can perform predictive decisioning in response to the dynamically changing traffic conditions. The different kind of traffic control methods can be broadly divided into three categories, 1) Fixed/Rule-based Control, 2) Actuated Control and 3) Adaptive Control. Traditional rule-based control strategies like fixed timing traffic signal control, use historical data to determine a signal plan under the assumption that traffic flows will always remain similar to the referred historical demand data. Since they do not account for lift or drops that deviate from the user data, these methods result in sub-optimal traffic flows and increased traffic congestion. Actuated traffic signal control methods make use of real-time measurements from traffic control infrastructure and uses heuristics to establish traffic control. Adaptive traffic signal control strategies that learn and predict future traffic state and perform predictive decisioning. However, these methods are modelled to respond to long-term changes in traffic flows and suffer under dynamic fluctuations. These systems also need the environment to be modelled extensively by domain experts and need manual intervention from time to time. To design intelligent systems that do not require the environment to be extensively modelled and learn with minimal manual intervention, co-operative multi-agent reinforcement learning based traffic signal control is being studied extensively in this paper. The main contributions in this paper are as follows:

1. We develop a co-operative multi-agent deep reinforcement learning framework that undertakes and ameliorates traffic congestion.
2. We use target policy smoothing, delayed target policy updates and double critics to enhance learning stability.
3. We observe that the reward obtained while following our method is much higher than independent control methods, which tells us that cooperation is better than independent behavior.
4. We assess the performance of our proposed strategy on larger road networks and different kind of traffic flows and observe that our solution generalizes well to the different scenarios.
5. We observe that our framework performs significantly better than adaptive and rule-based traffic control counterparts by effectively reducing the vehicular delay and average vehicular queues across different traffic flows and road networks.

The different sections of the paper have been arranged as follows: We present related work in Sect. 2. In this section, we perform a thorough literature review of the field and shed light on the landmark contributions in traffic signal control. In Sect. 3, we elaborate on the Traffic Signal Control problem at hand, by detailing the different vehicular traffic flows and the road networks studied in the paper. In Sect. 4, we provide an overview of the different multi-agent reinforcement learning algorithms that have been used in the paper. In Sect. 5, we develop the problem statement and formulate the problem as a Markov Decision Process by defining the state, action and reward functions. We also shed light on our proposed strategy (MATD3) for Traffic Signal Control of large scale real-world road networks. In Sect. 6, we discuss the results of the experiments conducted. We evaluate the performance of our method compared to other traffic signal control strategies, different traffic flows and road networks. In Sect. 7, we conclude our paper by summarizing the findings of our experiments and by suggesting possible future directions.

2   Related Work

Traffic signal control has gained a lot of research attention as the need to develop a robust traffic control strategy has been of increasing necessity with the increase in urban population and vehicles over the years. Traditionally, traffic signal control methods used strategies like fixed-duration control where fixed signal phases were executed in a round-robin manner for fixed phase duration based on rule-based assumptions derived from past traffic data. In [7], the authors develop a fixed duration traffic signal control method by specifying permissible ranges for the green phase splits and evaluate it on a 1×2 arterial road network. In [26], the authors use a fixed duration traffic control strategy and study the impact of drivers' route choice decisions on an isolated intersection. However, these methods could not efficiently control traffic as it cannot scale to changes in vehicular flows and throughput with time. Actuated Traffic Control methods which use real-time measurements from traffic infrastructure to develop simple heuristics for traffic signal control are also studied extensively, as these methods improved over fixed duration traffic control methods. In [6], the authors extend the duration of the green phase signal to allow for smooth traffic flow under the assumption that the traffic flow rate is constant. These methods rely heavily on assumptions and require extensive domain knowledge, unlike the Adaptive Traffic Control methods which use real-time measurements from traffic infrastructure to perform predictive decisioning based on future traffic states to optimize traffic throughput. Some algorithms like UTOPIA in [20], SCATS in [19] and RHODES in [10] are adaptive traffic control methods that have been adopted in various cities and countries. In [3], the authors use a type two fuzzy system to calculate the green light phase duration based on the input data collected from the road network. Some authors also use genetic algorithms to establish traffic signal control by using the inverse of the road network performance index as the fitness function to be optimized. The ability of reinforcement learning (RL) methods to learn an optimal control strategy under uncertainty makes it a great choice for traffic signal control problems. In [14], the authors use function approximations to make the state space tractable and use Q-Learning to learn a traffic signal control strategy. As artificial neural networks gained interest among researchers, deep reinforcement learning has also been studied widely in the traffic control domain. It is a better choice than the traditional RL controllers as they could efficiently handle high-dimension state and action spaces which closely model real-life traffic scenarios. For instance, in [25] the authors use Double Deep Q Network to establish traffic signal control on an isolated intersection for different time-varying vehicular flows. However, these methods cannot learn the dependence of certain intersections on other intersections of the road network or learn to co-operate between the different intersections of the road network. This drawback can be mitigated by extending these deep RL methods to multi-agent RL algorithms. There have been significant contributions in applying multi-agent reinforcement learning to traffic signal control in the past, see for instance [12] where the authors have used Multi-agent Q − Learning to efficiently learn traffic control. In [5], multi-agent advantage actor-critic has been used to enable phase selection for traffic control. In [8], the authors model cooperative traffic signal control using Deep Q learning and transfer learning. However, most applications to traffic signal control have been focused on using multi-agent $Q-$ learning and discrete-action settings. Other prior work in this area, see for instance, [13, 21] used centralized control strategies for a common decision maker again assuming a discrete set of available actions. In [24], authors propose a traffic signal control strategy in continuous action settings using Multi-agent Twin Delayed Deep Deterministic Policy Gradients (MATD3) [2]. We extend the work on [24] and study its robustness on larger road networks and different kind of traffic flows. We have considered a 5×5 road intersection with complex geometry to assess the generalization capability of our proposed strategy.

3   Traffic Signal Control

Real-world traffic scenarios are complex to model as they are a combination of various unpredictable factors like driver behavior and route choices. However, traffic signal control problems need to be simulated to closely model real-world traffic scenarios, so that control strategies can be studied. A reasonably accurate simulation can be obtained by a) modelling the road-networks and the route choices; b) modelling the density of vehicular traffic flows and the different kind of vehicles travelling on the network.

3.1   Road Networks

The arrival patterns, different routes and the interactions between the vehicles an traffic infrastructure are modelled mathematically to aid in the study of traffic flows and control strategies. We shed light on the different network topologies that have been used to study and evaluate the performance of our method compared to other state of the art control strategies in this section.

2 × 2 Grid Network. A 2×2 road network R_1 with four intersections denoted as $\{n_1, n_2, n_3, n_4\}$ was simulated on SUMO. The network has horizontal arms that have two lanes and the vertical arms that have a single lane. The length of the arms is $450m$, with a maximum allowed speed of 11 m/s on the horizontal arms and 07 m/s on the vertical arms. We have four agents in our road network, as there are four intersections and each intersection has a traffic light. The nodes n_1–n_3 and n_2–n_4 are the source-destination pairs (Fig. 1).

Fig. 1. 2×2 simulated road network (Source: [24]).

5×5 Grid Network. A large scale traffic grid network R_2 with twenty-five intersections denoted as $\{n_1, n_2, ..., n_{25}\}$ was simulated on SUMO as shown below in Fig. 2. The network has horizontal arms that have two lanes and the vertical arms that have a single lane. The length of the arms is $600m$, with a maximum allowed speed of 11 m/s on the horizontal arms and 07 m/s on the vertical arms. We have twenty-five agents in our road network which correspond to the traffic lights at the intersections. The diagonally opposite intersections like n_1-n_{21}, n_2-n_{22} and $n_{11}-n_{15}$ are the source-destination pairs.

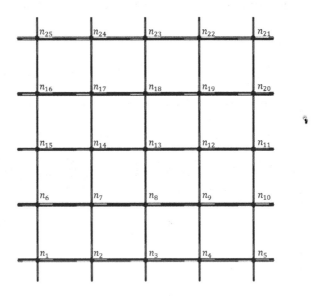

Fig. 2. 5×5 simulated road network.

3.2   Vehicular Traffic Flows

The arrival patterns, different routes and the interactions between the vehicles an traffic infrastructure are modelled mathematically to aid in the study of traffic flows and control strategies. In this section, we elaborate on the different traffic flows that have been used in our experiments to generate vehicles on the road networks and to analyse the robustness of our framework.

Major-Minor Flows.   Major-Minor Flows [5], which are time-displaced and alternating high density (major) flows F_1, F_2 are generated on the horizontal arms and lower density (minor) flows f_1, f_2 are generated on the vertical arms. The route of the vehicles are generated randomly, while the vehicular flows alternated between major and minor flows from a set of predefined origin and destination pairs (Fig. 3).

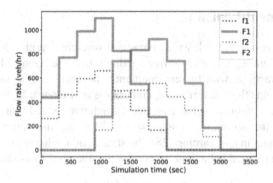

Fig. 3. Major-minor vehicular flows [24].

Weibull Flows.   The arrival of vehicles at intersections is a stochastic process. To generate vehicles in our traffic flow simulation, the time interval between the successive arrival of vehicles was modelled as Weibull Distributions as follows,

$$f(t) = \frac{\gamma_{flow}}{\alpha_{flow}} \left(\frac{t - \mu_{flow}}{\alpha_{flow}} \right)^{\gamma_{flow}-1} e^{-\left(\frac{t - \mu_{flow}}{\alpha_{flow}} \right)^{\gamma_{flow}}} \tag{1}$$

This probability distribution was chosen as it is a good fit for a wide range of traffic flows [23]. The parameters α_{flow}, γ_{flow} and μ_{flow} describe the scale, shape and location respectively. In our case, we have used the standard one-parameter Weibull Distribution where $\gamma_{flow} = 2$. Based on the arrival timing, we spawn the vehicles and assign routes randomly at the start of every episode (Fig. 4).

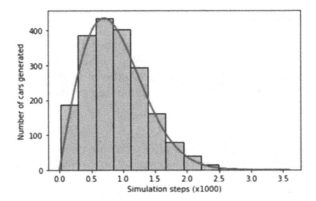

Fig. 4. Weibull vehicular flows.

4   Reinforcement Learning

Reinforcement Learning is the learning paradigm whereby learning for an agent happens dynamically through trial-and-error methods that the agent adopts during the course of its interactions with the environment. The agent learns optimal behaviour by performing actions that maximize the cumulative future rewards. State-action value function $Q(s_t, a_t)$ is defined as the expected cumulative reward that can be obtained when performing the action, a_t in state s_t and following the optimal policy subsequently. For example, in Q-Learning [28], the state-action value estimate is maximised iteratively to learn optimal behaviour by minimizing the cost J_Q as shown below,

$$y_Q = r_t + \gamma max_a Q(s_{t+1}, a) \tag{2}$$

$$J_Q = \mathbf{E}\left[(y_Q - Q(s_t, a_t))^2\right] \tag{3}$$

With the advent of Deep Learning, reinforcement learning tasks that required processing unstructured data, dealing with high dimensional vector spaces and increased computational needs became easier and tractable. However, a significant challenge in deep reinforcement learning methods is that the agents cannot learn to coordinate and share information with each other to optimize a collective objective. Multi-agent Deep Reinforcement Learning uses Deep Reinforcement Learning techniques to control multiple agents present in the environment and enable them to cooperate or compete so as to achieve a collective objective. Since traffic networks have many intersections that are dependent on each other, it is crucial to exploit multi-agent deep reinforcement learning techniques to enable the different intersections in the network to work collectively towards reducing traffic congestion. In this section, we given an overview of the multiagent reinforcement learning algorithms that have been used as benchmarks against which we evaluate the robustness of our proposed strategy.

4.1   MADDPG

In deep deterministic policy gradient (DDPG) [17], the RL agent learns the action value function Q and the policy μ hand in hand. The action value function $Q(s, a)$ parame-

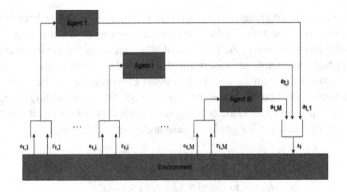

Fig. 5. Multiagent reinforcement learning (Source: [24]).

terized by θ_Q and the policy μ parameterized by θ_μ are learnt by neural networks. The algorithm is an extension of deep Q learning, which is a value-based method for discrete actions to an actor-critic based method for continuous actions. DDPG uses the deterministic policy gradient theorem, where the gradient of the policy is used to move the loss function in the form of a gradient ascent as opposed to the maximum operation over the discrete action space to obtain the optimal policy. The actor uses an Ornstein-Uhlenbeck noise to encourage exploration, by adding the OU Noise to the generated actions. DDPG is an off-policy algorithm which learns from a mini-batch of sample transitions obtained from an experience replay buffer D. There are copies of the above online actor and online critic networks called the target actor and target critic networks that slowly update the weights of the target network with that of the online network to ensure stability in learning updates (Fig. 5).

$$\theta_{Q'} = \tau\theta_Q + (1 - \tau)\theta_{Q'} \tag{4}$$

$$\theta_{\mu'} = \tau\theta_\mu + (1 - \tau)\theta_{\mu'} \tag{5}$$

The target actor μ' is parameterized by $\theta_{\mu'}$ and the target critic Q' is parameterized by $\theta_{Q'}$. The critic loss J_Q and actor loss J_π for an RL agent in the Deep Deterministic Policy Gradient case are described as follows,

$$y_Q = r + \gamma\left\{Q'(s, a)\right\} \tag{6}$$

$$J_Q = \mathbf{E}\left[[y_Q - Q(s, a)]^2\right] \tag{7}$$

$$\nabla_{\theta_\mu} J(\mu) = \mathbf{E}\left[\nabla_{\theta_\mu}\mu(a|o)\nabla_a Q(s, a)\right] \tag{8}$$

Multiagent Deep Deterministic Policy Gradients (MADDPG) [18] is an extension of the single agent DDPG algorithm to the multi-agent reinforcement learning setting. In MADDPG, a centralized critic is learnt which has access to the actions of all the agents. It implicitly models the other agents' behavior and predicts an action-value function $Q(s, a)$ given the knowledge about the actions of all other agents. However, the policy or the actor network μ learns to predict the action to be taken independently and based just on their independent states. Due to the loss function of the actor being dependent on the critic network, the action-value function acts as a feedback on the policy μ and thus eventually learns to model the behavior of other agents in the environment. During deployment phase, the actors act independent of the other agent's action choices. This is known as centralised training and decentralised execution [18]. The actor for agent i uses an Ornstein-Uhlenbeck noise to encourage exploration, by adding the OU Noise to the generated actions. The critic loss J_{Q_i} and actor loss for an agent i in the multi agent deep deterministic policy gradients case are described below,

$$y_{Q_i} = r_i + \gamma \left\{ Q'_i(x, a_1, ..., a_M) \right\} \tag{9}$$

$$J_{Q_i} = \mathbf{E}\left[[y_{Q_i} - Q_i(x, a_1, .., a_M)]^2 \right] \tag{10}$$

$$\nabla_{\theta_{\mu,i}} J(\mu_i) = \mathbf{E}\left[\nabla_{\theta_{\mu,i}} \mu_i(a_i|o_i) \nabla_{a_i} Q_i(x, a_1, .., a_M) \right] \tag{11}$$

where μ'_i is the target actor and $\theta'_{\mu,i}$ is the target critic with the corresponding weights $\theta'_{\mu,i}$ and $\theta'_{Q,i}$ for an agent i which are updated in a similar fashion as they were used in DDPG.

4.2 IDQN

In [27], the authors extend the Q Learning algorithm for a multi-agent problem setting. The rewards are modified to model different kinds of behavior like co-operation and competition. The presence of other agents in the environment possesses challenges to the stability of the learning updates due to the non-stationarity present in the environment. The authors propose in [27] an autonomous Q Learning algorithm for each agent, thereby completely relying on the environment for the interactions between agents. The proposed algorithm can handle discrete action spaces or discretized continuous action spaces as it derives from Q-Learning.

5 Problem Statement

A road network $R(n, l)$ is defined where n denotes a collection of M different intersections on the road network given as $\{n_i\}_{i=1,2,...,M}$ and l is the set of incoming lanes l_{jk} coming from the intersection j to an intersection k. It is assumed here that j and k are one-hop neighbouring junctions. The subset l_{n_i} is the set of incoming lanes coming to n_i given by $\{l_{jn_i}\}_{j=1,2,...,M,j\neq n_i}$. Each intersection has a traffic light that executes phases, which are a combination of red and green traffic signals that go green or red simultaneously for a finite duration. Phase p from a set of possible phases P_{n_i} for an intersection n_i, is executed in a round robin manner for a phase duration d. The phase duration for the green phases d_g, is learnt by our method, while the duration for the yellow phases d_y, remains fixed. There are induction loop detectors and lane area detectors on the incoming lanes in the road network, which provide traffic related information like queue length $q_{l_{n_i}}$ and vehicle delay $w_{l_{n_i}}$. The queue length $q_{l_{n_i}}$ can be defined as the number of vehicles that are present in the incoming lanes for the intersection n_i and have a speed of less than 0.1 m/s. The vehicle delay $w_{l_{n_i}}$ can be defined as the delay faced by the vehicle located at the end of the queue in incoming lanes l_{n_i}.

5.1 Markov Decision Process Formulation

Reinforcement learning systems can be modelled as Markov Decision Processes (MDP) [4,22], using the tuple (S, A, R, T) where S denotes the state space, A denotes the action space, R denotes the reward function and T denotes the transition probability function, respectively. At time t, the agent observes the state $s_t \in S$ of the environment and takes an action $a_t \in A$. This action decides on the amount of green light to allocate to the next phase at that instant and causes the agent to transition into a new state s_{t+1} and thereby receive a reward r_t, that then acts as a feedback signal on the action a_t. Since our framework uses model free algorithms, we will ignore the transition kernel T because even though state transitions indeed occur through T, it is assumed unknown to the agent who only has access to online data in the form of state, action, reward and next state tuples. Now, we represent the traffic signal control problem as an MDP where the agents are the traffic lights present on the intersections and define the state space, action space and reward function used in our solution.

State Space Definition. Choosing the correct state representation to use for an agent is dependent on the kind of control problem and is key to efficient learning. There are many frequently used state definitions in literature for traffic signal control like DTSE [9], camera images [16] and traffic parameters like queue length [1]. We have used the tuple of vehicle delay and queue length at the different incoming lanes at an intersection to define the state of our agent. Since there are multiple agents in the road network, each agent observes a local state o_t which is a subset of the global state s_t of the road network. The observation for the agent corresponding to the traffic light at an intersection n_i at time t, i.e., o_{t,n_i} is defined as,

$$o_{t,n_i} := \left\{ q_{t,l_{n_i}}, w_{t,l_{n_i}} \right\} \tag{12}$$

where $q_{t,l_{n_i}}$ and $w_{t,l_{n_i}}$ refer to queue length $q_{l_{n_i}}$ and vehicle delay $w_{l_{n_i}}$ at time instant t. This state information can be collected from SUMO at runtime and fed to our algorithm using TRACI, a python API.

Action Space Definition. As with regular junctions, we assume the various phases at any junction to go green in a round-robin manner. The decision to be made by each agent is the amount of green time to assign to any phase during a cycle. We thus define the actions to be the green phase duration d_g to be executed at an intersection when a green phase is enabled by the round-robin phase controller. The phase duration d_g is allowed to lie in the interval $(d_{g_{min}}, d_{g_{max}})$, where the upper and lower bounds $d_{g_{min}}$ and $d_{g_{max}}$ are suitably chosen. The precise value of d_g to be used is obtained from the actor network output a as follows:

$$mid := \left(\frac{d_g^{max} - d_g^{min}}{2} \right) + d_g^{min} \tag{13}$$

$$interval := (d_g^{max} - mid) \tag{14}$$

$$d_g := mid + (a * interval) \tag{15}$$

A fixed d_y is executed to ensure a smooth transition into green phase from red phase and to avoid any unexpected incidents.

Reward Function Definition. The reward is the most important ingredient in a reinforcement learning problem and it needs to be chosen in a way that it can easily achieve the goal of the optimization problem. Our objective here is to reduce traffic congestion and there are several widely used reward functions to achieve this in related works, like the delta in delay or queue length from last timestep [15], throughput in the lane and other linear combinations of traffic parameters like waiting time, density, etc. We use the following as our definition of the single stage reward:

$$q_{t,n_i} := \sum_{j=1, j \neq n_i}^{M} q_{t,l_{j,n_i}}, \tag{16}$$

$$w_{t,n_i} := \sum_{j=1, j \neq n_i}^{M} w_{t,l_{j,n_i}}, \tag{17}$$

$$r_t := -(q_{t,n_i} + c * w_{t,n_i}). \tag{18}$$

where, q_{t,n_i} and w_{t,n_i}, denote the cumulative queue size and cumulative vehicle delay faced due to the set of incoming lanes l_{n_i} at an intersection n_i. We have kept $c = 0.3$, a weight parameter used for the waiting time that indicates the relative importance of vehicle delay with respect to the queue length. As our goal is to minimize traffic congestion, the linear combination of queue length and vehicle delay in the traffic network is modelled as a negative function of these parameters Thus, maximizing the objective function defined in terms of the single-stage rewards defined as in (9) would amount to minimizing an analogous objective function defined via costs that are in turn defined by taking the negative of the rewards.

5.2   Multi-agent Twin Delayed Deep Deterministic Policy Gradients for Traffic Signal Control

Traffic flows in a road network R, are controlled by the traffic lights present at the different intersections. The control actions taken by a single traffic light at an intersection n_i not only affects the traffic congestion around it but also has a widespread effect across the network. Thus, it is of crucial importance to learn a control strategy that is robust to the actions taken by the other agents and improves the traffic congestion both locally and globally in the road network. Single agent reinforcement learning methods do not scale efficiently when the action spaces and state spaces expand to higher dimensions. Multi-agent reinforcement learning methods are an apt choice for our solution as they can learn a global objective by coordinating with other agents and can scale efficiently to high dimensional state and action spaces. The road network R can be defined using a multi-agent setting like in Fig. 2 with the M traffic lights as the agents present in the environment, at time t. The agents see a local state $o_{t,i}$, from the collection $o_t = (o_{t,1}, o_{t,2}, ..., o_{t,M})$ and perform actions $a_t = (a_{t,1}, a_{t,2}, ..., a_{t,M})$. These actions cause the environment to change and the agents receive a reward $r_t = (r_{t,1}, r_{t,2}, ..., r_{t,M})$ and observe the next local state $o_{(t+1),i}$ from the collection $o_{(t+1)} = (o_{(t+1),1}, o_{(t+1),2}, ..., o_{(t+1),M})$. The rewards act as feedback signals about the actions $a_{t,i}$ taken by the agent i in achieving the global control objective.

Multi-agent Twin Delayed Deep Deterministic Policy Gradient is a multi-agent actor-critic based algorithm, which uses the feedback from critic (state action value function) to improve the actor (policy). Overestimation bias is a common problem in reinforcement learning methods where the state action value function is maximised to learn the optimal policy. This causes the learned policy to become overoptimistic and unstable. Multi-agent Deep Deterministic Policy Gradient (MADDPG) suffers from maximisation bias as it maximises the estimate of a target critic and uses it to learn the optimal policy. MATD3 mitigates the bias by learning two critics and uses the minimum of their estimates to learn the optimal policy. Since, it now becomes an underestimation bias it does not propagate through the algorithm and results in stable learning. The critics are learnt by minimizing the cost function J_{Q_i} as below:

$$y_{Q_i} = r_i + \gamma min_{j=1,2} \left\{ Q'_{i,j}(x, a_1, ..., a_M) \right\} \tag{19}$$

$$J_{Q_i} = \mathbf{E} \left[[y_{Q_i} - Q_i(x, a_1, .., a_M)]^2 \right] \tag{20}$$

Each agent learns two centralized critics that use the actions of all the agents in the network and predict a state-action value function that describes how good the action of its agent was, given its knowledge about the actions of all the other agents. The actor uses the state-value function as feedback on its predictions and thus implicitly learns to model the behaviour of other agents in the network, as in (Ackermann et al., 2019).

$$\nabla_{\theta_i} J(\mu_i) = \mathbf{E} \left[\nabla_{\theta_i} \mu_i(a_i | o_i) \nabla_{a_i} Q_{1,i}(x, a_1, .., a_M) \right] \tag{21}$$

During the execution phase, the actors act independently as they have modelled the behaviour of other agents in the training phase. This enables centralized training and decentralized execution, thereby circumventing challenges that arise due to partial observability of agents. MATD3 learns a deterministic actor μ, which maps a state to a particular action rather than a probability distribution over actions. Ornstein Uhlenbeck noise is used to encourage exploration for deterministic policy. Overfitting of state-action value estimate is common in actor-critic methods like MADDPG, which work with deterministic policies. This causes the policy to exhibit high variance even for similar actions.

$$\epsilon \sim clip \left(G(0, \sigma), -k, k \right) \tag{22}$$

$$a'' = \mu' \left(o_{(t+1),i} \right) + \epsilon \tag{23}$$

MATD3 uses a regularization method which smooths out the target policy μ' by fitting an appropriately clipped Gaussian noise G with zero mean and a small standard deviation σ on the actions like in (23), so that the variance across similar actions can be minimized. Negative effects tend to multiply in actor-critic methods due to the feedback loop that exists between the actor and critic modules. The instability of one can affect the other resulting in sub-optimal overall performance. Thus, in MATD3, the actor network updates are delayed so that the critic can achieve reasonable reduction in residual error before the actor network is updated. It also uses other common methods like target networks and experience replay buffers to ensure stable learning. It uses two online critics Q_1, Q_2 and corresponding target critics Q'_1, Q'_2. The weights of the target actor μ' and the target critics Q'_1 and Q'_2 slowly follow the weights of their online counterparts as follows,

$$\theta_{Q'_1} = \tau\theta_{Q_1} + (1-\tau)\theta_{Q'_1} \tag{24}$$

$$\theta_{Q'_2} = \tau\theta_{Q_2} + (1-\tau)\theta_{Q'_2} \tag{25}$$

$$\theta_{\mu'} = \tau\theta_\mu + (1-\tau)\theta_{\mu'} \tag{26}$$

MATD3 improves the shortcomings of MADDPG by using techniques explained above like double centralized critics to minimize overestimation bias, target policy smoothing to reduce variance in deterministic policies and delayed policy updates to ensure stable learning updates. Thus, have chosen it to solve the traffic signal control problem at hand.

Algorithm 1. MATD3 For Traffic Signal Timing Control.

---

for *episode = 1 to E* **do**
    Initialize empty experience replay buffer D;
    Initialize online and target network weights θ and θ';
    Reset the traffic signal environment, the *OU* Noise N_0 ;
    Obtain initial observation from environment o_0;
    for *t = 1 to 3600* **do**
        Select action $a_i = \mu_i(o_i) + N_i$;
        Convert a_i to green phase duration d_{g_i} acc to (15);
        Execute green phase durations $d_{g_1}, d_{g_2},..., d_{g_M}$;
        Obtain vehicular queue length and delays to get reward $r_{t,1},..., r_{t,M}$;
        Observe next state $o_{t+1,1}, o_{t+1,2}, ..., o_{t+1,M}$;
        Store (o_t, a_t, o_{t+1}, r_t) in D;
        Set $o_t = o_{t+1}$;
        for *agent i = 1 to M* **do**
            Sample a random batch of S samples (o_t, a_t, o_{t+1}, r_t) from D;
            Set $y_i = r_i + \gamma \min_{j=1,2} Q_{i,j}{}^{\mu'}(o_t, a_1, ..., a_M)$;
            Minimize critic loss for both $j = 1, 2$
            $L(\theta_i) = \frac{1}{S} \sum_S (Q'_{i,j}(o_{t+1}, a_1, ..., a_M) - y_i)^2$;
            if $t \% d == 0$ **then**
                Update policy μ_i with gradient
                $\nabla_{\theta_i} J(\mu_i) = \nabla_{\theta_i}\mu_i(a_i|o_i)\nabla_{a_i}Q_{1,i}(x, a_1, .., a_M)$;
                Update target critic network parameters as $\theta_{Q'_j} = \tau\theta_{Q_j} + (1-\tau)\theta_{Q'_j}$;
                Update target actor network parameters as $\theta_{\mu'} = \tau\theta_\mu + (1-\tau)\theta_{\mu'}$;
            end
        end
    end
end

Deep Neural Network Architecture. In this section, we shed light on the deep neural networks that were used in the different algorithms considered in this paper. Each traffic light agent i for the road network requires six neural networks, one deterministic online actor, two centralized online critics and their corresponding target networks. The compute resource usage is maintained at a reasonable level as costly operations involving backpropagation are incurred only for the online networks. The deterministic actor network takes the current observation of agent i as input and returns the action a_i to be taken. The actor network has 4×400 hidden dense layers with ReLU activation. The output unit produces a Tanh activation to bound the continuous action generated within safe limits. The action a_i is then converted into the corresponding green phase duration d_g using (15). The critic networks take the current observation o_i and the concatenated actions of all the agents in the road network as input and return a state-action value for the input pair. The critic network has 3×400 hidden dense layers with ReLU activation. The output unit had linear activation and returned the centralised critic value. We used Adam optimizer [11], a discount factor $\gamma = 0.99$, learning rates $\alpha = 0.001$ and $\tau = 0.003$. We train the online network once every three steps along with the target networks for target policy smoothing. We train the neural networks for around 2000 episodes. Experience Replay buffer D which stores tuples of past experience has size $B = 50000$. The old samples are removed and new samples are stored in their place as the buffer becomes full. Mini Batches of size $S = 120$ are randomly sampled from the replay buffer and used in the training process.

6   Results and Discussion

In this section, we present results about the performance of our proposed control strategy and examine them for insights and improvement areas. First, we verify the ability of our proposed strategy in learning to alleviate traffic congestion. We also look at how our strategy impacts traffic parameters like average delay faced by the vehicles and the average queue length. Second, we evaluate the performance of our control strategy in comparison to strategies that belong to different levels of control complexity as follows:

1. Non-Adaptive control - Describes the class of control strategies that are static and predefined. We compare the performance of our method opposed to Fixed Duration (FD) control where the signal phases are changed in a round robin manner for a fixed green phase duration $d_g = 8\,\text{s}$;
2. Independent control - Control strategies that belong to this class act independently without co-operation according to their local state and optimize their individual reward functions. We choose IDQN [27], a widely used independent control strategy and compare its performance with the performance of our method; and
3. Co-operative control - This set contains state-of-the-art control strategies that are capable of cooperating with the different agents in the network and optimize individual performance in a way to achieve a global control objective. We have chosen MADDPG [18] which are multi-agent control strategies and compare their performance with our proposed strategy.

We compare our method's performance against the aforementioned algorithms on different grid road networks and over two different time varying traffic flows, namely

Major-Minor flows and Weibull Flows. We assess the robustness of our control strategy adapting to the different kinds of traffic flows and network topologies.

6.1 Simulation Settings

Phases can be defined as a combination of the red and green traffic lights that can be shown for the different movements in an intersection like moving straight, turning left or right, etc. The possible phases that can be executed are stored in arrays separately for the different intersections. When a phase changes from red to green for a particular link, we execute a yellow signal duration $d_y = 2$ s to avoid any crashes or unexpected incidents. The green duration is fixed at $d_g = 8$ s for FD controls. This duration was picked as a benchmark as it provided reasonable performance on our use case across the different traffic flows. The different phases are executed in a circular manner in the intersections. The green duration $d_g \in (5 \text{ s}, 25 \text{ s})$ for the different intersections. There are a total of 3600 steps in the SUMO simulation which constitutes an episode of environmental interactions.

6.2 Training Results

The phases are executed in a round robin fashion and the green phase durations are controlled by the different candidates we are comparing. In FD algorithm, the green phase duration is fixed at $d_g = 8$ s. This was picked as a benchmark as it provided reasonable performance on our use case across the different traffic flows. In the IDQN algorithm, the continuous action space of phase duration has been discretized and each of the integer durations between d_g^{min} and d_g^{max} are its actions. In MATD3 and MADDPG algorithms, the action space is continuous and the actions are the green phase durations. From Fig. 6 and Fig. 7 below, it can be seen that the proposed control strategy is able to successfully learn iteratively over episodes by performing actions that increase its reward. It is important to note that during the initial stages of learning, our strategy has lower average reward than the FD control and MADDPG algorithms. However, as learning continues, the average reward of our control strategy exhibits a strong rate of increase over episodes and settles after learning for 1,000 episodes. As FD control is static, it does not improve the congestion over episodes. It can be seen in Fig. 6 and Fig. 7, that MADDPG learns at a significantly slower pace than our strategy for the 2×2 intersection case, as it settles after learning for 1,600 episodes. IDQN suffers to learn over episodes as it cannot scale to address high dimensional discrete action spaces and does not coordinate with other agents in the network. As its performance deteriorates over episodes across the different kinds of traffic flows, it has been excluded from the Vehicle Delay and Queue Length comparisons.

The average reward of our strategy improves over MADDPG by 8% and 10% for the Major-Minor and Weibull traffic flows respectively. It also shows a significant improvement over FD control by 22% and 35% for the Major-Minor and Weibull traffic flows respectively. The efficiency of our framework in mitigating traffic congestion in the 2×2 road network can be inferred from the average episodic vehicle delay in Fig. 8 and Fig. 9. The vehicle delay in the initial phases was significantly higher than FD control, however as learning progressed, our control strategy effectively minimized it over the episodes by adapting incrementally.

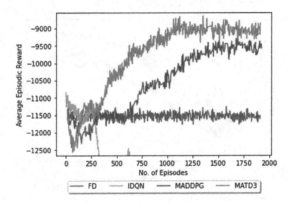

Fig. 6. Average episodic reward for major-minor flows on 2 × 2 road network (Source: [24]).

As our control strategy learns to adapt to the traffic conditions quickly, we can see that the average vehicle delay also reduces quickly compared to MADDPG. The average vehicle delays were reduced by 7% compared to MADDPG across the different traffic flows. The vehicle delays were reduced by 24% and 28% compared to FD control for the Major-Minor flows and Weibull Flows as shown in Fig. 8 and Fig. 9 respectively.

The final performance metrics of all the algorithms for 2 × 2 road network have been summarized in Table 1. These values denote the values of Average Episodic Reward, Average Episodic Vehicle Delay and Average Episodic Queue Length after the learning stabilises. We can see that our control strategy shows significant improvement over MADDPG and FD control strategies as explained above and shown below in Table 1.

Table 1. Performance metrics separated by TSC algorithms for 2 × 2 networks.

Major-minor flows				
Metrics	FD	IDQN	MADDPG	MATD3
Average reward	−11532	−23939	−9790	**−9214**
Average delay	36403	–	30126	**28233**
Average queue	719	–	752	**744**
Weibull flows				
Metrics	FD	IDQN	MADDPG	MATD3
Average reward	−2928	−17342	−2393	**−2176**
Average delay	9064	–	7871	**7012**
Average queue	209	–	110	**102**

To evaluate the robustness and generalizability of our proposed strategy to different network topologies, we studied its performance against the different kind of time-varying traffic flows. The average episodic reward of IDQN was very brittle and did not

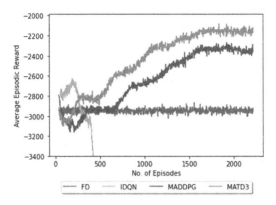

Fig. 7. Average episodic reward for Weibull flows on 2×2 road network (Source: [24]).

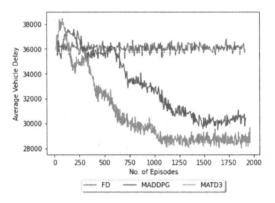

Fig. 8. Average episodic vehicle delay (veh) on major-minor flows on 2×2 road network (Source: [24]).

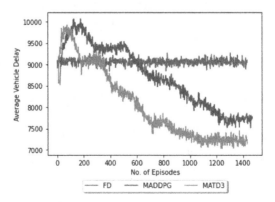

Fig. 9. Average episodic vehicle delay (veh) on Weibull flows on 2×2 road network (Source: [24]).

show capabilities to scale to larger networks which increase the state and action spaces. IDQN does not scale well to the increase in the number of agents/intersections in the network and exhibits erratic learning behavior. Thus, these two algorithm performances have not been included in comparison in Fig. 10 and Fig. 11.

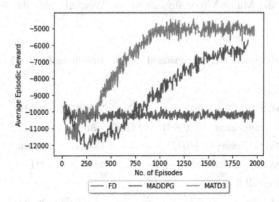

Fig. 10. Average episodic reward on major-minor flows on 5×5 road network.

The behavior of the different algorithms in the 5×5 road network are in-line with the performance of the algorithms on the 2×2 road network scenario. In Fig. 10, we can see that the episodic reward for MATD3 in the 5×5 road network starts initially at lower levels than that of the fixed duration control and MADDPG. However, it exhibits steady episode-over-episode learning behavior until around 1000 episodes, after which the agent's learning stabilises. MADDPG exhibits very slow learning as it ascends with much lower slope and takes until around 1600 episodes to have stabilised learning. The fixed duration control method does not improve the average episodic reward with more episodes as it is not an adaptive control strategy.

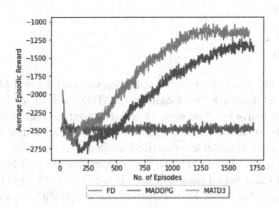

Fig. 11. Average episodic reward on Weibull flows on 5×5 road network.

Our proposed strategy shows around 16% improvement over MADDPG and around 50% improvement over the fixed duration control method for the major-minor flow case as shown in Fig. 10. For the weibull flow case, the proposed strategy shows 18% improvement over MADDPG and around 50% improvement over the fixed duration control strategy as shown in Fig. 11. The average episodic queue length and average vehicle delay for the Major-Minor flows and the Weibull vehicular flows are shown below in Table 2.

Table 2. Performance metrics separated by TSC algorithms for 5×5 networks.

Major-minor flows				
Metrics	FD	IDQN	MADDPG	MATD3
Average reward	-10007	-23426	-5983	**-5012**
Average delay	31077	–	18490	**15436**
Average queue	684	–	436	**381**
Weibull flows				
Metrics	FD	IDQN	MADDPG	MATD3
Average reward	-2474	-29538	-1265	**-1109**
Average delay	4963	–	2420	**2254**
Average queue	985	–	539	**433**

The proposed strategy is able to reduce the average delay and average queue length significantly. MATD3 improves over MADDPG by 16% and 7% over the major-minor flows and weibull vehicular flows respectively. Also, it outperforms the fixed duration control significantly across the different traffic flows as well. The improvement trend of our proposed strategy (MATD3) over MADDPG and FD control is consistent across the different network topologies and vehicular flows, elucidating that our method is robust and scalable to different kind of environments and significantly outperforms state of the art control strategies.

7   Conclusion

In this paper, we proposed co-operative traffic signal control using Multiagent Twin Delayed Deep Deterministic Policy Gradients (MATD3). Our method establishes traffic signal duration control in a road network where the traffic lights at each intersection learn cooperatively to reduce traffic congestion. We have shown that our method outperforms existing reinforcement learning traffic control strategies like Multiagent Deep Deterministic Policy Gradients (MADDPG), Independent Deep Q Networks (IDQN) and the traditional traffic signal control method Fixed Duration control (FD) across different time varying traffic flows. More experiments were conducted on larger networks using our algorithm with comparisons on different kinds of traffic flows. We studied the scalability of our solution to larger networks, using 5×5 road network and saw that our method was scalable to the larger network with around 25 intersections and was robust to different kind of time-varying traffic flows.

References

1. Abdulhai, B., Pringle, R., Karakoulas, G.J.: Reinforcement learning for true adaptive traffic signal control. J. Transp. Eng. **129**(3) (2003)
2. Ackermann, J., Gabler, V., Osa, T., Sugiyama, M.: Reducing overestimation bias in multi-agent domains using double centralized critics. arXiv preprint arXiv:1910.01465 (2019)
3. Balaji, P., Srinivasan, D.: Type-2 Fuzzy Logic based urban traffic management. Eng. Appl. Artif. Intell. **24**(1), 12–22 (2011). https://doi.org/10.1016/j.engappai.2010.08.007. https://www.sciencedirect.com/science/article/pii/S0952197610001624
4. Bellman, R.: A Markovian decision process. J. Math. Mech. 679–684 (1957)
5. Chu, T., Wang, J., Codecà, L., Li, Z.: Multi-agent deep reinforcement learning for large-scale traffic signal control. IEEE Trans. Intell. Transp. Syst. **21**(3), 1086–1095 (2019)
6. Dunne, M.C., Potts, R.B.: Algorithm for traffic control. Oper. Res. **12**(6), 870–881 (1964)
7. Gazis, D.C.: Optimum control of a system of oversaturated intersections. Oper. Res. **12**(6), 815–831 (1964)
8. Ge, H., Song, Y., Wu, C., Ren, J., Tan, G.: Cooperative deep q-learning with q-value transfer for multi-intersection signal control. IEEE Access **7**, 40797–40809 (2019)
9. Genders, W., Razavi, S.: Using a deep reinforcement learning agent for traffic signal control. arXiv preprint arXiv:1611.01142 (2016)
10. Head, L., Mirchandani, P., Shelby, S.: The Rhodes prototype: a description and some results (1998)
11. Kingma, D.P., Ba, J.: Adam: a method for stochastic optimization. arXiv preprint arXiv:1412.6980 (2014)
12. Prabuchandran, K.J., Hemanth Kumar, A.N., Bhatnagar, S.: Multi-agent reinforcement learning for traffic signal control. In: 17th International IEEE Conference on Intelligent Transportation Systems (ITSC), pp. 2529–2534 (2014). https://doi.org/10.1109/ITSC.2014.6958095
13. Prashanth, L.A., Bhatnagar, S.: Threshold tuning using stochastic optimization for graded signal control. IEEE Trans. Veh. Technol. **61**(9), 3865–3880 (2012). https://doi.org/10.1109/TVT.2012.2209904
14. Prashanth, L.A., Bhatnagar, S.: Reinforcement learning with function approximation for traffic signal control. IEEE Trans. Intell. Transp. Syst. **12**(2), 412–421 (2011). https://doi.org/10.1109/TITS.2010.2091408
15. Li, L., Lv, Y., Wang, F.Y.: Traffic signal timing via deep reinforcement learning. IEEE/CAA J. Automatica Sinica **3**(3), 247–254 (2016)
16. Liang, X., Du, X., Wang, G., Han, Z.: Deep reinforcement learning for traffic light control in vehicular networks. arXiv preprint arXiv:1803.11115 (2018)
17. Lillicrap, T.P., et al.: Continuous control with deep reinforcement learning. arXiv preprint arXiv:1509.02971 (2015)
18. Lowe, R., Wu, Y.I., Tamar, A., Harb, J., Pieter Abbeel, O., Mordatch, I.: Multi-agent actor-critic for mixed cooperative-competitive environments. In: Advances in Neural Information Processing Systems, vol. 30 (2017)
19. Lowrie, P.: Scats: Sydney co-ordinated adaptive traffic system: a traffic responsive method of controlling urban traffic (1990)

20. Mauro, V., Di Taranto, C.: Utopia. IFAC Proc. Volumes **23**(2), 245–252 (1990). https://doi. org/10.1016/S1474-6670(17)52678-6.   https://www.sciencedirect.com/science/article/pii/ S1474667017526786. iFAC/IFIP/IFORS Symposium on Control, Computers, Communications in Transportation, Paris, France, 19–21 September

21. Prashanth, L.A., Bhatnagar, S.: Reinforcement learning with average cost for adaptive control of traffic lights at intersections. In: 2011 14th International IEEE Conference on Intelligent Transportation Systems (ITSC), pp. 1640–1645 (2011). https://doi.org/10.1109/ITSC. 2011.6082823

22. Puterman, M.L.: Markov Decision Processes: Discrete Stochastic Dynamic Programming. Wiley, Hoboken (2014)

23. Riccardo, R., Massimiliano, G.: An empirical analysis of vehicle time headways on rural two-lane two-way roads. Procedia Soc. Behav. Sci. **54**, 865–874 (2012)

24. Shanmugasundaram, P., Bhatnagar, S.: Robust traffic signal timing control using multiagent twin delayed deep deterministic policy gradients. In: ICAART (2), pp. 477–485 (2022)

25. Shanmugasundaram, P., Sinha, A.: Intelligent traffic control using double deep q networks for time-varying traffic flows. In: 2021 8th International Conference on Signal Processing and Integrated Networks (SPIN), pp. 64–69 (2021). https://doi.org/10.1109/SPIN52536. 2021.9565961

26. Smith, M.: Traffic control and route-choice; a simple example. Transp. Res. Part B: Methodol. **13**(4), 289–294 (1979)

27. Tampuu, A., et al.: Multiagent cooperation and competition with deep reinforcement learning. CoRR abs/1511.08779 (2015). http://arxiv.org/abs/1511.08779

28. Watkins, C.J., Dayan, P.: Q-learning. Mach. Learn. **8**(3), 279–292 (1992)

Generating the Gopher's Grounds: Form, Function, Order, and Alignment

Jiayi Zhao[2](✉) [iD], Anshul Kamath[1] [iD], Nick Grisanti[1] [iD], and George D. Montañez[1] [iD]

[1] AMISTAD Lab, Department of Computer Science, Harvey Mudd College,
Claremont, CA, USA
{akamath,ngrisanti,gmontanez}@hmc.edu
[2] Department of Computer Science, Pomona College, Claremont, CA, USA
jzae2019@mymail.pomona.edu

Abstract. Previous work has shown that artificial agents with the ability to discern function from structure (intention perception) in simple combinatorial machines possess a survival advantage over those that cannot. We seek to examine the strength of the relationship between structure and function in these cases. To do so, we use genetic algorithms to generate simple combinatorial machines (in this case, traps for artificial gophers). Specifically, we generate traps both with and without structure and function, and examine the correlation between trap coherence and lethality, the capacity of genetic algorithms to generate lethal and coherent traps, and the information resources necessary for genetic algorithms to create traps with specified traits. We then use the traps generated by the genetic algorithms to see if artificial agents with intention perception still possess a survival advantage over those that do not. Our findings are two-fold. First, we find that coherence (structure) is much harder to achieve than lethality (function) and that optimizing for one does not beget the other. Second, we find that agents with intention perception do not possess strong survival advantages when faced with traps generated by a genetic algorithm.

Keywords: Structure and function · Agents · Genetic algorithms

1 Introduction

Imagine being placed in an unknown environment where you expect to encounter both treasures and dangers. Here you must rely on your instincts, observations, and ability to identify potential dangers. In nature, both humans and animals are equipped with the ability to perceive signals of risk, weigh their safety against possible rewards, and decide what actions to take; risk assessment is an essential aspect of survival. Recent work has revealed the potential advantage of *intention perception*, a particular kind of risk assessment ability to detect the intention of other agents, in artificial agents under a variety of adversarial situations [10, 14, 15].

In one such study, Hom et al. created a framework of simulated gopher agents surviving against a series of simple combinatoric traps, and they found that artificial

---

J. Zhao and A. Kamath—Have contributed equally.

© The Author(s), under exclusive license to Springer Nature Switzerland AG 2022
A. P. Rocha et al. (Eds.): ICAART 2022, LNAI 13786, pp. 143–168, 2022.
https://doi.org/10.1007/978-3-031-22953-4_7

gophers possessing the ability to perceive the environment as intentionally designed (to harm the gopher) had significantly higher survival rates than gophers without intention perception [10]. Specifically, they assumed that traps intentionally constructed by humans were more likely to be "coherent" (a property of trap structure defined in Sect. 3.1) than unintended traps generated uniformly at random, and used this coherence as a indicator of designed traps.

There are two limitations with Hom et al.'s work: first, their design of an intention perception algorithm implicitly assumed a correlation between trap structure and its functionality, a relationship that requires further evidence to affirm; second, their experimental framework only investigated the survival of gophers for two types of traps (human-designed traps and traps generated uniformly at random). Whether their results hold more broadly, for different trap-generating processes, remains a relevant question.

In the present study, we examine the correlation between trap structure and trap functionality in a more general context. The relationship between structure and function is central, as machines can generally be defined according to their structure and function. While Hom et al. proposed that trap coherence implies intentional design and intentional design implied functional lethality (so that coherence implied lethality), we test this chain of inference by looking at trap coherence and trap lethality for machines produced by *genetic algorithms*. Genetic algorithms are a metaheuristic search method modeled on natural selection, consisting of biologically-inspired operators like selection, crossover (recombination), and mutation [7, 16, 18]. Genetic algorithms are known for their ability to generate solutions to optimization and search problems defined on complex, high-dimensional discrete spaces, and have become a popular tool for solving *structural optimization* problems, which is the automated synthesis of mechanical components based on structural considerations [3, 21]. Generating traps with desirable characteristics (e.g., coherence and functionality) can be viewed as a simplified structural optimization problem on a high-dimensional discrete space. By simply changing fitness functions, one can obtain traps optimized for a variety of traits. Thus, we employ genetic algorithms as our primary trap-generation mechanism.

A second goal of this paper is to continue exploring the influence of intention perception on survival of artificial gophers, possibly drawing conclusions on intention perception more generally. We investigate whether intention perception can still provide gophers with survival advantages when gophers are faced with a variety of traps generated by genetic algorithms. In particular, we generate traps with structure (coherence) and with no function (no lethality), traps with function but no structure, and traps with both structure and function. We test whether the intention-perception algorithm of Hom et al. is able to distinguish such traps from human-designed traps, and how this affects the survival rates of gophers.

We find that while lethality requires some baseline level of coherence, the relationship is weak and the correlation between coherence and lethality is almost non-existent for traps generated by genetic algorithms. As such, the survival advantages of intention perception observed by Hom et al. no longer hold in this more general case. We also find that producing function (lethality) is much easier than producing coherence for trap-generating genetic algorithms. Lastly, we observe that local structure and clustering within fitness functions (*order*) is not sufficient to guarantee genetic algorithm success; biasing *alignment* with the target set is also necessary.

2 Related Work

One of the focuses of the present work is the correlation between trap coherence and trap structure, namely, the relationship between structure and function of simple, combinatoric machines. Given the general importance of the relationship between structure and function, there has been a wide range of research on this topic, with objects ranging from organisms to engineering products.

Weibel, for example, posited that all functions depend on structural design in biological organisms, specifically for the morphometric characteristics of the organs. He proposed a *theory of symmorphosis* and attempted to quantify the relationship between structure and function in different organ systems [22]. Bock and Wahlert similarly approached the relationship from an adaptationist perspective, suggesting that structure and function "constitute the two inseparable dimensions of biological features when considering morphology and evolutionary biology" and "must always be considered together" [2].

In contrast, Gero and Kannengiesser argued that no direct connection exists between structure and function for human-designed objects [6]. Instead, they proposed the *Function-Behaviour-Structure* ontology which asserts that for any object, function is "ascribed to" behavior, and behavior is "derived from" structure. Though structure and function may affect each other, they are not directly connected.

Building on a presumed correlation between structure and function, the notion of *intention perception* was introduced by Hom et al. [10] for a kind of risk assessment by artificial agents. More broadly, there has been rich array of work on risk assessment that may also provide insights to intention perception specifically. Vorhees and Williams studied rodents' spatial learning and memory as they tried to maneuver safely through environments [20]. They argued that rodent survival depends on the ability to learn and remember locations, and this ability relies on two systems: *allocentric* navigation that uses cues outside the organism and *egocentric* navigation that uses internal cues. In our work, the intention perception of simulated gophers relies only on allocentric navigation, as decisions are made based on observations of the environment.

As mentioned in Sect. 1, our choice of genetic algorithms is motivated by their ability to produce high-quality solutions to a variety of search and optimization problems [7, 16, 18]. However, traditional genetic algorithms face several difficulties. One such difficulty is uncertainty—fitness functions are often noisy or approximated, environmental conditions change dynamically, and optimal solutions may change over time [1, 13, 19]. A variety of techniques have been developed to combat such problems [11].

2.1 Relation to Kamath et al.

This paper is an expanded supplement to Kamath et al. [12], adding additional experiments to the work done there. In the present manuscript we investigate how changing the trap generation process affects the intention perception algorithm and the survival of gopher agents, along with revisiting the work done in the original paper.

3   Methods

Our goals are to investigate the link between structure and function in simple combinatorial machines, and to explore how an agent's survival is impacted by intention perception under more complicated scenarios. We adopt the "trap-gopher" framework of Hom et al., in which simulated gopher agents analyze a series of combinatorial traps containing food, and decide whether or not to enter the traps using their coherence-based intention perception algorithm [10]. Extending this framework, we introduce genetic algorithms that allow us to generate traps with different desirable traits, produced by a variety of fitness functions.

3.1   Traps

As mentioned, our trap framework is taken from Hom et al. [10]. Under this framework, each trap is a combinatorial machine embodying both structure and function.

Trap Structure.   A trap's structure is simple; each trap is designed as a 4×3 grid that contains 12 tiles. There are three fixed tiles for all traps: one in the middle of bottom row that acts as the "door," allowing gophers to enter and triggering the trap; a fixed blank "floor" tile directly above the "door" that is traversible; and a "food" tile, enticing the gopher to enter the trap. Besides the three fixed tiles, each remaining tile can be either: a laser gun that we call an **arrow** tile; a blank **floor** tile; or a **wire** tile meant to propagate pulses from the door to arrow tiles. The arrows and wires have various rotations and thicknesses, and accounting for all possible variations, there are a total of 91 possibilities each of these 9 tiles can take, with details of tile variations given in the Appendix of Hom et al. [10]. Hence, there are a total of $91^9 \approx 4.28 \times 10^{17}$ possible traps in this framework. We let $\mathcal{X}$ denote the set of all valid traps, with $|\mathcal{X}| \approx 4.28 \times 10^{17}$. Examples traps are shown in Fig. 1.

To quantify the structure of a given trap, we define the *coherence* of the trap, in agreement with Hom et al. [10], to represent how "connected" a given trap is. First, we say that a *coherent connection* exists between two non-empty (wire or arrow) tiles if: (1) the thicknesses of the two elements match, and (2) the two elements share an endpoint (i.e., the rotation of the elements align). The *coherence* of a trap is then defined as the number of coherent connections per non-empty (wire or arrow) tile.

Trap Function.   *Functional* traps have at least one arrow properly connected to the sensing door. That is, functional traps have an arrow directly connected to the door or connected to the door through a series of wires with matching orientations and thicknesses, for which the door will send a "pulse" to the arrow after sensing an entering gopher. Once an arrow receives the pulse it will fire a laser, and if the laser hits the gopher, it may kill the gopher with certain probability (decided by the thickness of the arrow). We associate a larger probability of killing gophers with thicker arrows: in particular, the probabilities of killing a gopher on a successful hit with a wide, normal, skinny arrow are $P_{k,w} = 0.45$, $P_{k,n} = 0.3$, and $P_{k,s} = 0.15$ respectively.

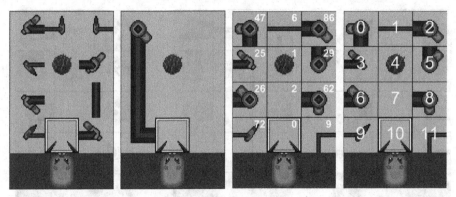

(a) Example of a functional trap created by the genetic algorithm. **(b)** Example of a designed trap created by Hom et al. **(c)** Encoding for the twelve trap tiles. **(d)** Indexing the twelve trap tiles.

Fig. 1. Example traps, trap encoding, and trap location indexing. Figures 1, 2, 3, 4, 5, 6 and 7 are reproduced from [12].

To quantify the function of a given trap, we define *lethality* of a trap as the probability that it kills a gopher entering it. We are able to compute the lethality, also referred to as functionality in this context, of a trap analytically and verify the analytical results through empirical simulation.

Trap Encoding. To generate traps using genetic algorithms, we introduce a genotypic trap representation called an *encoding*. We code each trap as a finite length vector of components, analogous to a chromosome, with the variable components corresponding to genes. We consider the 93 possible individual tiles as variable components and map each of them to a unique integer $x \in [0, 92]$. For instance, the door tile is given the code 0, the food tile the code 1, the floor tile the code 2, and the skinny arrow with right-acute angle rotated at $0°$ is represented by 33. The encoding of an example trap is given in Fig. 1c.

For convenience, we enumerate the twelve tiles in a trap as shown in Fig. 1d. Our next step is to consider how to order the twelve tiles in the genotypic representation of a trap. Though simply encoding a trap by listing the codes for its tiles in the order $(0, 1, 2, 3, 4, 5, 6, 7, 8, 9, 10, 11)$ is acceptable, we instead encode a trap by listing the codes for its tiles in the order $(9, 6, 3, 0, 1, 2, 5, 8, 11, 10, 7, 4)$, using the wrap-around pattern shown in Fig. 2. This genotypic representation better reflects the actual spatial layout of the trap.

3.2 Gophers

Gopher Basics. As with traps, we adopt the simulated gophers from Hom et al. as the artificial agents in our experiments [10]. These gophers have intrinsic goals: survive traps and eat more food. Thus, each gopher will encounter traps, decide whether or not

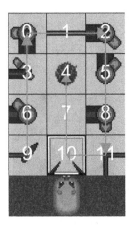  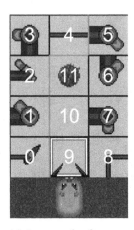

(a) Encoding with permutation (9, 6, 3, 0, 1, 2, 5, 8, 11, 10, 7, 4).

(b) Encoded trap: [72, 26, 25, 47, 6, 86, 29, 62, 9, 0, 2, 1].

(c) An example of recombining at the 5th cell with our encoding methods.

Fig. 2. (a) Second encoding permutation and (b) corresponding encoded trap, for Method 2. (c) A recombination example split, under Method 2.

to enter them, and attempt to eat the food once inside. A gopher will repeat this process until it gets killed by a laser strike, dies from starvation, or successfully finishes going through a predetermined number of traps.

Following Hom et al., we include *intention gophers* and *baseline gophers* in our experiments. Intention gophers possess intention perception—the ability to assess the coherence of the trap and then determine whether the trap is randomly generated or deliberately harmful, based on its coherence. If the intention gopher senses the trap as sufficiently coherent, it will conclude the trap is intentionally designed (rejecting the null hypothesis of random generation), and skip over the trap unless it is forced to enter due to starvation. Baseline gophers, in contrast, simply enter traps according to some predetermined probability.

To simulate behavior, we first assign each gopher (whether intention or baseline) with a hunger level $H \in [0, 1)$ to indicate how hungry a gopher is. We set Maximum Fasting Interval (MFI) as the maximal number of traps a gopher can endure without eating, and define the hunger level by $H(n) = \frac{n+1}{\text{MFI}}$, where n is the number of traps the gopher has already endured without food. The probability that a baseline gopher will enter an arbitrary trap is defined as $P'_e(H) = P_e \cdot (1 - H^{10}) + H^{10}$, where P_e is the default probability of entering and $P'_e(H)$ is the adjusted probability of entering. While the baseline gopher will decide whether to enter based on the adjusted probability of entering, the intention gopher will decide based on the intention perception algorithm described in the next section.

For convenience, we use discrete time steps, called *frames*. After entering a trap, a gopher will head directly toward the food in the center of the trap at the rate of 1 tile/frame and eat for a certain amount of time. As pulses take time to travel, eating longer puts gophers at higher risk of being hit. Thus, we design the eating time of a gopher to be based on its confidence of entering a trap, i.e., the default probability of entering a trap. Specifically, the eating time t_{eat} of the gopher is selected according to the probability vector $p = [p_1, p_2, p_3, p_4, p_5]$, calculated based on P_e through methods in [10], where p_j represents the probability that a gopher eats for j frames.

If no arrow in the trap fires, after eating for t_{eat} frames, the gopher will exit the trap from the way it came at the same speed. However, if any arrow in the trap fires a laser, the gopher will leave immediately regardless of its current hunger level, what it was doing, and whether it was hit. This allows us to model the "skittishness" of gopher, and it does not count as having eaten if a gopher leaves before it finishes eating.

Intention Perception. We simulate gophers' ability to determine whether the external agents intend to harm through assessment of trap structures using the intention perception framework adopted from Hom et al. [10]. The intention perception model is built upon the *functional information* model introduced by Hazen et al. [9] within Montañez [17], which "evaluates the surprise level (S) of a random configuration variable meeting or exceeding a given level of function" [10]. The intention perception model evaluates the surprise level S of any trap meeting a certain level of coherence. Following Hom et al., the surprise level S is computed as

$$S(x) = -\log_2 \left[|\mathcal{X}|(1 + \ln|\mathcal{X}|) \frac{p(x)}{F_g(x)^{-1}} \right] \tag{1}$$

where x is any trap configuration, $\mathcal{X}$ is the space of all possible traps, $g(x)$ is the coherence of a given trap x, $p(x)$ is a probability measure on space $\mathcal{X}$ (we set as $p(x) = 1/|\mathcal{X}|$ by default in experiments, namely, a uniform distribution), and $F_g(x)$ is the proportion of traps with at least the level of coherence of trap x. In other words, $F_g(x)$ is calculated by $F_g(x) = M_g(x)/|\mathcal{X}|$, where $M_g(x)$ is the number of traps with coherence greater or equal to $g(x)$. In order to implement the model, we use precalculated $M_g(x)$ terms for each possible coherence value $g(x)$, as given in the Appendix of Hom et al. [10].

After computing the surprise level S of a certain trap x, we reject the null hypothesis that a trap is randomly generated at a significance level of $\alpha = 0.0001$, which corresponds to a surprise level of $S = 13.29$ bits. That means that the probability of a trap with surprise level of at least 13.29 bits being generated by the null hypothesis process does not exceed 0.0001 [10, 17]. Rejecting the null hypothesis implies that the intention gopher regards the trap as being intentionally designed rather than generated uniformly at random, and therefore the gopher will try to avoid the trap.

3.3 Genetic Algorithms

While Hom et al. considered only two types of trap-generating processes (namely, human design and uniformly random generation), we investigate a wider variety of traps generated by genetic algorithms. Similar to natural selection, individuals in a genetic algorithm population reproduce at a rate proportional to their fitnesses, producing offspring that largely inherit the characteristics of their parents. Populations shaped by the algorithm will tend toward increased fitness. Thus, by defining different fitness metrics one can produce individuals that are optimized for different desired characteristics.

For our genetic algorithm, we begin with a search space $\mathcal{X}$, which is the set of all valid traps defined in Sect. 3.1, a randomly generated initial population $X \subseteq \mathcal{X}$, and a fitness function $f : \mathcal{X} \rightarrow \mathbb{R}$ that evaluates the fitness of each individual trap (details given in Sect. 3.4). As discussed in Sect. 3.1, we represent each individual in the search space by a string of variables known as *genes*, with the joint string being called a *chromosome*, using the genotypic representation system defined there. Concretely, each gene is an integer encoding a tile and a chromosome is a string of twelve such genes. At each step, the genetic algorithm will go through the process of *(roulette-wheel) selection*, *recombination*, and *mutation* to generate a new offspring population $X' \subseteq \mathcal{X}$. This process is repeated for ten thousand generations.

For recombination, we select (in a fitness-proportional, roulette-wheel manner) two elements from the population, splitting the chromosomes of both elements into two parts at the same position, and combine the first slice of the first element with the second slice of the second element. This generates a new trap that inherits genetic information from both parents. Figure 2c illustrates an example of how we might split a trap at a certain cell. Finally, each recombined new element will undergo a mutation step: for a single trap, the algorithm uniformly picks a gene (that is not the door or food) from its chromosome and switches that gene to some random gene $y \in [0, 90]$, mimicking a genetic point mutation. Each trap generated through the steps of selection, recombination, and mutation becomes an element of the new population $X' \subseteq \mathcal{X}$. We repeat the process until the size of the new generation matches that of the old.

We iteratively create new generations until a specific number of generations is generated. Finally, we output the single trap with highest fitness value from across all generations. The complete process of our genetic algorithm is described in Algorithm 1.

Algorithm 1. Sample Genetic Algorithm.

1: **procedure** GENETICALGORITHM
2:      *globalBest* ← none
3:      *population* ← generateRandomPopulation()
4:      **while** not terminationConditionsMet **do**
5:          *newPopulation* ← empty
6:          **for** *element* in *population* **do**
7:              *selectedPair* ← roulette(*population*)
8:              *combined* ← recombine(*selectedPair*)
9:              *mutated* ← pointMutate(*combined*)
10:             *newPopulation*.add(*mutated*)
11:         *popBest* ← bestTrap(*newPopulation*)
12:         **if** $f(popBest) > f(globalBest)$ **then**
13:             *globalBest* ← *popBest*
14:         *population* ← *newPopulation*
15:     **return** *globalBest*

3.4 Fitness Functions

Fitness functions are critical in generating desirable traps. They impose an ordering on all elements in the search space, based on certain criteria. When those criteria align with one's goals, it endows the genetic algorithm with the capacity to generate traps with particular traits as expected. However, not all fitness functions are valid and effective. We define two properties of fitness functions useful for discussing their effectiveness. First, we say a fitness function is **spatially ordered** if it assigns fitness values to individual elements based on some pattern or local clustering. Second, we say a fitness functions is **correctly aligned** if it is spatially ordered and embodies a preference for elements in a specific target set, which, in our setting, is the set of all traps that are either coherent, functional, or both.

We next introduce the set of fitness functions used in our experiments, and explore how the properties of each fitness function contribute to its effectiveness.

Random Fitness. Given any trap $x \in \mathcal{X}$, the random fitness function $r : \mathcal{X} \to \mathbb{R}$ is a function defined by $r(x) = n$ where n is a real number chosen uniformly at random from the interval $[0, 1]$. In other words, we assign each trap in the search space a random fitness value that is not based on any property of the trap itself. Thus, the random fitness function is neither spatially ordered nor correctly aligned, as the spatial distribution of its values reveal no regularities but only randomness.

Binary Distance (Hamming) Fitness. The hamming fitness function begins by picking a "target" trap $t \in \mathcal{X}$ uniformly at random from the search space. It then measures the distance between a given trap and the fixed target trap. Given any trap $x \in \mathcal{X}$, the hamming fitness function $h : \mathcal{X} \to \mathbb{R}$ is a function defined by $h(x) = \frac{\#_{\text{diff}}}{9}$, where $\#_{\text{diff}}$ is the number of differing genes in the chromosomes of x and t, while $9 = 12 - 3$ is the largest possible number of differing genes, as there are three fixed cells for all traps. Since the hamming fitness function imposes ordering on traps based on their distance to the target trap, it is spatially ordered. However, this criteria doesn't align with our target set, so this fitness function is not correctly aligned.

Coherent Fitness. Given any trap $x \in \mathcal{X}$, the coherent fitness function $c : \mathcal{X} \to \mathbb{R}$ returns the coherence of trap x defined in Sect. 3.1. This fitness function assign values based on trap coherence and gives higher values to more coherent traps, which are included in our target set. Thus, the coherent fitness function is both spatially ordered and correctly aligned.

Functional Fitness (Lethality). Given any trap $x \in \mathcal{X}$, the functional fitness function $f : \mathcal{X} \to \mathbb{R}$ is defined by $f(x) = \frac{P_{\text{kill}}(x)}{P_{\text{max}}}$, where $P_{\text{kill}}(x)$ is the probability of x killing an entering gopher, also known as *lethality* of x as defined in Sect. 3.1, and P_{max} is the largest probability of killing an enter gopher which is realized only in the case that two arrows both hit the gopher. Since this fitness function rewards lethal traps, and since lethal traps are often similar to other lethal traps, this indicates that it is both spatially ordered and correctly aligned.

Multiobjective Fitness. We now define a fitness function that evaluates both the coherence and lethality of any given trap. Moreover, it prioritizes traps that are both coherent and lethal instead of traps that are only coherent or only lethal by penalizing the gap between the trap coherence and lethality values.

We define two types of multiobjective fitness functions. The first is a *local multiobjective fitness function* $\varphi : \mathcal{X}^n \to \mathbb{R}^n$ ($n \in \mathbb{N}$ is the population size) that takes in a population of traps and outputs an array containing fitness values of all traps in that population. The local multiobjective fitness function imposes a proper ordering on the input population based on the relationships between traps, and this effectively boosts the performance of the genetic algorithm when optimizing for more than one objective. However, the local multiobjective fitness value of each trap only depends on its relative rank within the population, which implies that the same trap may have different fitness values in different generations. Therefore, we define an additional *global multiobjective fitness function* $g : \mathcal{X} \to \mathbb{R}$ as a universal measure of trap coherence and lethality. We employ the local fitness function during the selection process within the genetic algorithm and the global fitness function to record the quality of generated traps.

Local Multiobjective Fitness Function. This fitness function is a variation of a standard method for multiobjective evolutionary optimization which relies on the notion "dominance" among traps [4]. For any traps $x, y \in \mathcal{X}$, we say that x *dominates* y if x has both a greater coherence fitness and a greater functional fitness than y. Given a trap $x \in \mathcal{X}$, let $\#_{dominant}(x)$ denote the number of traps x dominates within the population. The base score for x is then $\#_{dominant}(x) + 1$.

Moreover, we wish to add more diversity into the selected population by disincentivizing sampling traps that are too similar to each other. Let $N(x) = \{y \in \mathcal{X} \mid \#_{dominant}(x) = \#_{dominant}(y), y \neq x\}$ be the set of neighbors of x containing traps that have same base value as x. Then, we compute the normalized distance between x and its closest neighbor $d_{normalized}(x) = \min_{y \in N(x)} \|x - y\|/\sqrt{2}$, where $\|x - y\|$ denotes the point-wise Euclidean distance between trap x and y, and $\sqrt{2}$ is the maximum possible distance between two traps. If $N(x) = \emptyset$, the normalized distance is set to be 1. Then, for each $x \in \mathcal{X}$, we add this normalized distance to its base score, obtaining the boosted score. Each boosted score is then divided by the maximum boosted score across the population, leaving the most fit trap with a fitness value of 1. Finally, we return the array of normalized boosted scores contained in range $(0, 1]$ as the fitness values of traps in the population.

In this way, the local multiobjective fitness function can not only serve as a good measure of relative fitness of traps within the population, accelerating the genetic algorithm, but also promotes diversity within the population.

Global Multiobjective Fitness Function. Given any trap $x \in \mathcal{X}$, the global multiobjective fitness function is defined as

$$g(x) = \begin{cases} \frac{f(x)+c(x)}{e^{2|f(x)-c(x)|}} & |f(x) - c(x)| \leq k_{\text{diff}}, \\ \frac{1}{10k_{\text{diff}}} \frac{f(x)+c(x)}{e^{2|f(x)-c(x)|}} & |f(x) - c(x)| > k_{\text{diff}}, \end{cases}$$

where $f(x)$ and $c(x)$ are the functional and coherence fitness values of x respectively, and k_{diff} is some pre-defined constant. The intuition behind this definition is to reward both coherence and lethality of a trap while penalizing the difference between coherence and lethality. The design of a threshold k_{diff} intends to disincentivize solely optimizing coherence or lethality alone (which would lead to large gaps between the functional and coherent fitness values). Furthermore, since the global multiobjective fitness function assigns higher values to traps that are both lethal and coherent, it is both spatially ordered and correctly aligned.

4 Experimental Setup

4.1 Generating Traps Through Genetic Algorithms

Our goal is to generate traps with specific traits using genetic algorithms equipped with different fitness functions. In the process, we observe the performance of each fitness function, in terms of their convergence speed and the quality of the traps produced.

For each fitness function (i.e., random, hamming, coherent, functional, or multiobjective) we generate 1,000 optimized trap examples. Since each run of the genetic algorithm outputs a single best trap as the final step, we run the genetic algorithm for 1,000 independent trials. For each run of the genetic algorithm, we set the population size to be constant 20, terminate the algorithm after 10,000 generations, and output the trap with best fitness value among all 200,000 traps generated in this run. After repeating this process for all five fitness functions, we also generate 1,000 traps uniformly at random and make use of the designed traps from Hom et al. [10] for comparison.

5 Results

5.1 Generating Traps Through Genetic Algorithms

First, we aim to understand how the genetic algorithm traverses through its solution space when optimizing for different attributes. Moreover, we use three methods to understand how the algorithm searches the space: we calculate the average number of generations until the best-fitness trap was found, the proportion of traps found with a given lethality/coherence, and an estimated probability distribution for traps over the range of lethality and coherence values.

Time to Optimal Trap. First, we calculate the average number of generations until the best-fitness trap is found. Figure 3 is a boxplot which shows the number of generations until the best trap was found in each of the 1,000 trials. As stated above, the experiment was split based on the fitness function used to generate the traps. The plot shows that the functional fitness function has a median at around 100 generations, along with a small interquartile range and some outliers up to 500 generations. On the other hand, the multiobjective and coherence fitness functions seem to have medians around 3,000 generations and ranges that span all 10,000 generations. The only notable difference between the multiobjective and coherence fitness functions is that the interquartile range of the coherence function is smaller than that of the multiobjective function. Specifically, it seems that the coherence boxplot has an interquartile range of around 1,200 generations to 5,200 generations, while the multiobjective fitness function seems to have an interquartile range of 200 generations to 6,200 generations. Hence, the coherence fitness function seems to more reliably find its optimal trap in the 2,500–5,000 generation range, while the multiobjective fitness function seems to be less reliable, finding its optimal trap in the 200–6,200 generation range. Since the range of the functional boxplot is so much smaller than that of the coherence and multiobjective boxplots, it is evident that finding a maximally lethal trap is much easier than finding a maximally coherent trap. Furthermore, it is evident that coherence is the bottleneck for the multiobjective fitness function as the multiobjective boxplot strongly resembles the coherence boxplot.

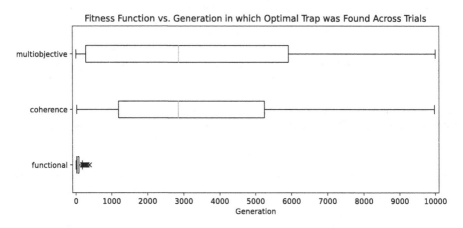

Fig. 3. Boxplot showing the distribution of when the optimal trap was found across all generations. Reproduced from [12].

Figure 4 shows two line plots depicting the average time to optimal trap. Figure 4a depicts the average fitness across all 1,000 trials for a given generation, and Fig. 4b depicts the cumulative average optimal fitness across all 1,000 trials for a given generation. Unlike the average fitness, the cumulative optimal fitness takes "the best trap seen until generation i" for each trial and averages those across all trials, whereas the average fitness just takes the average fitness of all traps in generation i across all trials. Additionally, the lack of visibility in the error bars can be attributed to the low variance in the data.

In Fig. 4a, notice that each of the functional, coherence, and multiobjective fitnesses plateau after around 300 generations. After this plateau, there were no deviations from the observed trend, and hence we focus on the first 500 generations of the plot. Notice that the functional, coherence, and multiobjective curves all settle at values around 0.75, 0.25, and 0.10, respectively. It makes sense that the functional fitness function converges at a high average fitness value, since this indicates that the function is able to find traps that are maximally lethal quickly (notice that the plot should not converge to 1, or maximal lethality, since we are averaging all traps in a given generation across all trials. By virtue of recombination and mutation, there are bound to be some defective traps within each generation, thereby lowering the total average fitness). However, it is interesting that the coherence and multiobjective functions converge at lower values of

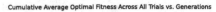

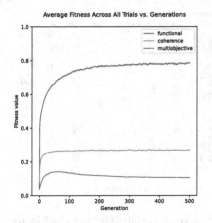

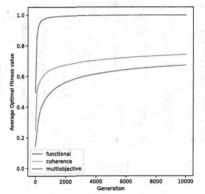

(a) Line plot showing the average fitness across all trials over generations. The (imperceptible) shaded region again represents the 95% confidence interval.

(b) Line plot showing the cumulative average optimal fitness across all trials over generations. The shaded region represents the 95% confidence interval.

Fig. 4. Line plots showing the trends of average fitness over generations, from [12].

0.25 and 0.10. Since the optimal solution likely wasn't found (an intuition we will soon confirm), we would expect the average fitness of these traps to generally increase since our genetic algorithm has the potential to generate coherent structures. Finally, note the peak in the multiobjective curve. This is likely due to the genetic algorithm choosing to sacrifice lethality in favor of coherence to generate traps with higher coherence and lethality. Such a choice would temporarily decrease overall fitness.

Next, consider Fig. 4b, the optimal cumulative fitness graph. Notice that the functional, coherence, and multiobjective lines converge to around 1.0, 0.75, and 0.60, respectively. Furthermore, since this is a graph of cumulative optimal fitness, notice that all of our plots depict monotonically increasing averages. The functional graph converges to 1.0 within about 500 generations. This tells us that all 1,000 trials were able to find a maximally lethal trap within that same period. Likewise, the coherence and multiobjective plots converge to values below 1, which tells us that these functions were not reliably able to find traps of maximal fitness (either maximally coherent or maximally coherent and lethal). In fact, this plot tells us that the highest value for coherence and multiobjective traps that we can find on average is 0.75 and 0.60. Such a disparity between the functional and coherence/multiobjective line plots is evidence that coherence is a much harder problem to solve than lethality (at least for this problem instance). Finally, after around 4000 generations, notice that there is another dramatic decrease in slope among all of the lines. Such a decrease indicates that most trials have found their optimal traps, and corresponds to the end of the interquartile range in the respective box plot.

Proportion Vectors. Figure 5 shows the proportion of traps with a given lethality and coherence. Each vector is separated by the method used to generate the trap. First, notice that the uniform random, (genetic algorithm) random, and hamming vectors are

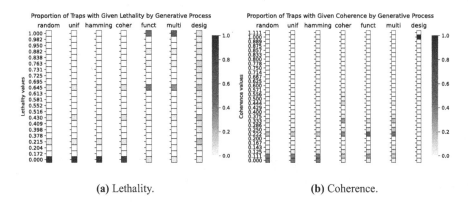

(a) Lethality.   **(b)** Coherence.

Fig. 5. Heatmap showing the proportion of traps with a given lethality/coherence, split by the parameter which the genetic algorithm was optimizing for (and designed traps). Reproduced from [12].

nearly identical in both figures. This supports the idea that all of these functions are equally effective at finding lethal and coherent traps. Specifically, this implies that the random and hamming fitness functions generate traps of similar quality to sampling our solution space uniformly at random (when using lethality and coherence as our proxy for success). Hence, sampling traps using a random fitness function is as effective as uniformly assigning fitness values to traps. Additionally, it is evident that being spatially ordered is not the only important aspect of our fitness function (contrary to [8])— there must also be correct alignment to encode some selection bias and guide the genetic algorithm to a target set of interest. In the case of the hamming function, notice that it is spatially ordered but not correctly aligned. Spatial-orderedness in the hamming case comes from optimization towards some random "goal" trap. Failing to align correctly can be seen in its inability to consistently generate traps with high lethality/coherence. Hence, spatial order is not sufficient for search success.

Additionally, notice that there are hot spots at non-zero values for traps generated uniformly at random. These hot spots are at lethalities 0.215, 0.430, and 0.645, and at coherences less than or equal to 0.333. The lethalities correspond to simple, lethal traps, such as traps where there is an arrow right by the door. Examples of such traps are shown in Fig. 6. The coherences correspond to random, coherent connections formed within cells. Note that it is not hard to form these connections by themselves, but it is the act of chaining long coherent connections together that becomes difficult.

Notice that the coherence vector resembles the uniform random vector in Fig. 5a and the lethality vector resembles the uniform random vector in Fig. 5b. As seen in the hamming case, this resemblance to the uniform random vector is indicative of a mismatch in alignment. In other words, optimizing for lethality does not beget coherence and vice versa, a trait that is attributable to our problem instance: the intersection of coherent and lethal target sets is too small.

In Fig. 5a, notice that there are a considerable proportion of traps that have achieved maximal lethality (namely, traps generated by the functional and multiobjective fitness functions). However, the same cannot be said for traps reaching maximal coherence in

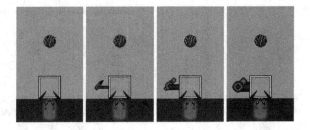

Fig. 6. Four simple traps of lethality 0, 0.215, 0.430, and 0.645, respectively, from [12].

Fig. 5b. Specifically, about 40% of the traps generated by the functional fitness function had maximal lethality, but only about 10% of the traps generated by the coherence fitness function had a coherence value of 0.556 (which corresponds to the last color of sufficient magnitude to be non-white). It is important to note that our genetic algorithm was able to find traps with higher coherence than 0.556, but there were not a significant enough proportion of those traps to show up in Fig. 5b. Hence, this is further evidence that finding lethal traps is significantly easier than finding coherent traps.

Finally, note that the proportion vectors for the designed traps are starkly different from the other vectors. Recall that these traps were created by the Hom et al. to zap gophers in a variety of ways—they were not intentionally designed to be maximally lethal or maximally coherent. Despite this lack of intentional effort, notice that every designed trap has a coherence of 1 and a near-randomly distributed lethality. Hom et al. attributed this unintended coherence to an innate sense of structure in human design. Furthermore, since coherence was an unintentional side-effect of construction, we see that form is a good indicator of intentional construction, as Hom et al. assumed. However, as shown by the inability for our genetic algorithm to reliably produce highly coherent traps directly, it is hard to reproduce this affinity for structure *in silico* [12].

Frequency Density Heatmaps. Finally, Fig. 7 shows the log proportion of traps generated with a given coherence and lethality. Again, each of the heatmaps are split by the method used the generate the traps. These heatmaps are similar to the proportion vectors shown in Fig. 7, but they plot both coherence and lethality as separate dimensions on the same graph (rather than being separate graphs). Note that all traps across all 1,000 trials and 10,000 generations are shown here, and hence we can see how the genetic algorithm traversed its search space among all iterations (again, using coherence and lethality as proxies for success).

First, notice that all distributions have hot spots at lethalities 0, 0.215, 0.430, and 0.645, which we have already noted correspond to simple, lethal traps (as shown in Fig. 6). Furthermore, notice that there is some baseline level of coherence for such simple traps, since having a firing arrow implies that there must be at least one coherent connection. This relationship can be seen for any trap with non-zero lethality, since these traps also have non-zero coherence in the heatmap. Additionally, notice that the lethalities 0.215, 0.430, and 0.645 are present in traps with coherence less than 0.222 (meaning that there is at most one coherent connection in the trap). On the other hand, when we consider lethalities larger than 0.645, notice that all of traps have coherence

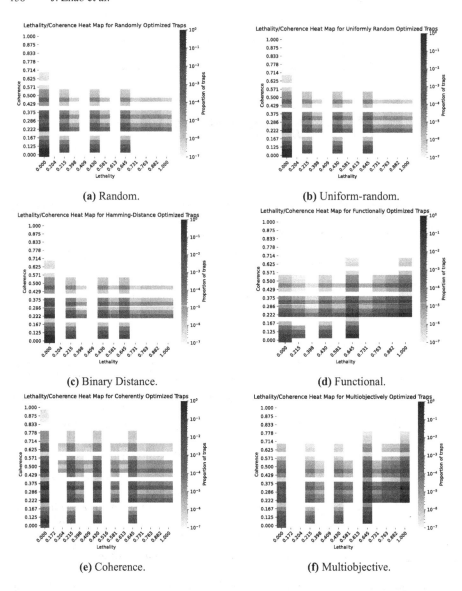

Fig. 7. Heatmaps representing the log proportion of traps with a given lethality and coherence value separated by optimization parameter from [12].

greater than 0.222, since these traps must have two firing arrows. Hence, since traps can only be lethal if they are built upon coherent connections, all lethal traps must have some baseline level of coherence. In other words, an absolute lack of coherence implies an absolute lack of lethality [12].

Next, notice that in Figs. 7a, 7b, and 7c have nearly identical distributions. Since these figures correspond to our unaligned fitness functions, the similarity of these distributions gives credence to the claim that these methods generate results of similar quality, and thus cannot reliably generate lethal or coherent traps.

Finally, in Figs. 7d, 7e, and 7f, we have functional, coherence, and multiobjective distributions, respectively. We can see that the multiobjective heatmap shares traits with both the functional and coherence heatmaps. Namely, notice that the multiobjective heatmap resembles the functional heatmap with some of the probability mass shifted towards higher coherence values. This is as expected, since the multiobjective function tries to find traps with high coherence and lethality. However, since lethality is easier to obtain, it makes sense that the multiobjective plot more closely resembles the functional plot; the algorithm seems to be finding highly lethal traps first, and then it tries to increase the coherence of those highly lethal traps.

6   Intention Perception and Genetic Algorithm Traps

6.1   Examining Generated Traps Under Intention Perception

Having generated a series of traps with genetic algorithms, we evaluate them in terms of intention perception. We note that while the significance value of $\alpha = 0.0001$ and uniform distribution probability measure $p(x) = 1/|\mathcal{X}|$ were used by default in both Hom et al.'s and our own previous work [10, 12], we add more variation to the intention perception model in the present paper. Considering that the traps in our study are generated by genetic algorithms rather than being selected uniformly at random from the sample space $\mathcal{X}$, a default, idealized uniform distribution model may affect the accuracy of intention perception. We test this claim.

Using the intention perception framework introduced in Sect. 3.2, we design four different intention perception models with varying probability measures $p(x)$ and significance levels α. Specifically, we use two different probability models: one representing an idealized uniform distribution and one estimating the real distribution of traps in the generating process, smoothed by the Simple Good-Turing (SGT) method [5]. We also test two significance levels, $\alpha = 0.0001$ and $\alpha = 0.05$. We then apply these intention perception models to the five classes of traps (random, functional, coherence, multiobjective, and designed) in an attempt to see whether gophers equipped with intention perception will regard the generated machines as designed traps, and if so, how this affects survival.

Survival of Gophers. We investigate the status of gophers with and without intention perception surviving against a series of traps generated by the genetic algorithms. For each class of traps, we randomly sample fifty traps, and a gopher will decide whether to enter a trap or skip to the next trap until it gets killed by a laser, dies from starvation, or successfully survives the fifty traps. Note that the gopher will behave exactly as described in Sect. 3.2: after deciding to enter the trap, the gopher will directly head toward the food and eat for some amount of time. However, if any arrow fires, the skittishness of the gopher will force it to leave immediately. We repeat this for 1,000 independent trials, record the status of the gophers as they progress through fifty traps, and analyze the results across availability of intention perception and types of traps. The parameters in the experiment are given in Table 1.

Table 1. Default values of experiment parameters.

Param.	Description	Value
P_e	Default prob. of entering	0.8
MFI	Maximum Fasting Interval	4
$P_{k,w}$	Prob. of kill w/ wide arrow	0.45
$P_{k,n}$	Prob. of kill w/ normal arrow	0.30
$P_{k,s}$	Prob. of kill w/ skinny arrow	0.15

Survival of Brave Gophers. Gophers are skittish by construction. However, we further investigate how the survival status of gophers is affected when the gophers are *brave*: instead of leaving a trap immediately whenever an arrow fires, a brave gopher will only leave the trap if it is hit or has finished eating. We re-run the same set of experiments for brave gophers as for default (skittish) gophers. That is, we run the experiment for each type of trap for 1,000 independent trials, average the measured outcomes, and analyze the results.

We investigate whether the generated traps are considered designed or randomly generated when gophers apply their intention perception algorithm. Moreover, by choosing different distributions and significance level parameters, we also study how varying of parameters affects the algorithm itself.

Table 2. Intention perception test results.

Fitness function	α	Unif. "Designed" %	SGT "Designed" %
Uniform random	0.05	0%	0%
Functional	0.05	0%	0%
Coherence	0.05	100%	8.9%
Multiobjective	0.05	97.5%	0.1%
Designed	0.05	100%	100%
Uniform random	0.0001	0%	0%
Functional	0.0001	0%	0%
Coherence	0.0001	100%	0.1%
Multiobjective	0.0001	58.2%	0%
Designed	0.0001	100%	100%

Table 2 shows the results of the intention perception algorithm for the uniform distribution model ($p(x) = 1/|\mathcal{X}|$) and the Simple Good-Turing (SGT) model. We test for α levels of 0.05 (corresponding to a surprise level of 4.33 bits) and 0.0001 (corresponding to a surprise level of 13.29 bits). As seen, for uniform random generated traps and functional traps, 0% of them are regarded as intentionally designed at both significance levels, under both distribution models. In other words, they are never mistaken for designed traps. In contrast, the designed traps themselves are judged as designed 100% of the time, at both significance levels under both models. For coherence and multiobjective traps, the results become more interesting. Under the uniform distribution model, coherence traps are deemed designed 100% of the time at both significance levels. Multiobjective traps are deemed designed 97.5% of the time at $\alpha = 0.05$, and 58.2% of the time at $\alpha = 0.0001$. However, once the more accurate SGT distribution model is used, the percentages drop precipitously for both types of traps.

We conclude that the intention perception algorithm finds coherence-optimized traps to be very similar to designed traps, but that there is a clear threshold between human-designed traps and others under the SGT model, at roughly the $\alpha = 0.0001$ level, where the intention perception algorithm becomes nearly perfect at distinguishing between human-designed traps and the others. Thus, changing the probability model from a misspecified uniform model to a more accurate SGT estimated model greatly improves the accuracy of the intention perception algorithm. Even though most of the coherence-optimized traps are considered to be intentionally designed under a assumed uniform distribution, very few of them are considered designed under the estimated SGT distribution model.

6.2 Survival of Gophers in Generated Traps

We investigate whether the intention perception algorithm of Hom et al. continues to confer significant survival advantages for artificial gophers when confronted with traps generated by a wider variety of processes. For these experiments we used the default parameter values of Hom et al. [10], including the misspecified uniform distribution probability model discussed in the previous section.

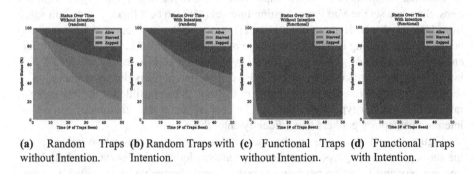

(a) Random Traps (b) Random Traps with (c) Functional Traps (d) Functional Traps
without Intention.   Intention.   without Intention.   with Intention.

Fig. 8. The effects of intention perception on the status of (skittish) gophers progressing through random and functional traps.

Figures 8a and 8b show the status of gophers with and without intention perception as they progress through fifty random traps, and these fifty random traps are selected from among the random traps generated by the genetic algorithm equipped with the random fitness function. We observe that only about 21.8% of baseline gophers survive all fifty traps while around 30.8% intention perception gophers do. The greater survival rate for intention perception gophers can be attributed to the sharp decline in percentage of gophers starved (40.6% starved for baseline gophers compared to 18.7% starved

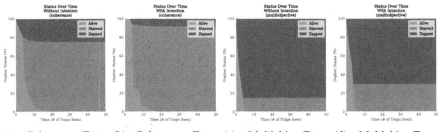

(a) Coherence Traps without Intention. **(b)** Coherence Traps with Intention. **(c)** Multiobj. Traps without Intention. **(d)** Multiobj. Traps with Intention.

Fig. 9. The effects of intention on the status of (skittish) gophers progressing through coherence and multiobjective traps.

for intention gophers). This is mainly because intention perception gophers are more likely to enter random traps and eat, confidently judging them as safe. However, intention gophers also have a higher probability of being killed by lasers (37.6% zapped for baseline gophers compared to 50.5% zapped for intention gophers). Thus, their confidence has a cost. Overall, intention perception gives gophers a survival advantage on random traps.

Figures 8c and 8d show how intention perception influences the survival of gophers as they progress through functional traps generated by the genetic algorithm optimizing for lethality. In this case, both baseline gophers and intention perception gophers have similar lifespans of around 5 traps. This is due to the high lethality of functional traps. Since we set the Maximum Fasting Interval (MFI) to be 4 (using the default value from Hom et al. and Kamath et al. [10, 12]), every gopher will enter at least one trap before the 5th, leading to a high percentage of death from lethal lasers. The only difference between baseline gophers and intention perception gophers is that while 99.2% of intention gophers are killed by lasers, 3.3% of baseline gophers die from starvation as shown in Fig. 8c. While the high lethality of the traps is responsible for the low survival rate for both gopher types, the relatively low coherence of the functional traps causes intention perception gophers to confidently enter them.

Figures 9a and 9b reveals another case in which intention perception fails to boost the survival rate of gophers even when traps are not lethal. We observe that both baseline gophers and intention perception gophers only survive through around 17 traps. Both baseline gophers and intention perception gophers die mainly from starvation, but intention gophers are even more likely to starve (73.5% starved for baseline gophers compared to 91.0% starved for intention gophers). As seen in Sect. 5, coherence traps usually have only low levels of lethality, resembling the lethality levels of traps generated uniformly at random. However, the high coherence implies a high probability of proper connectedness, which leads to a higher probability of firing. Even though the lasers may not hit the gophers, they can still frighten the skittish gophers and cause them to leave before finishing eating. This leads to the high percentage of gophers dying from starvation for both gopher types. However, the decrease for baseline gophers is relatively smooth, but the decrease for intention gophers is more periodic. We observe a sharp decline in the surviving gopher population at around 4 traps, corresponding to the Maximum Fasting Interval (MFI) of 4. This is because, as the name suggests, coherence-optimized traps have high coherence, leading intention perception gophers to treat them as designed traps and thus they refuse to enter them. For coherence traps, the intention perception algorithm becomes a liability, as the largely non-functional coherence confuses the decision apparatus, leading to increased, unnecessary starvation.

Finally, Fig. 9c and 9d show the status of baseline and intention gophers when attempting to survive against series of multiobjective traps that are optimized for both coherence and functionality. In this case, intention perception again provides no survival advantage to gophers. Though intention perception gophers have a lower percentage of dying from lasers (88.1% zapped for baseline gophers compared to 71.3% zapped for intention gophers), they have an increased likelihood of starvation (11.9% starved for baseline gophers compared to 28.7% starved for intention gophers). The average lifespan for both gophers types is again approximately 4. Similar to case of functional traps, this means gophers are forced to enter at least one trap before the 5th. Once they entered the trap, they are either directly zapped by a laser or frightened to leave the trap without consuming food since the traps are both lethal and coherent. Thus, before entering the 5th trap they typically die from either laser strike or starvation.

6.3   Survival of Brave Gophers in Generated Traps

In contrast to Sect. 6.2, Figs. 10 and 11 show the status of **brave** gophers with and without intention perception as they progress through fifty random traps generated by our genetic algorithms, beginning with the random fitness function results in Figs. 10a and 10b. Notice that the number of gophers that starve has now sharply decreased, regardless of intention perception. Furthermore, notice that gophers with intention (seemingly) do not starve at all. Both of these observations make sense since random traps are likely non-lethal. Even if these random traps are firing traps, it is unlikely that the orientation of such a trap would hit the gopher. Furthermore, if a gopher is hit by a rogue arrow, the probability that it will be hit in successive traps is equally small. Due to their bravery, these gophers will keep eating even when aberrant arrows fire. Starvation is still possible, though, such as when a gopher without intention perception decides not to enter MFI - 1 traps, and is hit by a rogue arrow in the final trap.

Notice that Figs. 10c and 10d are nearly identical to Figs. 8c and 8d, respectively. Effectively nothing changes in the setup since every trap is maximally lethal. Thus, having brave gophers does not make much of a difference, since any entering gopher will be shot immediately and then leave. Hence, the only factor in what proportion of gophers starve or are zapped is the probability of entering, which remains constant between the previous experiment and this one.

In Figs. 11a and 11b the gophers survive much longer than in Figs. 9a and 9b, respectively. This is expected, since these gophers are brave. We saw in the previous experiment that high connectedness implied a higher probability of firing, which would scare off skittish gophers. However, brave gophers are rewarded for their bravery—since the probability of a trap being lethal is low (as coherence does not necessarily beget lethality [12]), if a gopher enters a trap it will most likely be able to eat unharmed.

However, the probability of entering a trap now causes a larger discrepancy between the intention perception and non-intention gophers. Since these traps are highly coherent, gophers with intention perception are more likely to consider these traps designed, and will not enter them until they are forced to (namely, every 4 traps). Furthermore, if these gophers get hit on the 4th trap, then they starve. Hence, we see sharp drops every 4 traps in Fig. 11b. On the other hand, gophers with no intention perception are rewarded for their ignorance, and hence we see much smoother curves (since there is a fixed 80% probability that a non-intention gopher will enter a trap). This is another case where intention perception slightly helps gophers through genetic algorithm traps.

Finally, consider Figs. 11c and 11d. Again, these plots are nearly identical to Figs. 9c and 9d. This is due to the same reasoning as the functional case—all traps are somewhat lethal. Furthermore, note that these traps may not be maximally lethal, since we penalize large differences in coherence and lethality (thereby artificially lowering lethality in favor of coherence). Hence, we expect traps to fire, but not necessarily kill the gophers. Thus, when a gopher enters a multiobjective trap, it is likely to get either killed or starve before the 5th trap, and the gopher's boldness is unable to save it.

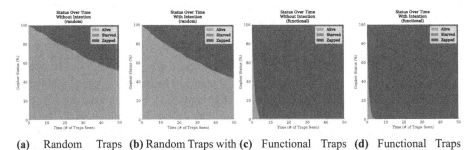

(a) Random Traps without Intention. **(b)** Random Traps with Intention. **(c)** Functional Traps without Intention. **(d)** Functional Traps with Intention.

Fig. 10. The effects of intention perception on the status of (skittish) gophers progressing through random and functional traps.

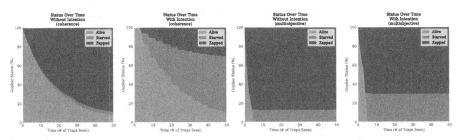

(a) Coherence Traps without Intention. **(b)** Coherence Traps with Intention. **(c)** Multiobj. Traps without Intention. **(d)** Multiobj. Traps with Intention.

Fig. 11. The effects of intention on the status of brave gophers progressing through coherence and multiobjective traps.

7   Discussion

7.1   Genetic Algorithm

First, we saw that it is easier to optimize for lethality than for coherence. This could be seen in Fig. 4 since the average cumulative optimal fitness of the functional fitness function reaches a maximal lethality of 1.0, while the coherence fitness function was only able to reach a coherence of 0.75 on average. Furthermore, every trial for the functional fitness function converged to a maximal lethality within 500 generations, as per Fig. 3. Additionally, we saw a considerable proportion of traps generated reach a maximal lethality under the functional fitness function in Fig. 5, and we saw that the multiobjective heatmap shared a much stronger resemblance with the functional heatmap than the coherence heatmap in Fig. 7. However, even though we saw highly lethal traps within 200 generations (when optimizing for lethality), we noted that these traps were only simple, lethal traps, where there were one or two arrows by the door. If we wanted to generate traps with only these 2 arrows by the door (and everything else as floor cells), then that would be a much harder problem. In other words, it is hard to generate highly coherent traps with just these two arrows, just as it is hard to generate long chains of coherent connections.

Next, we saw that most coherence-optimized traps did not reach their optimum fitness until around 2,500 generations, as per Fig. 3. This can be attributed to a lack of "shortcuts" in optimizing for coherence, unlike lethality [12]. Specifically, when optimizing for lethality, the algorithm exploited the shortcut of putting two arrows near the door. There is no such shortcut for coherence—the only way to create highly coherent traps is to place the correct tiles with the correct thickness in the correct orientation at the correct position on the board. This discrepancy in problem difficulty is reflected in the target set sizes: among all possible traps, there are only 26,733 traps with a coherence of 1, while there are at least $91^7 \approx 5.1 \times 10^{13}$ traps with lethality 1. Furthermore, according to a uniform sampling of one million traps, 2.27% of those traps had a lethality greater than 0.5, whereas only 0.0037% of traps had a coherence greater than 0.5.

Finally, we note that the coherence of a trap is solely dependent on the connectedness of the wire, which is not a property that is preserved under recombination [12]. Since we encode our traps as an array, when we recombine and mutate, we effectively cut the trap in two. Thus, we can cut the coherence by up to a factor of one half if we cut along a coherent connection, and we can further lower the coherence if we then mutate a cell that is a coherent connection. On the other hand, if we only have arrows by the door, mutation and recombination are much less likely to affect these traps. Modifying the genetic algorithm to allow for coordinated mutations and recombination may overcome the current barriers to achieving high coherence levels.

7.2   Intention Perception

We tested gophers against traps generated by our genetic algorithms. Some of the gophers were equipped with intention perception algorithms, using a default, misspecified uniform distribution probability model. We saw that under the uniform model the gophers would always enter the trap, unless the trap was coherence-optimized. In the event that the trap was optimized for both lethality and coherence, we saw that a majority of multiobjective traps were thought to be designed. This suggests that intention perception may no longer confer strong survival advantages when presented with such traps under a misspecified model. Furthermore, as we saw in Sects. 6.2 and 6.3, intention perception gophers no longer survive at a significantly higher rate than those without intention perception. When presented with traps optimized for only coherence, intention perception gophers actually starved more often, since they become too scared to enter traps they deem harmful. On the other hand, intention perception gophers enter every trap optimized for lethality, thereby dying instantly (and never starving). Hence, the gophers were confidently wrong in both cases, losing their survival advantage.

8   Conclusions

As discussed in the introduction, we set out to investigate two potential limitations of Hom et al.'s work. First, we conclude that the link between lethality and coherence is weak. We saw that while an absolute lack of coherence implies an absolute lack in lethality (cf. Fig. 7), this is where the correlation ended. As noted by Kamath et al., even though highly lethal traps imply a baseline level of coherence, the genetic algorithm does not produce high coherence as a side product of high lethality [12]. Similarly, high coherence does not beget high lethality. However, high coherence may boost the probability of finding firing traps, but firing traps may not necessarily hit the gopher (and hence may not be lethal).

Second, we found that while intention perception helps intention gophers survive as they progress through random traps, the strong survival advantage disappears under other conditions. When traps are lethal, all gophers are killed quickly, within 5 traps. When gophers progress through traps that are coherent and traps that are both coherent and lethal, intention perception leads to more gophers dying from starvation, but the average lifespan of intention gophers is the same as that of baseline gophers. Even if we attempt to reduce of number of gophers dying from starvation by abandoning the skittishness of gophers, intention perception does not significantly benefit gophers' chances of survival in any of the situations. Therefore, we can conclude that Hom et al.'s finding that intention perception provides significant survival advantage to artificial agents doesn't always hold. This is because the implicitly assumed correlation between trap coherence and trap lethality doesn't hold generally.

Finally, we explored the capacity of genetic algorithms to generate traps with specific traits. We saw that they were efficient in creating highly functional traps in a small number of generations, but the genetic algorithms struggled to optimize for coherence. The inability of genetic algorithms to directly generate highly coherent traps implies that trap coherence may still remain a plausible sign of intentional construction. Moreover, we conclude that generating traps with specific traits of interest requires our fitness functions to be both spatially ordered and correctly aligned. Being spatially ordered allows the genetic algorithm to perform a meaningful local search with neighborhood constraints on the elements of the search space, but simply being spatially ordered is not enough. Additionally, alignment allows us to target a specific set using selection bias.

Acknowledgements. This research was supported in part by the NSF under Grant No. 1950885. Any opinions, findings, or conclusions are those of the authors alone, and do not necessarily represent the views of the National Science Foundation.

References

1. Bhattacharya, M., Islam, R., Mahmood, A.N.: Uncertainty and evolutionary optimization: a novel approach. In: 2014 9th IEEE Conference on Industrial Electronics and Applications, pp. 988–993 (2014). https://doi.org/10.1109/ICIEA.2014.6931307
2. Bock, W.J., Wahlert, G.V.: Adaptation and the form-function complex. Evolution **19**, 269–299 (1965)
3. Chapman, C.D.: Structural topology optimization via the genetic algorithm. Ph.D. thesis, Massachusetts Institute of Technology (1994)
4. Fonseca, C.M., Fleming, P.J., et al.: Genetic algorithms for multiobjective optimization: formulation discussion and generalization. In: ICGA, vol. 93, pp. 416–423 (1993)
5. Gale, W.A.: Good-Turing smoothing without tears. J. Quant. Linguist. **2**, 217–237 (1995)
6. Gero, J.S., Kannengiesser, U.: A function-behavior-structure ontology of processes. Artif. Intell. Eng. Des. Anal. Manuf. **21**(4), 379–391 (2007). https://doi.org/10.1017/S0890060407000340
7. Golberg, D.E.: Genetic Algorithms in Search, Optimization, and Machine Learning. Addison-Wesley, Boston (1989)
8. Häggström, O.: Intelligent design and the NFL theorems. Biol. Philos. **22**(2), 217–230 (2007)
9. Hazen, R.M., Griffin, P.L., Carothers, J.M., Szostak, J.W.: Functional information and the emergence of biocomplexity. Proc. Natl. Acad. Sci. **104**(Suppl. 1), 8574–8581 (2007). https://doi.org/10.1073/pnas.0701744104. https://www.pnas.org/doi/abs/10.1073/pnas.0701744104
10. Hom, C., Maina-Kilaas, A., Ginta, K., Lay, C., Montañez, G.D.: The Gopher's gambit: survival advantages of artifact-based intention perception. In: Rocha, A.P., Steels, L., van den Herik, H.J. (eds.) Proceedings of the 13th International Conference on Agents and Artificial Intelligence: ICAART, vol. 1, pp. 205–215. INSTICC, SciTePress (2021). https://doi.org/10.5220/0010207502050215
11. Jin, Y., Branke, J.: Evolutionary optimization in uncertain environments - a survey. IEEE Trans. Evol. Comput. **9**(3), 303–317 (2005). https://doi.org/10.1109/TEVC.2005.846356
12. Kamath, A., Zhao, J., Grisanti, N., Montañez, G.: The Gopher grounds: testing the link between structure and function in simple machines. In: Proceedings of the 14th International Conference on Agents and Artificial Intelligence: ICAART, vol. 2, pp. 528–540. INSTICC, SciTePress (2022). https://doi.org/10.5220/0010900900003116
13. Krink, T., Filipic, B., Fogel, G.: Noisy optimization problems - a particular challenge for differential evolution? In: Congress on Evolutionary Computation, CEC 2004, vol. 1, pp. 332–339, June 2004. https://doi.org/10.1109/CEC.2004.1330876
14. Maina-Kilaas, A., Hom, C., Ginta, K., Montañez, G.D.: The predator's purpose: intention perception in simulated agent environments. In: 2021 IEEE Congress on Evolutionary Computation (CEC). IEEE (2021)
15. Maina-Kilaas, A., Montañez, G.D., Hom, C., Ginta, K.: The hero's dilemma: survival advantages of intention perception in virtual agent games. In: 2021 IEEE Conference on Games (IEEE CoG). IEEE (2021)
16. Mitchell, M.: An Introduction to Genetic Algorithms. MIT Press, Cambridge (1998)
17. Montañez, G.D.: A unified model of complex specified information. BIO-Complexity **2018**(4) (2018)

18. Reeves, C., Rowe, J.: Genetic Algorithms: Principles and Perspectives: A Guide to GA Theory. Kluwer Academic Publishers, Amsterdam (2002)
19. Then, T., Chong, E.: Genetic algorithms in noisy environment. In: Proceedings of 1994 9th IEEE International Symposium on Intelligent Control, pp. 225–230 (1994). https://doi.org/10.1109/ISIC.1994.367813
20. Vorhees, C., Williams, M.: Assessing spatial learning and memory in rodents. ILAR J. Natl. Res. Council Inst. Lab. Anim. Resour. 55, 310–332 (2014). https://doi.org/10.1093/ilar/ilu013
21. Wang, S., Wang, M., Tai, K.: An enhanced genetic algorithm for structural topology optimization. Int. J. Numer. Methods Eng. 65, 18–44 (2006). https://doi.org/10.1002/nme.1435
22. Weibel, E.R.: Symmorphosis: On Form and Function in Shaping Life. Harvard University Press, Cambridge (2000)

Domain Dependent Parameter Setting in SAT Solver Using Machine Learning Techniques

Filip Beskyd[ID] and Pavel Surynek[(✉)][ID]

Faculty of Information Technology, Czech Technical University, Thákurova 9,
160 00 Praha 6, Czech Republic
{beskyfil,pavel.surynek}@fit.cvut.cz

Abstract. We address the problem of variable and truth-value choice in modern search-based Boolean satisfiability (SAT) solvers depending on the problem domain. The SAT problem is the task to determine truth-value assignment for variables of a given Boolean formula under which the formula evaluates to true. The SAT problem is often used as a canonical representation of combinatorial problems in many domains of computer science ranging from artificial intelligence to software engineering. Modern complete search-based SAT solvers represent a universal problem solving tool which often provide higher efficiency than ad-hoc direct solving approaches. Many efficient variable and truth-value selection heuristics were devised. Heuristics can usually be fine tuned by single or multiple numerical parameters prior to executing the search process over the concrete SAT instance. In this paper we present a machine learning approach that predicts the parameters of heuristic from the underlying structure of a graph derived from the input SAT instance. Using this approach we effectively fine tune the SAT solver for specific problem domain.

Keywords: SAT problem · Boolean satisfiability · Solver · Graph structure · Machine learning · Heuristic · Parameter tuning

1 Introduction

The Boolean satisfiability (SAT) problem, the task of finding a truth-value assignment of a given Boolean formula, is one of the fundamental computer science problems [6]. Concretely; the SAT problem was the first one to be proven to belong to the NP-Complete class of problems [10]. Major direct use-cases of SAT come from industries such as software testing [12], automated planning [20], hardware verification [17] or cryptography [33], as well as many other. Moreover, many other problems of computer science are often reduced to SAT.

Standard and in practice often used way of solving a given problem is to compile it, in some way, to a concrete SAT instance which is then given to another program as an input, so called a SAT Solver. The SAT solver solves the instance and answers whether there exists a truth-value assignment by which it can be satisfied or not, with the concrete proof, that is either variables assignment which satisfy the formula or conflict.

A. P. Rocha et al. (Eds.): ICAART 2022, LNAI 13786, pp. 169–200, 2022.
https://doi.org/10.1007/978-3-031-22953-4_8

There exist many solvers to the SAT problem. Solvers are divided into two major groups, **local search** and **systematic search** solvers. This work is focused on systematic search solvers based on the Conflict-driven clause-learning (CDCL) algorithm [24] whose implementations come as variants of the Minisat [29] solver.

CDCL SAT solvers have witnessed dramatic improvements in their efficiency over the last 20 years, and consequently have become drivers of progress in many areas of computer science such as formal verification [28]. There is a general agreement that these solvers somehow exploit structure inherent in industrial instances due to the clause learning mechanism and its cooperation with variable and value selection heuristics.

Typically, implementations of CDCL SAT solvers have many parameters, such as variable decay, clause decay and frequency of restarts, which need to be set prior to the solver being executed. Depending on how various parameters are set for an input instance often has significant impact on the running time of the solver. Hence it naturally makes sense to try to set these parameters automatically.

The paper is organized as follows: Sect. 3 provides theoretical minimum, in Sect. 4 we introduce related works, Sect. 5 states which parameters will be tuned and briefly explains their meaning, Sect. 6 measures the impact of each parameter on solving time, Sect. 7 presents how we applied machine learning to our problem and finally in Sect. 8 we evaluate our machine learning parameter setting in various benchmarks.

2   Contribution

In this work we apply **machine learning** techniques [26] to predict the values for the parameters of SAT solver which reduce solving time, based on the type of an input instance. This step is motivated among else by notion that many instances for a fixed domain are in some way similar thus formula's hidden structure will be similar as well.

For example the structure of most industrial SAT instances are vastly different from the structure of the random SAT instances [3] or instances constructed for planning problems, and these are different from instances encoding puzzles like the pigeon-hole problem. Problems that belong to the same domain tend to have similar structure within the domain and specific values of the parameters work better for them, than having the default parameter setting globally for every instance.

Our contribution presented in this paper consists in:

1. Visual summary of dependencies of solving time on setting of various parameters of the SAT solver.
2. Extending the set of usual features extracted by SAT solvers from instances, by computing graph related features on clause graph (CG), and variable–clause graph (VCG), which ought to better capture the underlying structure of the instance.
3. Building a machine learning mechanism based on the extended set of features that sets the SAT solver's parameters according to the input instance.

This paper substantially extends the conference paper [5]. Specifically we provide more formal background and extended set of experiments.

3 Background

3.1 Boolean Formula

The language of Boolean formula (in this paper we will refer to a boolean formula simply as formula) consists of Boolean variables, Boolean operators and parentheses.

Definition 1. Boolean formula *is formed by connecting Boolean variables by Boolean operators, these interconnections are enclosed in parentheses into logical sentences.*

3.2 Satisfiable Formula

Definition 2. *Formula* ϕ *is said to be* satisfiable *if and only if there exist a truth assignment to all of its variables such that the formula evaluates to TRUE.*

3.3 Conjunctive Normal Form

A simple structure is advantageous for algorithmic manipulation. The most common choice for SAT solving is the *conjunctive normal form* (CNF).

The usefulness of the conjunctive normal form for SAT solving was first highlighted by Davis and Putnam in [11]. A formula in conjunctive normal form consists of a conjunction of clauses. This allows a simple representation as a set of sets of literals.

Definition 3. *A* conjunctive normal form (CNF) *of a formula is a conjunction* $(\wedge)$ *of clauses.*

Any propositional logic formula can be transformed to CNF. Common way to obtain CNF of the formula is to use Tseitin transformation [34].

For satisfiability testing its not necessary to obtain equal formula, but rather *equisatisfiable* formula. The Tseitin transformation is a linear transformation from an arbitrary propositional formula to CNF, preserving satisfiability.

Definition 4. *Two formulas* ϕ *and* ψ *are* equisatisfiable *if and only if* ϕ *is satisfiable when* ψ *is satisfiable.*

3.4 Complexity of SAT Problem

SAT problem is one of the fundamental computer science problems. Concretely SAT problem was the first one to be proven to belong to NP-Complete class of problems [10].

3.5 CDCL Solver

The CDCL [24] paradigm extends DPLL with a series of techniques and heuristics such as conflict-driven branching, clause learning, backjumping, and frequent restarts that dramatically improve its performance over the plain DPLL solver [27], which makes them so useful for solving real-life industrial problems.

3.6 CDCL Pseudo-code

Algorithm 1. CDCL with restarts.

```
 1: function CDCL(φ)
 2:     υ = ∅                                                    ▷ Empty assignment
 3:     loop
 4:         υ = BCP(φ, υ)                                        ▷ Try solve by unit propagation
 5:         if ∃conflictingClause ∈ φ such that
              FALSIFIED(conflictingClause, υ) then
 6:             if CURRENTDECISIONLEVEL(υ) = 0 then
 7:                 return false
 8:             end if
 9:             learntClause = CONFLICTANALYSIS(conflictingClause, υ)
10:             φ = φ ∪ learntClause                             ▷ Clause learning
11:             υ = BTTOLEVEL(GetBTLevel(learntClause), υ)
12:         else if |υ| = |VARIABLESOF(φ)| then
13:             return true
14:         else if RestartCondition = true then
15:             υ = BTTOLEVEL(0, υ)                              ▷ Restart
16:         else
17:             OPTIONALCLAUSEDELETION                           ▷ Remove not-so-useful clauses
18:             var = BRANCHINGHEURISTIC                         ▷ Select next variable
19:             value = POLARITYHEURISTIC(var)                   ▷ Pick its value
20:             υ = υ ∪ {var → value}                            ▷ Branch
21:         end if
22:     end loop
23: end function
```

Important parts for us happening on lines 14, where the restart happens when the condition is met, on lines 18 and 19 variable selection heuristic and choosing its value. These heuristics are controlled in minisat by its parameters `-var-decay`, `-rfirst` and `-rinc` respectively.

4 Related Work

4.1 Portfolio Solver: SatZilla

SatZilla [35] is a portfolio solver, which won many awards in SAT Competition [2]. It introduces new approach of using many other solvers (portfolio) in the background. The solvers are used as-is, and SatZilla does not have any control over their execution.

Machine learning was previously shown to be an effective way to predict the runtime of SAT solvers, and SatZilla exploits this. It uses machine learning to predict hardness of the input instance, and then based on this prediction select a solver from its portfolio which will be assigned to solve the problem. Machine learning technique for predicting is ridge regression.

This works because different solvers are better for different types of instances, there is no universal solver which would perform very good on every category of instances, thus the key is to predict what kind of input instance it is and determine which solver would suit best to solve it.

First step is to identify one or more solvers to use for pre-solving instances. These pre-solvers are then ran for a short amount of time before features are computed, in order to ensure good performance on very easy instances and to allow the hardness predicting models to choose solver exclusively on harder instances.

Predicting hardness of an instance is done by first extracting various features from the input. To be usable effectively for automated algorithm selection, these features must be relatively cheap to compute.

To train the model, SatZilla will first compute some features on training set of problem instances and run each algorithm in the portfolio to determine its running times. If feature computation cannot be completed for some reason (error or timeout), backup solver will be determined and used for solving this instance.

In summary, when the model for predicting the runtime of the solvers has been already trained, SatZilla is ready to be used in practice. When the new input instance comes, it computes its features. These are then used as input for predictive model which predicts the best solver to be used. That particular solver is then used to solve instance.

4.2 Parameter Tuning: AvatarSat

AvatarSat [16] is a modified version of Minisat 2.0. AvatarSat introduced two key novelties. The first one is that it used machine learning to determine the best parameter settings for each SAT formula. The machine learning technique used is Support Vector Machine.

Second novelty in AvatarSat is the "course correction" as it dynamically "corrects" the direction in which solver is searching. Modern SAT solvers store new learnt clauses and drop input clauses during the search, which can change the structure of the problem considerably. AvatarSat's argument is that the optimal parameter settings for this modified problem may be significantly different from the original input problem.

AvatarSat therefore first selects values of parameters for MiniSat to use during the initial part of the search. When the number of new clauses accumulated during the search crosses a threshold, the "course correction" procedure examines the new clauses to select a new set of parameters for MiniSat to use after the restart. This is the principle of AvatarSat which dynamically adapts the parameter settings to the potentially changing characteristics of the SAT problem.

Input SAT instances are classified using features extracted from the instance. Each class corresponds to the best configuration for the SAT-formulas belonging to the domain. The approach is similar as we applied in this paper.

AvatarSat uses 58 different features of SAT formulas such as ratio between variables and clauses, number of variables, number of clauses, positive and negative literal occurrences etc. Features used are very similar to those of SatZilla, which were originally designed to measure hardness of the instance and not its structure.

The classifier is trained by running a number of configurations of Minisat on a number of sat instances, then each instance is paired with the optimal configuration and that data is used to train the classifier with Radial Basis Function. When the classifier is trained, Minisat can be configured for any SAT formula by classifying the formula and then retrieving the configuration associated with that domain.

AvatarSat is tuning only two parameters, -var-decay and -rinc, Nine values for the first one and three for the second one, so the number of examined configurations is 27.

4.3   Iterated Local Search

The key idea underlying iterated local search is to focus the search not on the full space of all candidate solutions but on the solutions that are returned by some underlying algorithm, typically a local search heuristic [23].

Iterated local search is a local search algorithm that optimalizes parameters but only one dimension at a time, it is a one-dimensional variant of hill climbing. It checks configurations differing in one single change from the current configuration until it finds a better one. Iterative first improvement are repeated until no improvement can be made by a single change. This is most likely to be a local extreme. To escape the local extreme a fixed number s of random changes are made, and the process of making iterative first improvements is resumed until a new local maximum is reached and the process of perturbation and iterative first improvements are repeated until some termination criterion is reached [30].

In [30] author has used this algorithm for MiniSat's parameter tuning. There was not feature extraction approach as in AvatarSat, SatZilla and this thesis, but it was an attempt to tune SAT solvers parameters and therefore we mention his solution in this chapter. Results were measured only on cryptographic instances, concretely factorization problem instances, but this approach performed surprisingly well. As author has mentioned, it is an open question how the tuned solver would perform on bigger instances.

5   Tuned Parameters

We will tune the following heuristics settings of MiniSat solver as these have the most significant impact on the solver's running time.

– -var-decay the VSIDS's decay factor
– -cla-decay the clause decay factor
– -rfirst base restart interval
– -rinc restart interval increase factor

5.1   VSIDS

VSIDS is an abbreviation of *variable state independent decaying sum*. VSIDS has become a standard choice for many popular SAT solvers, such as MiniSat [29] which we employed as default solver for this paper.

The main idea of VSIDS heuristic is to associate each variable with an *activity*, which signifies a variable's frequency of appearing in recent conflicts via the mechanism of *bump* and *decay*.

Bump is a number which is incremented by 1 every time this variable appears in conflict.

Decay factor $0 < \alpha < 1$ is a number by which each of the variable's activity is multiplied after each conflict and thus decreased.

5.2 Clause Decay

In MiniSat, similar principle as in VSIDS is applied to clauses. When a learnt clause is used in the conflict analysis, its activity is incremented. Inactive clauses are periodically removed from the *learnt clauses database* [29]. Since a set of unsatisfiable clauses generates many conflicts, and therefore many conflict clauses, the high activity of a clause can be seen as a potential sign of unsatisfiability [13].

5.3 Restart Frequency

Frequency of restarts in MiniSat is determined by two parameters, the *base restart interval* and *restart interval increase factor*. One round of search will take as long until the search encounters given number of conflicts L. For example, `minisat(120)` will be searching space of assignments as long as it reaches count of conflicts equal to 120. After that, the algorithm will pause, determine new number of needed conflicts to force next restart, and continue searching.

Number of needed conflicts to restart L is determined as follows:

$$L = \texttt{restart\_base} \cdot \texttt{restart\_inc\_factor}^{\#restarts}.$$

6 Impact of Parameters

The term "structure", due to its vagueness, leaves much room for interpretation, though, and it remains unclear how this structure manifests itself and how exactly it should be exploited [32].

However, research has advanced since then, and nowdays the structure of some instances can be exploited.

Base idea of our work comes from paper [3], where it was shown that industrial instances exhibit "hidden structures" based on which solver is learning clauses during search. In [31] researchers have shown that formulas with good community structure tend to be easier to solve.

Variables form logical relationships and we hypothesize that VSIDS exploit these relationships to find the variables that are most "constrained" in the formula. The logical relationship between variables are concretized as some variation of the variable incidence graph (VIG) [22].

Our idea is to exploit this fact, so we will construct a graph which is representing each instance, compute various properties of this graph which will be used as features of instances for machine learning, in addition to standard features of the instance like number of variables, clauses, their ratios etc.

In this section we will present results of our initial data exploration. We performed several observations on four different domains. On these domains we observe how the solver's parameters affect then number of conflicts, and thus solving time.

6.1 Domains of SAT Instances Selected

For this paper we limited our problem to four SAT domains for which we will use machine learning to set solvers parameters. We have chosen these:

- Random SAT/UNSAT
- Pigeonhole problem
- Planning
  - sliding tiles problem
  - Hanoi towers
- Factorization

We have selected these because they are **structurally diverse**, and we expect them to have different demands on parameters.

Random SAT/UNSAT are instances of 3-SAT problem, generated randomly. This domain is also part of SAT category in which various solvers are compared by efficiency they achieve. In SAT competition context the category is simply called *RANDOM*.

Definition 5. Phase transition *is the ratio of the number of clauses to variables.*

As we approach to this number, the phase transition point, the hardness of a problem is varied. Experiments have shown that an easy-hard-easy pattern for SAT occurs as this ratio is increased and that the hard instances occur in the phase transition [25] (Fig. 1).

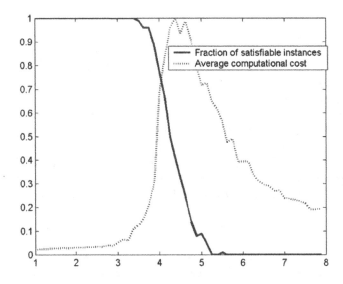

Fig. 1. Phase transition.

Pigeonhole problem involves showing that it is impossible to put $n + 1$ pigeons into n holes if each pigeon must go into a distinct hole. It is well known that for this combinatorial problem there is no polynomial-sized proof of the unsatisfiability [18]. Combinatorial problems are also part of SAT competition category, known as *crafted*. We chose pigeonhole problem as one representative, because it can be generated easily with random starting positions with fixed size.

Planning problems representatives, we chose planning problem known as *sliding tiles problem*, or in its fixed size form *Lloyd's fifteen*. We generate numbered tiles order randomly, and aggregate these instances always within fixed size, for example, We never combine problem of size 4×4 with 5×5. Another representative of planning is Hanoi towers problem, this problem is not possible to "randomize" because initial state is always given, this problem We added out of curiosity to observe if it will exhibit some similarities to sliding tiles planning problem.

Factorization problem is a numeric problem containing multiplication thus it is assumed to be hard for SAT solvers, more specifically the problem is to determine whether a big number is a prime or otherwise if it can be factored. This is an example of typical *INDUSTRIAL* instance from SAT competition. We chose factorization because its easy to generate random instances, by simply generate one big random number and build SAT formula. We will observe for MiniSat deals with satisfiable and unsatisfiable instances. When factorization instance is satisfiable, it means that the number is not prime.

6.2 Correlation of the Number of Conflicts and Solving Time

For the initial dataset building process, it is necessary to find close to optimal solver parameters for which the solving time is lowest possible.

Since some of the harder instances take several tens of seconds to solve, it would be unfeasible to generate dataset from solving each of these instances by brute force search on grid of parameter values, thus We decided to build this dataset from small instances from SATLIB. These instances are usually solved within fraction of second by Minisat solver, but this approach has a downside, it is hard to capture real solving time, because for these small instances overhead usually outweigh useful computation time.

Solving time varies a bit with every run and solving time captured by MiniSat also includes several system-originated factors which are not desired to take part in the dataset. However, computation is deterministic with fixed initial random seed, and number of conflicts for concrete parameters stays always the same for every run, so it is natural to use number of conflicts as other metric instead of actual solving time.

The following scatter plot shows strong correlation between number of conflicts and solving time on randomly selected instance from SATLIB, thus it is correct to use conflict count as measurement of performance of the parameters.

The implication from this observation for this thesis is, that we decided to measure conflicts instead of time, in this chapter and also in the final chapter about experiments.

6.3 Observed Parameters

Each of the subsections shows how the parameter's value depends on number of conflicts for each of aforementioned domains. Note that axes do not have same values in each of the examples. Before we made these plots we first analyzed at what intervals should we chose to discretize. For example we observed that *variable decay* parameter for values in $(0, 0.4)$ always gave bad results so we avoided those and only examined $[0.4, 1)$. For space-saving purposes we have omitted label of vertical axis, and it will always be **number of conflicts** (Fig. 2).

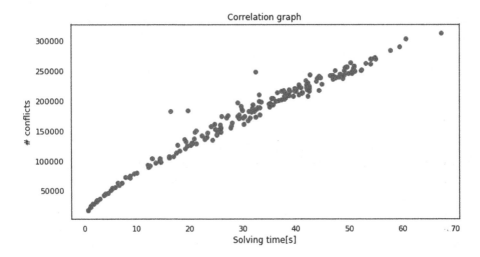

Fig. 2. Correlation between number of conflicts and solving time [5].

Following plots are results of several measurements of impact of one parameter at the time. For each domain we have gathered multiple instances, either downloaded or generated by myself. We ran MiniSat on every instance, with concrete parameter value and recorded number of conflicts encountered during the search with that value. Then we repeated the same with different initial random seed and computed mean of number of conflicts for each instance. Lastly We aggregated results from previous step for each domain by computing mean of conflicts for every parameter's value.

Variable Decay. For random SAT instances in (a) and (b) it is obvious that variable decay around 0.95 gives best results in terms of least conflicts. For unsatisfiable instances the plot line is also "smoother", this is probably because the solver has to search entire space so there are not many backjumps which would cut "heavy" branches.

Factorization instances seem to require -var-decay close to 1 for fastest solving. Again the plot for unsatisfiable instances – prime numbers (b) is smoother.

Obviously plots for planning instances are very different from previous instances. As -var-decay increases from 0.9 higher number of conflicts rises rapidly, this might mean that planning instances have variables which are more-less independent, because setting variable decay factor close to value of 1, effectively means algorithm will decay activity of variables very slowly.

Behavior of pigeonhole problem instances seems to be similar to factorization.

Clause Decay. Plots show that for random instances the fastest solving time is when parameter is set to value very close to 1.

Similar results as for random instances can be seen here, but the trend starts to decrease at approximately value of 0.93 (Figs. 3, 4, 5, 6 and 7).

These rather chaotic plots are suggesting that -cla-decay parameter is of little significance for planning instances.

From the plot it can be seen that there is a decreasing trend from clause decay. This is similar result as for random and factorization instances.

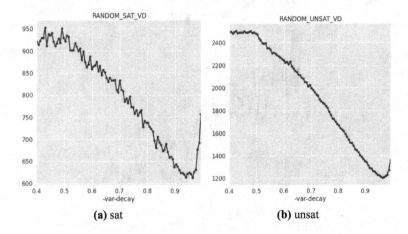

Fig. 3. Variable decay on random SAT instances.

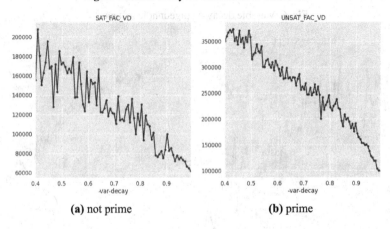

Fig. 4. Variable decay on factorization instances.

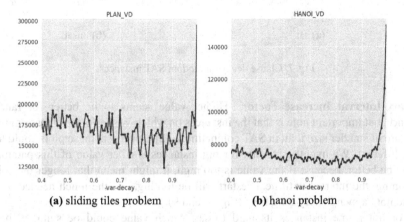

Fig. 5. Variable decay on planning instances.

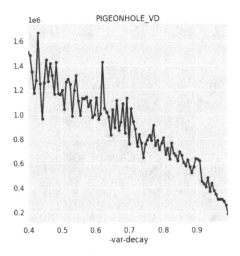

Fig. 6. Variable decay on pigeonhole instances.

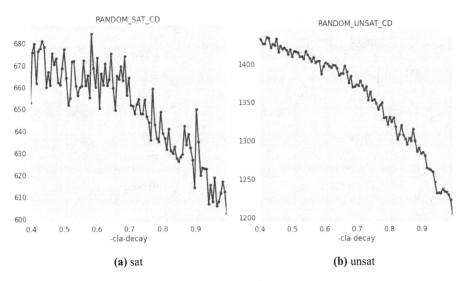

(a) sat   **(b)** unsat

Fig. 7. Clause decay on random SAT instances.

Restart Interval Increase Factor. Higher value seems to be better for random instance, but important note is that the instances on which We performed these aggregations are of smaller size than in SAT competitions [2]. For those, these plots could look very different. We hypothesize that for big instances smaller value of this parameter would be better, because if the value is too high, it might mean that longer the solver is running, the interval until next restart will be too high, so the much needed restart would not happen in very long time (Figs. 8 and 9).

For not prime instances its hard to say which value could be suitable, prime instances show that values over 10 seems like fastest.

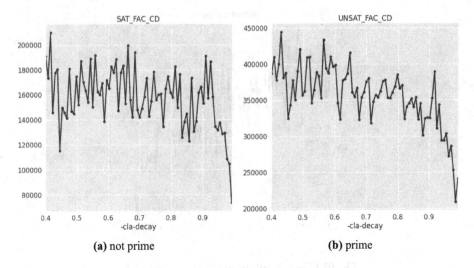

Fig. 8. Clause decay on factorization instances.

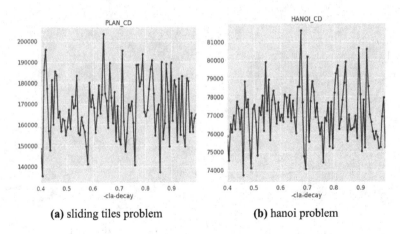

Fig. 9. Clause decay on planning instances.

For planning instances it is clear that lower values are faster that higher, (b) graph is clear, and on (a) there is slightly raising trend. But again we thought this was dependent on instance size. Note that x axis have different values on (a) and (b). Lower value means more frequent restarts, that is suggesting that solver is often in some local optima, which eventually will not lead to solution.

Plot shows that for value 5 and higher impact of this parameter does not show very significant improvement. Higher values are preferred for pigeonhole problem, this means that the problem demands less restarts because it is doing some useful work, in other words, the path to solution is narrow so there are not many branches which lead to nowhere (Figs. 10 and 11).

Restart Interval Base. Initial restart interval around 200 conflicts seems best for random instances.

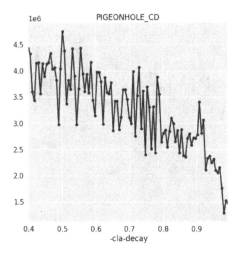

Fig. 10. Clause decay on pigeonhole instances [5].

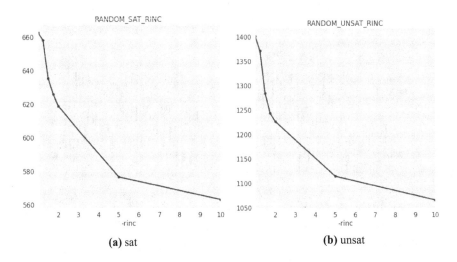

(a) sat   **(b)** unsat

Fig. 11. Restart interval increase factor on random SAT instances [5].

Nothing can be really drawn from this, apart from that this parameter does not matter for factoring instances.

On both (a) and (b) there is increasing trend, so for planning instances smaller initial interval is needed, and thus more frequent restarts (Figs. 12 and 13).

Decreasing trend suggests that less frequent intervals perform better for pigeonhole instances, this further confirms the hypothesis made with restart increase factor in previous section.

Random Variable Frequency. It is evident that that higher the probability the solver chooses random variable, the worse. The same is observed for all of the other domains, thus we will only provide plots without further comments.

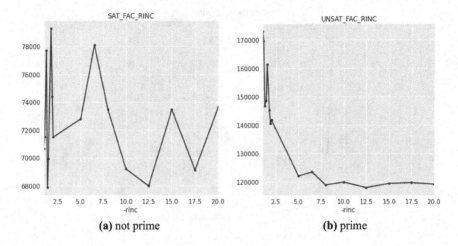

(a) not prime   **(b)** prime

Fig. 12. Restart interval increase factor on factorization instances.

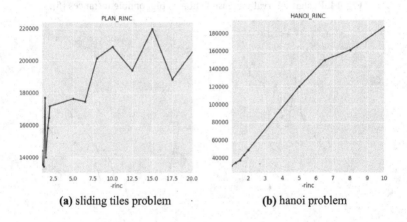

(a) sliding tiles problem   **(b)** hanoi problem

Fig. 13. Restart interval increase factor on planning instances.

6.4   Implications for Parameter Tuning

The results show that there are some dependencies among parameters and solving time, thus it makes sense to try and implement machine learning system to set these parameters automatically depending on input instance (Figs. 14 and 15).

It is debatable whether we should include parameter -cla-decay in the list of parameters which will be learned by machine learning technique, since for all domains value close to 1 was best. We included this parameter nevertheless.

The parameter -rnd-freq we will not include, because it is clear from the smooth lines on the presented graphs in previous section, that in every instance higher value yielded only worse results, and thus we take it as good suggestion that value of 0 of this parameter is best.

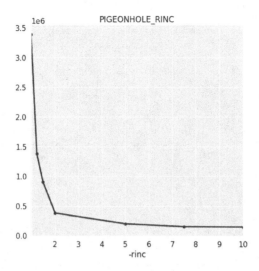

Fig. 14. Restart interval increase factor on pigeonhole instances [5].

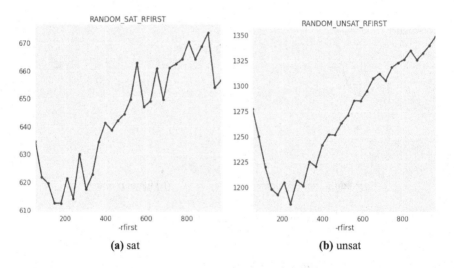

(a) sat   **(b)** unsat

Fig. 15. Restart interval base on random SAT instances.

Later when creating dataset for machine learning technique, for each domain we will use grid-search to find optimal parameters. For each instance of one of the domains, we will set up the grid of parameters to be searched. The values in this grid will be those, for which we observed to be successful individually. For example, for random SAT instances we will search the space of -var-decay $\in [0.8, 0.95]$ and -rfirst $\in [50, 400]$, because we saw that values from these intervals showed the best results (Figs. 16 and 17).

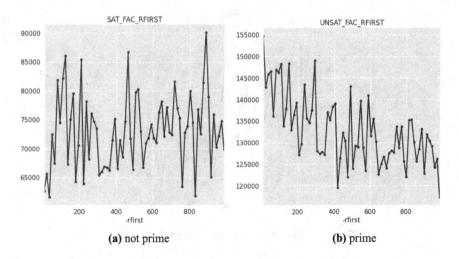

(a) not prime

(b) prime

Fig. 16. Restart interval base on factorization instances.

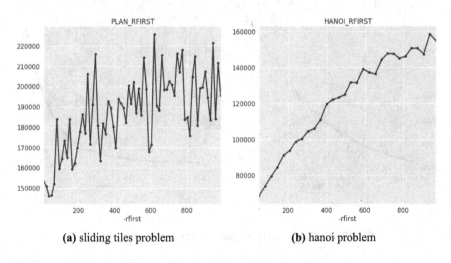

(a) sliding tiles problem

(b) hanoi problem

Fig. 17. Restart interval base on planning instances.

7 Parameter Tuning

In this section we will describe each of the components of the process of parameter tuning for MiniSat solver.

Starting with overview of features extracted from SAT instances which try to describe the structure of the instance as closely as possible.

Next stage is to prepare a dataset for machine learning technique.

In comparison to related works in Sect. 4, we took a different path in the process of actual learning, instead of treating this problem as classification task, where features are used for classifying each instance into a domain of the problem it most likely belong to, and only then set parameter values, which are predetermined for each domain; we will

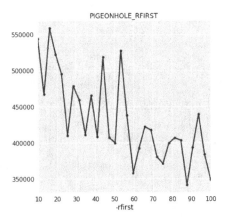

Fig. 18. Restart interval base on pigeonhole instances.

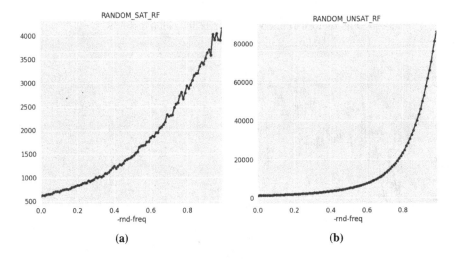

Fig. 19. Random variable frequency on random SAT instances.

directly predict values this is an attempt to choose the best parameters for each instance, even if the instances belong to same domain, a slight difference in parameter values can cause significant difference in running time (Figs. 18 and 19).

The dataset constructed will have n features, where n is number of extracted features, and four target features (parameters: -var-decay, -cla-decay, -rinc, -rfirst). Thus, the approach we implemented is doing an multi-output regression.

7.1   SAT Instance Features

Basic Formula Features. By basic features we mean characteristics of the instance which were used in SatZilla's [35] feature extractor which we have used with an option -base (Fig. 20).

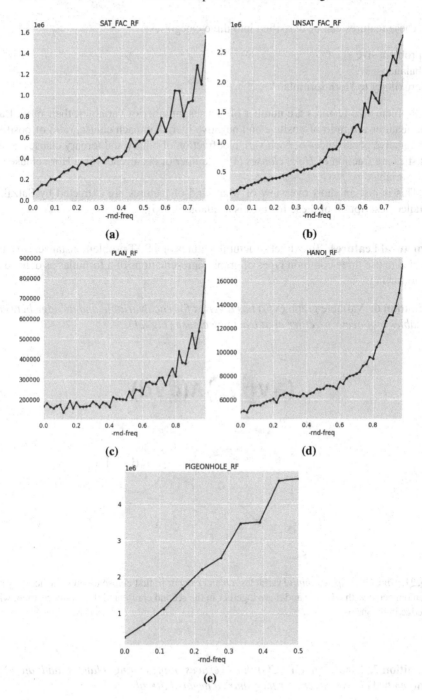

Fig. 20. Random variable frequency on factorization, planning and pigeonhole instances.

These features can be classified into three categories:

1. problem size
2. balance
3. proximity to Horn formula

Problem size features are number of clauses, number of variables, their ratio. Balance features are ratio of positive and negative literals in each clause, ratio of positive and negative occurrences of each variable, fraction of binary and ternary clauses. Horn statistics are fraction of *Horn clauses* [19], number of occurrences in a Horn clause for each variable.

This is just an short overview of what kind of features are extracted by SatZilla. Detailed description of these features is available in [35].

Structural Features. To extract structural features of a SAT problem instance, we have decided to use three common types of graph representations of a formulas as defined in the following.

Definition 6. Variable graph (VG) *has a vertex for each variable and an edge between variables that occur together in at least one clause (Fig. 21).*

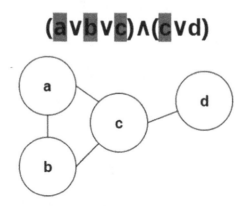

Fig. 21. *Variable graph example*, variables *a b* and *c* occur in first clause together, hence they are interconnected with edges, *c* and *d* are together in the second clause and that connects them with an edge in the graph.

Definition 7. Clause graph (CG) *has vertices representing clauses and an edge between two clauses whenever they share a negated literal.*

Definition 8. Variable-clause graph (VCG) *is a bipartite graph with a node for each variable, a node for each clause, and an edge between them whenever a variable occurs in a clause.*

From the input instance we construct each VG, CG and VCG, which correspond to constraint graphs for the associated *constraint satisfaction problem (CSP)*. Thus, they encode the problem's combinatorial structure [4] (Fig. 22).

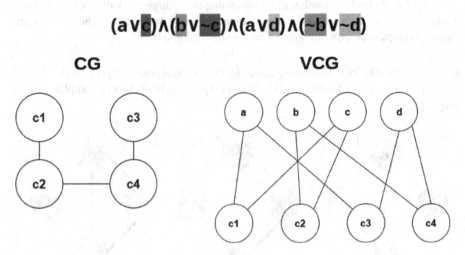

Fig. 22. *Clause graph & variable-clause graph,* let us name clauses in the example formula respectively c to c. In clause graph there is an edge between first and second clause because they share c and $\neg c$, respectively for other 2 edges. In bipartite variable-clause graph there are edges between a $c1$ and c, because first clause ($c1$) contains variables a and c.

For these three types of graphs, we used basic node degree statistics from [35].

Additionally, we computed several graph properties which we thought could help describe instance's structure more closely, and at the same time are not too much time expensive.

- Variable graph features
  - diameter
  - clustering coefficient
  - size of maximal independent set (approx.)
  - node redundancy coefficient
  - number of greedy modularity communities
- Clause graph
  - clustering coefficient
  - size of maximal independent set (approx.)
- Variable-clause graph
  - latapy clustering coefficient
  - size of maximal independent set (approx.)

- node redundancy coefficient
- number of greedy modularity communities

The VG is usually smallest in terms of number of nodes, thus we could afford to compute more properties on this graph, such as modularity communities and diameter.

In contrast CG is the biggest graph (there are more clauses than variables) and thus we limited the number of features extracted from this graph to only two, relatively easy–to–compute features.

VCG has the highest number of nodes among these three types of graphs ($|Vars| + |Clauses|$), but as defined earlier, it is a bipartite graph and some of the features are easier to compute on bipartite graph than on standard graph.

Clustering Coefficient. Clustering coefficient can be computed for every node. It measures how close its neighbors are to being in a clique (neighbors form a complete graph) (Fig. 23).

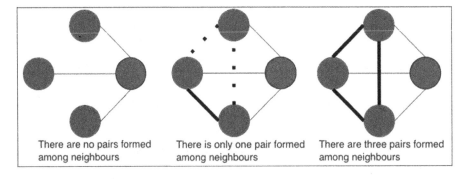

|There are no pairs formed among neighbours|There is only one pair formed among neighbours|There are three pairs formed among neighbours|

Fig. 23. Clustering coefficient example [1].

On the left graph the clustering coefficient of a red node is 0, because none of his neighbors share an edge, middle graph has only 1 edge so the coefficient would be $C_{red} = 1/3$, right graph has all 3 edges in the neighborhood of red node so $C_{red} = 3/3 = 1$.

For undirected graphs is it formally defined as:

$$C_i = \frac{2|\{e_{jk} : v_j, v_k \in N_i, e_{jk} \in E\}|}{k_i(k_i - 1)}$$

Where N_i is a set of neighbors of a vertex v_i, k_i is a number of neighbors of a vertex v_i. Computing clustering coefficient, if implemented properly, has the complexity of $O(n^2 \log n)$.

Because VCG graph is bipartite, we need to compute clustering coefficient there too, but for bipartite network this formula would not make much sense as the coefficient would be always 0 because neighbor of a vertex is from other partity and by definition there is no edge between nodes in same partity. For bipartite graphs there exist a redefinition called "Latapy clustering coefficient" [21].

Maximal Independent Set

Definition 9. *An* independent set *sometimes called* anticlique *is a set of vertices in a graph, no two of which are adjacent.*

Definition 10. Maximal independent set (MIS) *is an independent set that is not a subset of any other independent set.*

The problem of finding maximum independent set is called the *maximum independent set problem* and is an NP-hard optimization problem itself. However its approximation can be computed in $O(|V|/\log^2 |V|)$ [7], which we have used here.

Greedy Modularity Communities. We used Clauset–Newman–Moore algorithm [9] for finding communities in a graph.

Greedy modularity maximization begins with each node in its own community and joins the pair of communities that most increases modularity until no such pair exists.

The principle of this algorithm is similar to hierarchical agglomeration algorithm for detecting community structure which is faster than many competing algorithms.

Its running time on a network with n vertices and m edges is $O(md\log n)$ where d is the depth of the dendrogram describing the community structure.

Many real-world networks are sparse and hierarchical, with $m \sim n$ and $d \sim \log n$, in which case the algorithm runs in essentially linear time, $O(n\log^2 n)$.

7.2   Constructed Dataset

Constructing training dataset for learning consists of few steps.

For each instance we ran SatZilla's feature extractor, then ran our extractor and combined the computed features into one sample row.

We determined the optimal values for every parameter of MiniSat for the given instance, using the brute-force *grid-search* [15]. Grid-search is used to find the optimal hyperparameters of a model which results in the most 'accurate' predictions. The idea is that the 'grid' of parameters is created, meaning that each point in 'grid' represents a certain configuration of parameters values, this grid is exhaustively evaluated (hence why it is called brute-force) and the results are saved, the point with best results is then chosen to be used in evaluation practice.

Final step of compiling single sample for the dataset was to add the corresponding optimal parameters to the data row of extracted features.

Extraction Complexity. Building variable graph BUILDVG is $O(n^2)$, it iterates over every clause and then over every literal in that clause. Building variable clause graph has the same complexity as VG. Building Clause graph is the most expensive operation, for every pair of clauses, that is $O(n^2)$ operation, it checks for intersection of literals. Intersection of two sets is quadratic in worst case, thus the complexity of BUILDVG is $O(n^4)$.

7.3 Learning

As underlying machine learning technique we have chosen *random forest* [8], as this
is multi-output regression and also data are from four distinctive domains which have
different optimal parameter demands, and we believe random forest suits best for this
task.

Random forest is an ensemble learning method for classification that operates by
constructing a multitude of decision trees at training time. For classification tasks, the
output of the random forest is the class selected by majority of trees.

8 Evaluation

This section presents the results we have achieved. From the following demonstration
it is evident that the tuned parameters outperform MiniSat defaults.

All plots of this section only show pure solving time, time spent computing features
was excluded.

All instances are pre-processed by SatELite instance pre-processor [14] which is
very fast and the time spent preprocessing can be neglected in any evaluations.

In the following plots there are two columns for each instance next to each other.
Blue columns are performances on tuned parameters, green ones on the default MiniSat's parameters. Instances are sorted by number of conflicts yielded by default parameter.

8.1 Performance on Training Instances

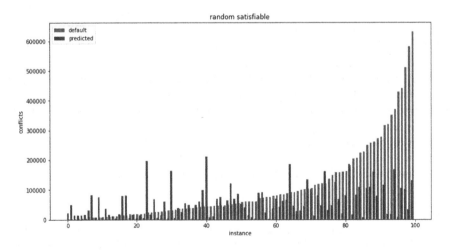

Fig. 24. 100 training instances, random, satisfiable (Color figure online) [5].

Instances used for training are from SATLIB, they have constant number of variables,
250 before preprocessing.

In Fig. 24 it can be seen that tuned parameters (blue), are faster for some of the instances but in fact slower for those instances that can be solved very fast with default parameters, those are instances which are solved within single digit number of restarts.

This is probably because the model tends to choose wider restart interval (in comparison to default's value of 2, which is quite low), because it was also trained on the factorization instances, which require less frequent restarts. On those random instances which take considerable time to solve by default parameters, the efficiency rises dramatically, and thus tuned parameters should be used on random instances which have larger number of variables, because for small instances default parameters perform better.

This could be fixed by including random instances of different sizes in the training set, so the model could adapt to the size of the instance better, for example, for small instances restart frequency should be also much smaller (Fig. 25).

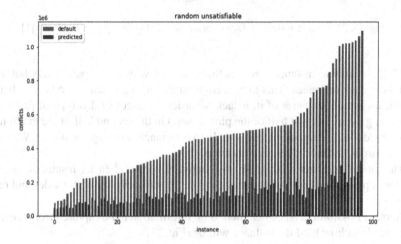

Fig. 25. 97 training instances, random, unsatisfiable [5].

For every random unstatisfiable instance from training set (SATLIB) the tuned parameters are much faster.

This plot proves that it is worth tuning solver's parameters in particular for unsatisfiable instances. There is a slight correlation between heights of green and blue bars on the graph, unlike for random satisfiable instances.

The hardest instances are from so called *phase transition* which is a ratio of clauses to variables around value 4.26, so roughly 4x more clauses than variables.

The computation of features is very fast for random instances as they have balanced ratio of clauses and variables (Fig. 26).

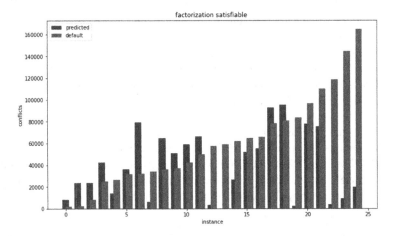

Fig. 26. 25 training instances, factorization, satisfiable (not prime numbers) [5].

12/25 satisfiable instances were actually slower with tuned parameters but 10 of them were easy instances. This may seem a bit disturbing result as first sight, but our hypothesis is that the cause of it, is lack of easier instances of this type of problem in the training dataset as first half of the plot shows. On the second half of the graph it can be observed that for harder instances, only two instances are slightly slower. We would say, for harder instances these results are positive.

The model does not distinguish well between hard and easier instances, and as a result it is predicting restart frequency parameters similarly for both harder and easier instances.

Another possibility can be that there is no information to be captured from the graph structure about how hard the instance will be (Fig. 27).

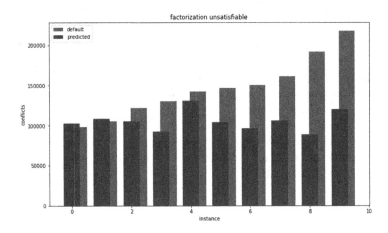

Fig. 27. 10 training instances, factorization, unsatisfiable (prime numbers) [5].

Majority of eight out of ten instances are favoring tuned parameters, for two easiest instances the default parameters perform better but only by a tiny bit of 500–1000 conflicts less which is small enough count to be neglected.

The improvement is only moderate, nowhere near the improvement observed on random unsatisfiable instances (Fig. 28).

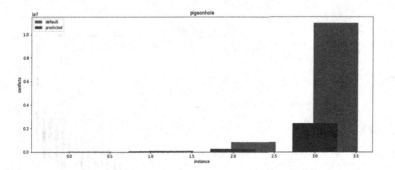

Fig. 28. Training instances, pigeonhole problem [5].

First two bars are insignificant, but on the remaining two the big improvement can be seen. Even though the training dataset contained only four instances of pigeonhole problem (because higher order of this problem is very difficult and it was infeasible to perform grid-search on many parameters values), the model was able to predict values correctly.

8.2   Performance on Testing Instances

As a testing set for random instances we generated instances randomly but with 300 variables in comparison to SATLIB's 250, to observe whether the model will be able to predict values correctly also for instances which are much harder than the ones it was trained on (Fig. 29).

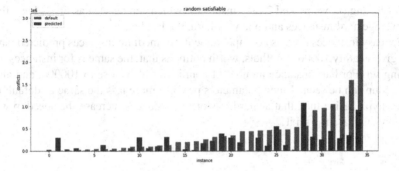

Fig. 29. 36 testing instances, random, satisfiable.

Plot shows very good results, this verifies our hypothesis, that even model trained on smaller instances can perform well for larger instances.

For harder instances (right half of the plot), there is only one instance which takes almost twice as much with tuned parameters as with the default ones. This is probably because the structures of the random instances are homogeneous regardless of their size (Fig. 30).

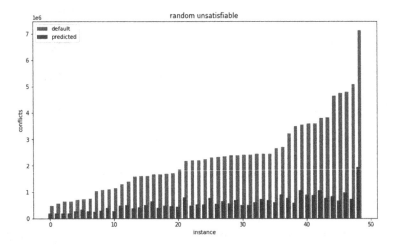

Fig. 30. 60 testing instances, random, unsatisfiable [5].

Observed results are remarkable, all instances are faster on tuned parameters by at least 2x, on some instances, mostly harder ones, 3x faster.

The key takeaway is that the parameter tuning is very effective way to improve SAT solvers performance on unsatisfiable instances.

Similar results as on training set can be seen here for factorization, satisfiable instances. Performance is better on harder instances, from harder instances only one is outperformed by default settings. Easier instances are solved faster by default settings, most likely because of low base restart interval (Figs. 31 and 32).

For testing set we picked 2 easy instances, which can be seen as first 2 bars, then a few average hard instances and one very hard, the last bar.

For easy instances there is no improvement, for medium instances predicted parameters give steadily 100000 conflicts, worth noting is that, the same is for instances in the training set. For hard instance number of conflicts is also close to 100000, and almost 2x speedup can be seen. Tuned parameters perform more less the same as default ones but we hypothesize that, that as hardness of the instances increase the speedup would get more significant with it.

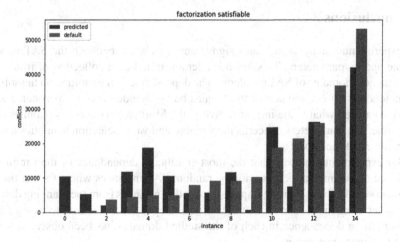

Fig. 31. 15 testing instances, factorization, satisfiable [5].

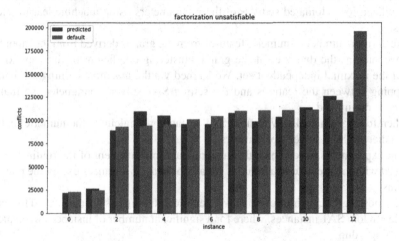

Fig. 32. 13 testing instances, factorization, unsatisfiable.

8.3   Planning Instances

It is unfortunate that we were unable to train the model for planning problems. This is due to computational burden that we encountered later, in the process of extracting features.

Constructing clause graph which is usually very big due to the nature of planning instances and computing features on it was not feasible.

If we were to start over, we would not include clause graph for planning instances, and focus more on graph properties of corresponding VG and VCG graphs.

9   Conclusions

Our experimental analysis indicates significant correlation between the SAT solver's runtime and its parameters. This has been demonstrated on a collection of four structurally diverse domains of SAT problems. The dependence of the runtime on the solver's parameters was observable across all domains being included in our experimentation.

We measured what is the impact of five of the MiniSat SAT solver's parameters on its runtime. The parameters concerns the variable and value selection heuristics and the restart policy of the solver.

Our experiments indicate that the most significant dependence of the runtime on the choice of parameters occurs with the random SAT instances where four of the five parameters tend to have a strong impact. Except the instances from the planning domain, every other domain has shown significant dependency on the clause decaying factor. Another strong dependence in each of the studied domains has been observed for the restart frequency parameter.

The observed dependencies of the runtime on selected SAT solver's parameters has been utilized for automated settings of these parameters using machine learning techniques.

We derive a number of numeric features from the graphs derived from the input SAT instance such as the diameter of the graph, clustering coefficient or the approximate size of the maximal independent set. We learned via the machine learning mechanism a mapping between the features and the setting SAT solver's parameters so that the runtime is minimized.

Then for a given (unknown) input SAT instance we calculate the numeric features and predict the SAT solver's parameters.

Our experiments have shown that a significant improvement of the runtime can be achieved with the predicted parameters for all domains of instances except the planning domains.

The most significant improvement via parameter tuning has been achieved for unsatisfiable random SAT instances, where for a significant number of instances we achieved up to 3x speedup.

As a suggestion for a future work, we plan to focus on computing features from the VG and VCG graph and omit calculation of the features from the CG as CG graph that turned out to be very computationally expensive and often causes feature extractor execution time to outweigh actual solving time.

Acknowledgements. This research has been supported by GAČR - the Czech Science Foundation, grant registration number 22-31346S.

References

1. Clustering coefficient example [image]. https://www.oreilly.com/library/view/mastering-python-data/9781783988327/ch07s02.html. Accessed 25 May 2022
2. SAT competition website. http://www.satcompetition.org/

3. Ansótegui, C., Giráldez-Cru, J., Levy, J.: The community structure of SAT formulas. In: Cimatti, A., Sebastiani, R. (eds.) SAT 2012. LNCS, vol. 7317, pp. 410–423. Springer, Heidelberg (2012). https://doi.org/10.1007/978-3-642-31612-8_31

4. Bennaceur, H.: A comparison between SAT and CSP techniques. Constraints **9**, 123–138 (2004). https://doi.org/10.1023/B:CONS.0000024048.03454.c0

5. Beskyd, F., Surynek, P.: Parameter setting in SAT solver using machine learning techniques. In: Proceedings of the 14th International Conference on Agents and Artificial Intelligence, ICAART, vol. 2, pp. 586–597. INSTICC, SciTePress (2022). https://doi.org/10.5220/0010910200003116

6. Biere, A., Biere, A., Heule, M., van Maaren, H., Walsh, T.: Handbook of Satisfiability: Volume 185 Frontiers in Artificial Intelligence and Applications. IOS Press (2009)

7. Boppana, R., Halldórsson, M.M.: Approximating maximum independent sets by excluding subgraphs. In: Gilbert, J.R., Karlsson, R. (eds.) SWAT 1990. LNCS, vol. 447, pp. 13–25. Springer, Heidelberg (1990). https://doi.org/10.1007/3-540-52846-6_74

8. Breiman, L.: Random forests. Mach. Learn. **45**, 5–32 (2001). https://doi.org/10.1023/A:1010933404324

9. Clauset, A., Newman, M., Moore, C.: Finding community structure in very large networks, p. 066111 (2005). https://doi.org/10.1103/PhysRevE.70.066111

10. Cook, S.A.: The complexity of theorem-proving procedures. In: Proceedings of the Third Annual ACM Symposium on Theory of Computing, STOC 1971, pp. 151–158. Association for Computing Machinery, New York (1971). https://doi.org/10.1145/800157.805047

11. Davis, M., Putnam, H.: A computing procedure for quantification theory. J. ACM **7**(3), 201–215 (1960)

12. Dennis, G., Chang, F.S.H., Jackson, D.: Modular verification of code with SAT. In: Proceedings of the 2006 International Symposium on Software Testing and Analysis, ISSTA 2006, pp. 109–120. Association for Computing Machinery, New York (2006). https://doi.org/10.1145/1146238.1146251

13. D'Ippolito, N., Frias, M.F., Galeotti, J.P., Lanzarotti, E., Mera, S.: Alloy+HotCore: a fast approximation to unsat core. In: Frappier, M., Glässer, U., Khurshid, S., Laleau, R., Reeves, S. (eds.) ABZ 2010. LNCS, vol. 5977, pp. 160–173. Springer, Heidelberg (2010). https://doi.org/10.1007/978-3-642-11811-1_13

14. Eén, N., Biere, A.: Effective preprocessing in SAT through variable and clause elimination. In: Bacchus, F., Walsh, T. (eds.) SAT 2005. LNCS, vol. 3569, pp. 61–75. Springer, Heidelberg (2005). https://doi.org/10.1007/11499107_5

15. Feurer, M., Hutter, F.: Hyperparameter optimization. In: Hutter, F., Kotthoff, L., Vanschoren, J. (eds.) Automated Machine Learning. TSSCML, pp. 3–33. Springer, Cham (2019). https://doi.org/10.1007/978-3-030-05318-5_1

16. Ganesh, V., Singh, R., Near, J., Rinard, M.: AvatarSAT: an auto-tuning Boolean SAT solver (2009)

17. Gupta, A., Ganai, M.K., Wang, C.: SAT-based verification methods and applications in hardware verification. In: Bernardo, M., Cimatti, A. (eds.) SFM 2006. LNCS, vol. 3965, pp. 108–143. Springer, Heidelberg (2006). https://doi.org/10.1007/11757283_5

18. Haken, A.: The intractability of resolution (complexity). Ph.D. thesis, USA (1984). aAI8422073

19. Horn, A.: On sentences which are true of direct unions of algebras. J. Symbolic Logic (1), 14–21 (1951). https://projecteuclid.org:443/euclid.jsl/1183731038

20. Kautz, H., Selman, B.: Planning as satisfiability, pp. 359–363 (1992)

21. Latapy, M., Magnien, C., Del Vecchio, N.: Basic notions for the analysis of large two-mode networks. Soc. Netw. **30**, 31–48 (2008). https://doi.org/10.1016/j.socnet.2007.04.006

22. Liang, J.H.: Machine learning for SAT solvers. Ph.D. thesis, University of Waterloo (2018)

23. Lourenço, H., Martin, O., Stützle, T.: Iterated local search: framework and applications. In: Gendreau, M., Potvin, J.Y. (eds.) Handbook of Metaheuristics. ISOR, vol. 146, pp. 363–397. Springer, Boston (2010). https://doi.org/10.1007/978-1-4419-1665-5_12

24. Marques Silva, J.P., Sakallah, K.A.: Grasp-a new search algorithm for satisfiability. In: Proceedings of International Conference on Computer Aided Design, pp. 220–227 (1996)

25. Mitchell, D., Selman, B., Levesque, H.: Hard and easy distributions of SAT problems. In: Proceedings of the Tenth National Conference on Artificial Intelligence, AAAI 1992, pp. 459–465. AAAI Press (1992)

26. Mitchell, T.M.: Machine Learning. McGraw-Hill, New York City (1997)

27. Moskewicz, M.W., Madigan, C.F., Zhao, Y., Zhang, L., Malik, S.: Chaff: engineering an efficient SAT solver. In: Proceedings of the 38th Design Automation Conference (IEEE Cat. No.01CH37232), pp. 530–535 (2001)

28. Newsham, Z., Lindsay, W., Ganesh, V., Liang, J.H., Fischmeister, S., Czarnecki, K.: SATGraf: visualizing the evolution of SAT formula structure in solvers. In: Heule, M., Weaver, S. (eds.) SAT 2015. LNCS, vol. 9340, pp. 62–70. Springer, Cham (2015). https://doi.org/10.1007/978-3-319-24318-4_6

29. Eén, N., Sörensson, N.: An extensible SAT-solver. In: Giunchiglia, E., Tacchella, A. (eds.) SAT 2003. LNCS, vol. 2919, pp. 502–518. Springer, Heidelberg (2004). https://doi.org/10.1007/978-3-540-24605-3_37

30. Pintjuk, D.: Boosting SAT-solver performance on fact instances with automatic parameter tuning (2015). https://www.diva-portal.org/smash/get/diva2:811289/FULLTEXT01.pdf

31. Pipatsrisawat, K., Darwiche, A.: A lightweight component caching scheme for satisfiability solvers. In: Marques-Silva, J., Sakallah, K.A. (eds.) SAT 2007. LNCS, vol. 4501, pp. 294–299. Springer, Heidelberg (2007). https://doi.org/10.1007/978-3-540-72788-0_28

32. Sinz, C., Dieringer, E.-M.: DPVIS – a tool to visualize the structure of SAT instances. In: Bacchus, F., Walsh, T. (eds.) SAT 2005. LNCS, vol. 3569, pp. 257–268. Springer, Heidelberg (2005). https://doi.org/10.1007/11499107_19

33. Soos, M., Nohl, K., Castelluccia, C.: Extending SAT solvers to cryptographic problems. In: Kullmann, O. (ed.) SAT 2009. LNCS, vol. 5584, pp. 244–257. Springer, Heidelberg (2009). https://doi.org/10.1007/978-3-642-02777-2_24

34. Tseitin, G.S.: On the complexity of derivation in propositional calculus. In: Siekmann, J.H., Wrightson, G. (eds.) Automation of Reasoning. Symbolic Computation, pp. 466–483. Springer, Heidelberg (1983). https://doi.org/10.1007/978-3-642-81955-1_28

35. Xu, L., Hutter, F., Hoos, H.H., Leyton-Brown, K.: SATzilla: portfolio-based algorithm selection for SAT, pp. 565–606 (2008)

More Sustainable Text Classification via Uncertainty Sampling and a Human-in-the-Loop

Jakob Smedegaard Andersen[✉] and Olaf Zukunft

Department of Computer Science, Hamburg University of Applied Sciences,
Hamburg, Germany
{jakob.andersen,olaf.zukunft}@haw-hamburg.de

Abstract. Text classification by large deep learning networks achieves high accuracy, but uses a lot of computing power and requires high resource investment. In the age of climate change, sustainable solutions are sought that can attain acceptable accuracy with less resource investment. In this paper, we investigate lightweight text classifiers and combine them with a human-in-the-loop approach. Our solution identifies instances that are uncertain to classify and assigns them preferentially to a human domain expert. Experiments performed with nine classifiers on six datasets show that with manually labelling less than 30%, an F1-score between $\sim$95% and 99% is achievable for five of six datasets. The inference on energy-efficient GPU-less infrastructure with only 4 GB can be done in less than 1 s.

Keywords: Text classification · Human-in-the-loop · Sustainability

1 Introduction

The rise of transformer based classifiers like BERT [13] and XLNet [50] has shown that the accuracy of machine learning (ML) [30] approaches to text classification is largely acceptable in different domains [13,43,50]. The impressive performance is nevertheless accompanied by a high level of complexity of the underlying deep learning network. Millions of parameters do not only limit the understandability of the classifier, but also require high-performance infrastructure for training and deployment of the models. In the face of the global climate crisis, green IT initiatives [45,49] investigate how resource-efficient approaches can be adopted. In this context, the reduction of energy consumption by using less compute intensive algorithms is desirable. Additionally, such algorithms also enable the use of edge devices that are typically not able to efficiently train and deploy large transformer based models.

However, it has been shown that resource-saving algorithms are not able to reach the same results as state-of-the-art models like BERT. Detecting hate speech with a traditional non transformer based approach results in an F1-score of only 82% [10]. This is typically not acceptable for e.g. social media companies which are required to block hate speech. One solution to this problem is to not fully automate the classification task,

A. P. Rocha et al. (Eds.): ICAART 2022, LNAI 13786, pp. 201–225, 2022.
https://doi.org/10.1007/978-3-031-22953-4_9

but to include human experts in the classification process. Using the human-in-the-loop approach [24], the task of text classification is sensibly divided between human experts and ML-based algorithms. The division is intended to shift boring routine tasks to the machine learning algorithms while the human expert handles the complex borderline cases. This requires reliable and trustful classifiers [42] that support the identification of borderline cases [27]. One idea is to use the uncertainty of predictions to determine those cases that should be allocated to domain experts [20, 21]. In the media industry, this approach has shown to be useful [26] in order to reach an acceptable accuracy of text classification [37].

This leads to a new problem for the text classification task: How do we obtain a reliable uncertainty estimation of the used text classification algorithm? The answer is required in order to determine the text that should be given to the domain expert for manual classification. Unfortunately, it is known that the uncertainty estimation is hard [22] for neural-net based classifiers. Additionally, state-of-the-art text classifiers like BERT require lots of resources that are not available in low-end and sustainable computational infrastructure environments. Hence, another approach is to use a traditional classifier that may reach similar F1-Scores if combined with a domain expert who is labelling a limited number of instances. These more traditional classifiers [5, 18] may also enable a more frequent re-training of the ML model, as they are not as compute-expensive as transformer based approaches. Studies reveal [2] that re-training the model using the labels acquired from the domain experts is beneficial, but also requires a low latency.

Our contributions in this paper are twofold: First, we perform experiments to evaluate the F1-scores and the quality of uncertainty for nine machine learning text classification algorithms. These models are more sustainable than the current transformer based approaches, as all of them are by far less resource-intensive. We aim at reaching similar F1-scores as a BERT by hand-labelling a limited amount of data through domain experts. For our experiments, we use six widely known datasets. Second, we demonstrate that the runtime for both training and inference is acceptable for sustainable low-end computing environments. This acceptable runtime also supports a highly interactive labeling process.

In this paper, we try to answer the following research questions:

- **RQ1:** How accurate do different lightweight classifiers estimate predicted probabilities?
- **RQ2:** Which lightweight classifier can capture the highest proportion of misclassifications via uncertainty-sampling, which after removal leads to the highest macro F1-score?
- **RQ3:** How much of the most uncertain classification outcomes have to be manually annotated to reach a certain level of macro F1-score?
- **RQ4:** What is the difference in performance between BERT and SBERT encodings?
- **RQ5:** How efficient are different classifiers regarding their training and inference time?
- **RQ6:** How much time is saved in training and inference when 8 GB of main memory is used instead of 4 GB?

This paper builds on and extends our previously published paper [4]. In contrast to our prior work, we focus on sustainability aspects in this paper. We have included three new datasets into the experimental evaluation and discuss the usage of BERT vs. SBERT encodings. Finally, we assess the results of different main memory sizes on the runtime, as this is known to have less effect on power-consumption, when compared with higher CPU-frequencies or more CPU/GPU.

The remainder of the paper is structured as follows. First, we outline related work in Sect. 2 and describe the problem solved in this paper in Sect. 3. In Sect. 4 we introduce our evaluation criteria including the used datasets, text features and algorithms. Afterwards, the results of the experiments for each research question are given in Sect. 5. In Sect. 6, we discuss our results. Finally, we give a conclusion and take a look at future work in Sect. 7.

2 Related Work

Current state-of-the-art deep learning approaches are highly accurate, but computational intensive, slow and impractical on low-end systems [13]. There is a growing demand for resource-efficient machine learning [1,52] and interactive real-time processing [2, 14,51]. Novel approaches are needed that enable sustainable yet highly accurate text classification. The human-in-the-loop paradigm [24] proposes a promising direction that includes algorithms that interact with human agents to optimize their behavior - a rapidly growing area of machine learning research.

Rattigan et al. [40] initially investigated the objective of maximizing the accuracy of classifiers post-training while limiting human efforts. Based on this goal, several approaches have been investigated to detect unreliable classification outcomes and finally improve the predictive performance of text classifiers through human intervention. Recent papers facilitate thresholds of conditional class probabilities to separate unreliable class outcomes. Pavlopoulos et al. [37] suggest identifying upper and lower class probability thresholds to determine a fixed sized slice of data instances which maximizes the accuracy of a model when manually annotated. He et al. [20] seek to improve the quality of uncertainty estimates to enable a more efficient separation of probable wrong and correct predictions. However, their approach is only applicable to deep neural networks, which requires a high computational effort. Andersen and Maalej [3] suggest a saturation based approach, which aims to maximize the accuracy of a classifier while spending human efforts most efficient. Besides uncertainty-based approaches, training a rejection function is another common approach to delegate unreliable instances to human annotators [11,16]. Abstaining from predictions aims to reduce the classification error, while keeping the coverage as high as possible. An abstention option can be modelled as an additional class result or achieved by training a separate classifier. However, the sustainability of semi-automatic approaches remains largely unexplored.

Manual annotation of classification results can also be considered a special case of *algorithm-in-the-loop decision-making* [17], where humans and not algorithms make the final classification decision. In contrast, we aim to involve humans only when the model cannot provide reliable classification results. Another area closely related to human-in-the-loop classification is *Active Learning* [31]. Active learning aims to minimize human efforts in generating training data to obtain highly accurate classifiers. In

Active Learning classifiers query labels from human annotators, which are added to their training data. By re-training the classifier from time-to-time, the learning behavior is improved. Active learning facilitates uncertainty sampling to guide human participation. In contrast to human-in-the-loop classification, Active Learning is applied during the training of the initial model, while the former aims to further improve the accuracy of an already trained model during its deployment. We aim to exceed the maximum achievable accuracy [6] of a pre-trained classifier at the cost of human involvement during the classification process.

3   Problem Statement

We first outline the task of semi-automatic text classification by introducing the field of text classification and outlining human involvement in the classification process. We then introduce the problem of increasing the maximum achievable accuracy of a deployed classifier by including humans in the classification loop.

Text classification [39] aims to predict the class labelling $y \in Y \subset \mathbb{N}$ of text instances $x \in X \subset \mathbb{R}^n$, which are related in a certain manner, e.g. distinguish between hate-speech and none-hate-speech in social media or assigning predefined sentiment-levels to user reviews. Machine learning classifiers are trained on specific tasks to learn conditional class probabilities $p(y = c|x)$ between labels x and text instances y. The unknown classification function has the shape $f : X \to Y$ or $f : X \to p(Y|X)$. The training process of automatic classifiers is guided by a corpus of already labelled text instances $D \subset X \times Y$ usually minimizing a loss function. Classification models are finally used to infer the labelling of new text instances by reporting the class which receives the highest conditional probability $y^* = f(x) = \arg\max_c p(y = c|x)$ over all classes c. Classification algorithms usually rely on majority votes or scaling techniques to transform classification outcomes, e.g. distance or activation functions, into probability distributions [38].

Uncertainty estimation aims to quantify the lack of confidence in the prediction of a classifier. Shannon's Entropy [46] is a common and well-performing approach to estimate the predictive uncertainty of class probabilities, that is:

$$H(x) = -\sum_c P(y = c|x) \log_2 P(y = c|x) \tag{1}$$

Shannon's Entropy gives high uncertainty values when all class outcomes are equally certain, e.g. $p(0|x) = p(1|x) = 0.5$ and small uncertainties when either $p(0|x)$ or $p(1|x)$ are equal to 1 in a binary classification task. The most uncertain instance u is the one that maximizes Eq. 1, i.e. $u = \arg\max_x H(x)$. Sampling a subset of the most uncertain data instances is commonly referred to as *uncertainty sampling* [31].

Text classification can be carried out both automatically and manually. The latter requires human labor and task-specific background knowledge. Here, humans are asked to judge the labelling of text instances. Human efforts are commonly expensive to offer, time-consuming and rarely available. Manual classification scales poorly with increasing workload. To be applicable, it is reasonable to maximize the efficiency and limit the amount of human participation [3]. To accomplish the most efficient human participation, manual efforts should be focused on the most uncertain predictions, which are highly unreliable and probable wrong [21]. To this end, an automatic classifier shall provide an appropriate misclassification ranking with respect to the reported uncertainty estimates in order to reliably distinguish between instances that are likely to be correct and those that would be better decided manually.

4   Experimental Evaluation

4.1   Evaluation Criteria

To answer RQ1, we evaluate the ability of classifiers to provide high quality class probabilities. First, we compare the mean class probability of all wrong and correct predictions exemplarily for one dataset. A separation between these means is necessary to reliably determine which predictions are likely to be correct or wrong. Second, we calculate the Brier score [9], a proper scoring rule to measure the accuracy of predicted probabilities. The Brier score is calculated as the squared error of predicted probabilities and true class outcomes, that is:

$$BS = |Y|^{-1} \sum_{y \in Y} \sum_{c \in C} \left(p(y = c|x) - I(\hat{y} = c) \right)^2 \tag{2}$$

where $I(\hat{y} = c) = 1$ if the true class of x represented by $\hat{y}$ is equal to c else 0. Lower Brier scores indicate better calibrated conditional class probabilities. A good calibration of class probabilities is desirable to reliably assess the actual probability of predictions, ultimately leading to a more accurate quantification of prediction uncertainties. To answer RQ2, we compare the macro F1-score of these classifiers when a certain amount of the most uncertain data instances, in our case 0, 10, 20, and 30%, are excluded from the test dataset. We use the macro-average, as many of the datasets used are very unbalanced and we aim to treat all classes with the same importance. For RQ3, we estimate the manual effort a human has to spend, e.g. by correcting classifier results, to reach a certain macro F1-score. We measure human effort by the number of cases in which instances have to be decided manually. Working with fully labelled datasets enables us to simulate human annotations by selecting the ground truth label for each annotation request. This is a common approach in the evaluation of interactive machine learning approaches [47]. Since human annotations are known to be noisy, we also simulate four different levels of noise. We assign a randomly selected class label to each annotation request with a probability of either 0, 5, 10 or 15%, respectively, instead of the ground truth label. The macro F1-score of a combined human-automatic classifier is calculated based on the unified sets of manually corrected and automatically derived labels. Regarding RQ4, we conduct all experiments with BERT and SBERT encodings to determine which one is most suitable for our approach. For RQ5, we examine the time required for training and inference to evaluate the computational efficiency of each classifier. All experiments were performed on an Intel® Xeon® Gold 5115 CPU @ 2.40 GHz using 1 core. Lastly, for RQ6 we investigate the time needed for training and inference when 4 GB and 8 GB of main memory are used. Reported measurements refer to the mean of five stratified cross fold datasets with a 50% train-test split. In the following, we abbreviate the term "macro F1-score" by "F1-score".

Table 1. Dataset details including size, number of classes, class distribution and the mean and standard deviation of words per text instance.

Dataset	Size	$|C|$	Class Distribution	#Words ($\mu \pm \sigma$)
App Store	5752	3	3472:1286:994	24 ± 29
News	13919	4	4891:3979:2625:2424	198 ± 711
Hate Speech	24783	2	19190:5593	15 ± 7
Issues	29998	3	10000:10000:9998	54 ± 59
Reuters	8614	8	3930:2319:527:499:458:425:290:166	117 ± 129
TREC	5952	6	1344:1300:1288:1009:916:95	10 ± 4

4.2 Datasets

We conduct our experiments with six publicly available, fully labelled, English datasets covering a variety of real-world domains. The datasets include binary and multi-class classification tasks which are originally skewed. The datasets are summarized in Table 1.

The **App Store** dataset [35] covers user written app reviews from app stores. The reviews are manually annotated as *feature request*, *bug report* or *praise*. Second, **News** refers to the 20NewsGroups dataset [29] that originally contains messages with 20 categories. We reorganize the dataset into its 4 most frequent classes which are *comp*, *politics*, *rec*, and *religion* [23]. The **Hate Speech** dataset [12] comes with a binary classification task of detecting toxic messages (hate speech or offensive language) from Twitter. **Issues** [25] contains of software issues extracted from heterogeneous GitHub projects. Issues were queried from 12,112 projects and labelled as *bug*, *enhancement* i.e. an improvement or new features request and *question*. The **Reuters** dataset consists of newswires from the Reuters financial newswire service [32]. The task is to classify instances to one of 8 topics. For our experiments, we choose a subset of the 8 most common topics with unique labels. The **TREC** dataset [33] is a collection of questions which refers to one of six different answer types which are: *person*, *location*, *number*, *abbreviation* and *entity*. For each dataset we employ a 5-fold stratified 50/50 split for training and testing data.

4.3 Evaluation Scope

Many classification algorithms have proven to perform well in the domain of text classification [28,34,48]. However, previous studies have mainly focused on investigating the predictive performance of pure automatic classifiers without computational constraints. It remains unknown which classifier performs best in a semi-automatic setting (as discussed in Sect. 3) while focusing on edge devices. In this work we investigate nine lightweight classification algorithms for text classification [7,19].

We consider the following classification algorithms: (1) A **Decision Tree (DT)** classifier which is a tree-like structure of decision rules inferred from the training data. Decision Trees can estimate conditional class probabilities by reporting pre-calculated fractions of correct class outcomes during training. (2) A **Random Forest (RF)** classifier is an ensemble of decision trees, each voting for a particular class outcome. The conditional class probability can be derived as the proportion of trees that vote for a particular class outcome. (3) A **k-Nearest Neighbor (kNN)** classifier builds on the assumption that the labelling of similar documents is the same. A new document is classified according to the k most similar documents of the training dataset. A majority vote is taken to determine the final class result. We consider the proportion of votes as the conditional class probability. (4) A **Native Bayes (GNB)** classifier which is based on the assumption of feature independence. A Naive Bayes classifier uses Bayes' rule to derive the conditional probability of a class. Textual feature representations such as BERT and SBERT (see Sect. 4.4) consist of continuous and also negative attributes. Therefore, we apply Gaussian Native Bayes, a variant that assumes that the attributes of the feature vector are normally distributed. (5) **Support Vector Machines (SVM)** classify data by finding an optimal linear hyperplane that separates features with a maximum margin. The classification rule is based on which side of the hyperplane a data point lies. In this work, we apply Platt scaling [38] to obtain conditional probabilities from SVM classification results. (6) **Logistic Regression (LR)** is a classification approach that can directly output conditional class probabilities. A Logistic Regression classifier uses a sigmoid function to squeeze the output of a linear predictor function between 0 and 1. (7) A **Multilayer Perceptron (MLP)** is a lightweight neural network that consists of several interconnected layers. Each layer is a computational unit that performs summation and thresholding. Similar to Logistic Regression, the conditional class probability can be derived by applying a sigmoid function, e.g. softmax, to the network's output layer.

Finally, we consider a Bayesian approach that allows for a comprehensive interpretation of uncertainty [15,47]. A Bayesian classifier replaces the models' weights ω with distributions, i.e. a Gaussian prior $\omega \sim N(0, 1)$. Since the posterior probability $p(\omega|X, Y)$ cannot be evaluated analytically, various approximation techniques are used in practice [8,15]. Sample-based approximations aim to fit the posterior $p(\omega|X, Y)$ with a simple to compute distribution $q^*(\omega)$. The conditional class probability can then be approximated by averaging T Monte Carlo samples over possible weights. In this paper, we consider (8) a **Bayesian** variation of the **Multilayer Perceptron (B-MLP*)**. Bayesian models are of particular interest because they capture the uncertainty inherent in the model parameters [27]. Conventional deterministic classifiers can only capture the uncertainties inherent in the data. A holistic assessment of the uncertainty of Bayesian classifiers can be performed by calculating Shannon's entropy (Eq. 1) for the mean conditional class probabilities of several model runs.

4.4 Implementation Details and Text Features

For most classifiers, we rely on the commonly used default implementation provided by the Scikit-learn[1] library. We have implemented classifiers that are not available in Scikit-learn via TensorFlow[2].

The parameters used for each classifier are the following: For the Decision Tree we use Scikit-learn's non-parametric implementation. The Random Forest classifier uses $T = 100$ Decision Trees with bootstrap enabled. For the kNN classifier we set $k = 25$

---

[1] https://scikit-learn.org/stable/index.html.

[2] https://www.tensorflow.org/.

as the number of considered neighbors. A linear kernel is used for the Support Vector Machine. The structure of the MLP takes the shape [768, 500, 500, C]. Since Scikit-learn does not offer a Bayesian-MLP, we employ TensorFlow version 2.4.1 to implement a Bayesian Multilayer Perceptron (B-MLP*). The posterior is approximated by using a dropout variational distribution [15]. Further, we approximate the class probability by applying $T = 100$ forward passes. We additionally implement a second (9) **non-Bayesian-MLP (MLP*)** using TensorFlow to compare only the impact of Bayesian modelling. In comparison to Scikit-learn's MLP implementation, our MLP* model applies dropout as performed by the Bayesian MLP, but only during the training process. We use 10% of the training data as validation data for all MLP implementations to enable early stopping.

In our experiments, we rely on lightweight text classifiers that require numerical feature vectors as input. Text documents consist of character sequences that must first be transformed to a vector space in order to apply machine learning classifiers. In this paper, we consider two pre-trained language models that provide text representations, i.e. encodings, for unlabeled text documents. First, we consider the *pre-trained Bidirectional Encoder Representations from Transformers* (BERT) [13] model. BERT is intended to be fine-tuned to obtain state-of-the-art text encodings. However, fine-tuning is very computational intensive and requires a lot of memory that is not available on weak infrastructures. For this reason, we consider out-of-the-box BERT encodings as a baseline for our approach. Second, we use Sentence-BERT (SBERT) [41], a modification of BERT designed to provide semantically meaningful encodings without domain-specific fine-tuning. Moreover, SBERT encodings are much more resource-efficient to compute than BERT encodings. BERT and its variations encode a text document d as a n-dimensional vector of continuous attributes $x = (a_i, ..., a_n)$. We use the pre-trained *bert-base-uncased*[3] model for BERT and the *all-mpnet-base-v2*[4] model for SBERT, both of which compute encodings of length $n = 768$.

5   Experimental Results

In this section, we present the results of our experiments and answer our six research questions.

5.1   Quality of Predicted Probabilities

First, we examine the quality of the predicted probabilities of the individual classifiers. Figure 1 shows the mean class probability of all wrong and correct predictions using the App Store dataset. Each box shows the lower and upper quartiles, with a line at the median. Whiskers illustrate the range of the data. The figure demonstrates that the probability distributions of wrong and correct classified text documents generally differs. Only the DT and the GNB classifier show no differences in their means. For example, using SBERT encoding the mean class probability of all wrong and correct predictions is 66.4% and 89.42% respectively. Thus, for the majority of classifiers, reported class probabilities allow us to detect whether predictions are likely to be wrong or correct. BERT and SBERT show no significant differences on average.

---

[3] https://huggingface.co/bert-base-uncased.

[4] https://huggingface.co/sentence-transformers/all-mpnet-base-v2.

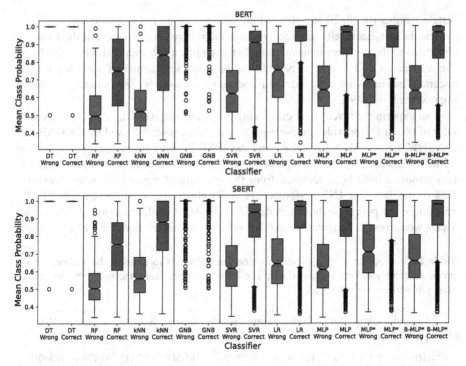

Fig. 1. Distribution of mean class probability for all wrong and correct classifications results for the App Store dataset.

Second, the Brier scores of all nine classifiers and six datasets are shown in Table 2. The lower the Brier score, the more accurate the conditional class probabilities. A Brier score of 0 means that the classifier is perfectly accurate, while a score of about 1 indicates a very inaccurate classifier. The table shows large differences between the classifiers in terms of the quality of their predicted probabilities. A DT and GNB provide on average the worst calibrated probabilities with a Brier score of 0.70 and 0.40 respectively using SBERT encodings. RF and kNN reach nearly equally calibrated probabilities, with an average of >0.27. The best average Brier scores (<0.25) were reached by SVM, LR and MLP as well as its variations. Across all datasets, MLP and MLP* receive the best scores using BERT encodings and LR, MLP and MLP* using SBERT. MLP* provide the most accurate probabilities with an average Brier score of ~0.22 (BERT) and ~0.20 (SBERT). Overall, SBERT encodings lead to much better calibrated probabilities across all classifiers and datasets compared to BERT.

5.2   Classifier Performance Under Stepwise Removal of Uncertain Instances

Next, we examine the F1-score of the automatic classifiers when a certain proportion of the most uncertain instances are removed from the test dataset. Tables 3 and 4 display the F1-scores of the nine classifiers applied to each of the six datasets using BERT and SBERT encodings respectively. The columns represent the F1-scores obtained when a certain number (0, 10, 20 and 30%) of the most uncertain instances are removed from the test dataset. Each cell additionally shows the relative improvement of the F1-score compared to the previous removal ratio. For example, a LR with SBERT on the News dataset reaches an F1-score of 88.90% on the entire test dataset. If 10% of the most uncertain instances are removed, the F1-score increases to 93.78% which is a relative improvement of 5.49%.

Our experiment reveals that classifying the whole test dataset, i.e. using a removal ratio of 0%, a DT provides on average the worst F1-score, followed by the GNB, RF and kNN. LR, SVM, MLP, MLP* and the B-MLP* achieve on average the highest initial F1-scores as well as the highest scores when a certain number of the most uncertain instances have been removed from the test dataset, e.g. +4.7% when removing 10% of the data. The kNN performs very well only on the News dataset with SBERT encodings, but poorly on the others datasets. The MLP implementation of Scikit-learn yields worse results compared to our TensorFlow implementation. Bayesian modelling

Table 2. Brier scores of the different classifiers and datasets to measure the accuracy of the predicted conditional class probabilities. The lower the Brier score, the better the conditional class probabilities are calibrated.

	Classifier	App Store	News	Hate Speech	Issues	Reuters	TREC	AVG
BERT	DT	0.6639	0.6983	0.5230	1.0166	0.5699	1.0181	0.7483
	RF	0.3344	0.3392	0.2549	0.5041	0.2632	0.4764	0.3620
	kNN	0.3105	0.3021	0.2717	0.4992	0.2065	0.3805	0.3284
	GNB	0.6100	0.4206	0.4605	0.7668	0.4148	0.6990	0.5620
	SVM	0.2686	0.2097	0.2118	0.4392	0.1125	0.2208	0.2438
	LR	0.2551	0.1858	0.2089	0.4320	0.1009	0.2151	0.2330
	MLP	0.2419	0.1920	0.2212	0.4385	0.1098	0.2336	0.2395
	MLP*	0.2390	0.1760	0.2046	0.4259	0.1028	0.2086	0.2262
	B-MLP*	0.2322	0.1728	0.2000	0.4209	0.1005	0.2060	0.2221
	AVG	0.3506	0.2996	0.2841	0.5492	0.2201	0.4065	0.3517

	Classifier	App Store	News	Hate Speech	Issues	Reuters	TREC	AVG
SBERT	DT	0.6534	0.6126	0.4551	1.0478	0.4182	1.0234	0.7018
	RF	0.3174	0.2779	0.2137	0.5191	0.1748	0.4931	0.3327
	kNN	0.2871	0.1292	0.2151	0.5099	0.0790	0.4437	0.2773
	GNB	0.4418	0.2286	0.3506	0.6958	0.1986	0.4929	0.4014
	SVM	0.2469	0.1546	0.1699	0.4115	0.0519	0.1872	0.2037
	LR	0.2381	0.1410	0.1671	0.4081	0.0489	0.1848	0.1980
	MLP	0.2427	0.1453	0.1822	0.4422	0.0533	0.1992	0.2108
	MLP*	0.2361	0.1377	0.1681	0.4139	0.0495	0.1792	0.1974
	B-MLP*	0.2309	0.1349	0.1629	0.4055	0.0483	0.1768	0.1932
	AVG	0.3216	0.2180	0.2316	0.5393	0.1247	0.3756	0.3018

Table 3. F1-scores of different classifiers when a certain number of the most uncertain predictions are removed from the test dataset using BERT embeddings.

Classifier	App Store				News				Hate Speech			
	0%	10%	20%	30%	0%	10%	20%	30%	0%	10%	20%	30%
DT	56.74	56.58	56.30	56.26	61.29	62.23	62.21	62.33	63.12	63.22	63.22	63.13
		-0.27	-0.50	-0.07		1.52	-0.03	+0.20		+0.16	+0.0	-0.14
RF	65.40	66.97	66.60	64.33	78.64	82.72	86.78	90.11	68.40	66.21	62.69	58.96
		+2.41	-0.54	-3.41		+5.19	+4.91	+3.84		-3.20	-5.31	-5.95
kNN	69.73	72.72	74.61	76.03	76.23	80.99	84.77	88.36	57.51	53.53	53.30	53.45
		+4.30	+2.60	+1.90		+6.25	+4.66	+4.25		-6.93	-0.41	+0.28
GNB	63.69	66.34	68.83	71.41	76.34	80.00	83.71	86.55	69.94	72.44	74.48	76.82
		+4.16	+3.75	+3.75		+4.79	+4.64	+3.40		+03.57	+2.82	+3.14
SVM	74.22	77.79	80.76	83.73	83.23	88.11	92.11	95.44	76.70	79.00	80.98	82.59
		+4.81	+3.82	+3.68		+5.86	+4.55	+3.61		+3.00	+2.51	+1.99
LR	77.01	81.13	84.84	88.19	85.13	90.42	94.52	97.11	78.17	81.08	83.63	85.57
		+5.35	+4.57	+3.95		+6.22	+4.53	+2.74		+3.72	+3.15	+2.31
MLP	77.55	81.68	85.70	89.53	85.36	90.63	94.73	97.34	78.25	81.40	84.03	86.15
		+5.33	+4.93	+4.47		+6.17	+4.53	+2.75		+4.01	+3.23	+2.53
MLP*	78.08	82.05	85.80	88.96	86.16	91.30	95.35	97.63	79.19	82.61	85.40	87.82
		+5.08	+4.57	+3.69		+5.97	+4.43	+2.39		+4.32	+3.38	+2.83
B-MLP*	77.96	81.97	85.53	88.88	86.03	91.18	95.18	97.56	79.10	82.46	85.18	87.43
		+5.13	+4.35	+3.91		+5.98	+4.38	+2.51		+4.25	+3.30	+2.63
AVG	71.15	74.14	76.55	78.59	79.82	84.18	87.71	90.27	72.26	73.55	74.77	75.77

Classifier	Issues				Reuters				TREC			
	0%	10%	20%	30%	0%	10%	20%	30%	0%	10%	20%	30%
DT	48.96	49.01	48.89	48.85	50.23	50.28	49.99	50.18	46.02	45.81	45.72	45.42
		+0.09	-0.24	-0.08		+0.10	-0.58	+0.39		-0.45	-0.21	-0.65
RF	63.44	65.74	67.78	69.93	72.89	77.75	82.16	82.47	67.71	69.97	72.11	73.96
		+3.61	+3.11	+3.17		+6.67	+5.68	+0.37		+3.33	+3.06	+2.57
kNN	62.02	64.21	66.24	68.19	73.94	79.45	82.91	83.02	72.26	74.80	76.96	79.36
		+3.53	+3.17	+2.93		+7.46	+4.36	+0.13		+3.52	+2.88	+3.12
GNB	60.42	62.38	64.01	65.58	68.64	74.66	80.53	84.96	61.55	63.90	66.10	68.33
		+3.25	+2.62	+2.45		+8.77	+7.86	+5.49		+3.82	+3.44	+3.37
SVM	67.71	70.44	72.52	74.70	87.26	93.67	96.82	98.43	83.60	87.48	89.74	92.38
		+4.03	+2.95	+3.02		+7.34	+3.36	+1.66		+4.65	+2.58	+2.94
LR	68.38	71.09	73.42	75.84	87.70	94.60	97.41	98.86	84.92	88.42	90.75	92.90
		+3.96	+3.28	+3.30		+7.87	+2.97	+1.49		+4.13	+2.63	+2.36
MLP	67.92	70.49	72.92	75.13	86.81	94.17	97.30	98.44	86.39	90.31	93.13	94.36
		+3.77	+3.45	+3.04		+8.48	+3.32	+1.17		+4.53	+3.13	+1.31
MLP*	69.27	72.02	74.48	76.97	87.48	94.97	97.69	98.95	86.72	90.23	92.21	93.61
		+3.97	+3.41	+3.35		+8.56	+2.86	+1.28		+4.05	+2.19	+1.52
B-MLP*	69.31	72.05	74.48	76.82	87.27	94.51	97.75	99.15	86.76	89.72	92.03	93.52
		+3.96	+3.37	+3.14		+8.29	+3.43	+1.43		+3.40	+2.57	+1.63
AVG	64.16	66.38	68.30	70.22	78.02	83.78	86.95	88.27	75.10	77.85	79.86	81.54

Table 4. F1-scores of different classifiers when a certain number of the most uncertain predictions are removed from the test dataset using SBERT embeddings.

Classifier	App Store				News				Hate Speech			
	0%	10%	20%	30%	0%	10%	20%	30%	0%	10%	20%	30%
DT	58.48	58.58	58.47	58.40	66.25	67.28	67.21	67.15	67.64	67.59	67.72	67.56
		+0.16	-0.18	-0.13		+1.55	-0.10	-0.08		-0.07	+0.19	-0.24
RF	63.44	65.30	65.86	65.34	87.24	91.44	94.80	96.24	76.82	76.93	74.07	67.97
		+2.93	+0.86	-0.80		+4.82	+3.68	+1.51		+0.14	-3.72	-8.24
kNN	69.42	70.47	69.94	69.41	89.67	94.63	97.73	99.06	71.05	71.07	71.83	73.88
		+1.50	-0.75	-0.75		+5.53	+3.28	+1.37		+0.03	+1.07	+2.85
GNB	74.11	77.35	80.45	83.33	86.55	91.94	95.48	96.80	77.19	80.71	83.94	86.88
		+4.37	+4.01	+3.59		+6.22	+3.85	+1.39		+4.56	+4.00	+3.51
SVM	76.46	80.13	83.68	87.66	88.51	92.92	96.20	97.43	82.79	86.25	88.67	89.87
		+4.80	+4.43	+4.76		+4.98	+3.53	+1.28		+4.18	+2.81	+1.35
LR	77.29	81.41	85.34	89.27	88.90	93.78	96.92	98.11	82.90	86.78	89.51	90.88
		+5.32	+4.83	+4.60		+5.49	+3.35	+1.22		+4.68	+3.15	+1.53
MLP	78.31	82.21	85.29	87.95	89.16	94.42	97.46	98.62	83.14	86.92	89.95	92.12
		+4.98	+3.74	+3.12		+5.89	+3.22	+1.19		+4.55	+3.48	+2.41
MLP*	78.75	82.99	86.43	90.44	89.28	94.64	97.60	98.85	83.71	87.63	90.96	93.02
		+5.38	+4.14	+4.65		+6.00	+3.13	+1.28		+4.68	+3.80	+2.27
B-MLP*	78.68	82.72	86.43	90.25	89.27	94.53	97.58	98.79	83.69	87.61	90.75	92.69
		+5.12	+4.50	+4.42		+5.90	+3.22	+1.24		+4.68	+3.59	+2.14
AVG	72.77	75.68	77.99	80.23	86.09	90.62	93.44	94.56	78.77	81.28	83.04	83.87

Classifier	Issues				Reuters				TREC			
	0%	10%	20%	30%	0%	10%	20%	30%	0%	10%	20%	30%
DT	47.38	47.36	47.38	47.41	65.12	65.42	65.43	65.22	46.02	45.81	45.72	45.42
		-0.05	+0.04	+0.07		+0.45	+0.01	-0.32		-0.45	-0.21	-0.65
RF	62.68	64.99	66.64	67.94	86.85	91.48	92.61	94.27	69.51	72.10	73.92	76.32
		+3.70	+2.54	+1.95		+5.33	+1.24	+1.79		+3.71	+2.53	+3.24
kNN	60.60	62.91	64.76	66.81	88.73	95.12	99.45	99.70	69.53	72.03	74.07	76.37
		+3.81	+2.96	+3.16		+7.20	+4.55	+0.25		+3.59	+2.83	+3.11
GNB	61.79	63.44	64.97	66.53	88.49	95.02	98.44	99.47	74.33	77.52	80.45	82.76
		+2.67	+2.41	+2.39		+7.38	+3.60	+1.05		+4.30	+3.77	+2.88
SVM	70.32	73.08	75.28	77.61	93.85	98.19	99.65	99.92	86.21	89.17	91.72	93.84
		+3.92	+3.01	+3.11		+4.62	+1.49	+0.28		+3.43	+2.86	+2.31
LR	70.45	73.24	75.68	78.04	93.93	99.05	99.84	99.84	86.11	89.12	91.64	93.75
		+3.96	+3.33	+3.12		+5.45	+0.80	-0.00		+3.49	+2.82	+2.31
MLP	69.47	72.33	74.86	77.33	93.33	98.52	99.66	99.62	86.40	90.33	93.14	94.36
		+4.11	+3.50	+3.30		+5.57	+1.16	-0.04		+4.55	+3.11	+1.31
MLP*	70.99	73.93	76.47	79.12	93.96	99.15	99.81	99.90	86.51	89.79	92.14	92.46
		+4.14	+3.44	+3.47		+5.53	+0.67	+0.09		+3.78	+2.62	+0.34
B-MLP*	71.01	73.87	76.31	78.72	94.03	99.22	99.80	99.92	86.45	89.41	91.77	91.53
		+4.03	+3.30	+3.16		+5.52	+0.58	+0.12		+3.42	+2.63	-0.26
AVG	64.97	67.24	69.15	71.06	88.70	93.46	94.97	95.32	76.79	79.48	81.62	82.98

(B-MLP*) does not improve the F1-score compared to a deterministic MLP. Using SBERT encodings compared to BERT, all classifiers achieve up to 20% higher F1-scores at the same removal ratio.

The F1-score generally increases substantially when a certain proportion of the most uncertain instances are removed from the test dataset. Only the uncertainty estimates of a DT are consistently not able to detect misclassifications. Here, the F1-score does not improve with larger removal ratios. Moreover, the relative F1-score improvements decrease with larger removal ratios. This indicates decreasing human efficiency. Especially when large amounts of removed data are given to human annotators. On average, classifiers with high initial F1-scores attain the best F1-scores after removing uncertain instances.

5.3 Semi-automated Classification Performance

In the next step, we examine the overall classification performance when a certain proportion of the classification results were performed by human annotators. Tables 5, 6, 7 and 8 display how many of the most uncertain instances from the unseen test set need to be manually classified to raise the semi-automatic classification results to a given F1-score. Each sub-table represents a different level of human noise, as introduced in Sect. 4. For example, on the News dataset 12.76% of the most uncertain predictions need to be manually corrected to improve the F1-score of the SVM (from the original 88.51%) to 95% using SBERT encodings.

An accurate human annotator can achieve a strong F1-score of 95 to 99% by manually labeling less than 23.5% of the News, Hate Speech, Reuters, and TREC datasets. For the App Store dataset, 29.32% is required. The Issues dataset has the worst F1-score using purely automatic classification. Here, an F1-score of 83% is achieved when 24.47% of the data is manually annotated, which corresponds to an absolute F1-score improvement of 10.01%. The tables further illustrate that models with a high initial F1-score require less manual efforts to raise the F1-score to a certain target level. Overall, models with lower initial F1-score scores rarely outperform the more accurate classifiers in regard to the final F1-score. Human annotators with higher noise require more manual effort to achieve a certain F1-score. This is because higher noise results in more misclassifications. However, our results suggest that human-in-the-loop text classification can obtain a higher F1-score than the pure machine and human parts alone. For example, an LR classifier with an initial F1-score of 88.90% on the News dataset and a 10% noisy human can attain an F1-score of >95% (max. 96.47%) when >13.56% of the dataset is manually classified.

We show that lightweight classifiers with a human in the loop can achieve strong accuracies even when the annotator makes multiple classification errors. In our experiments, the best performing classifier reach an F1-score of 89% (+10.92), 95% (+8.84), 91% (+11.81) 79% (+9.73) 99% (+11.52) and 91% (+4.61) with a manual effort of 19.74, 11.44, 14.24, 18.34, 5.08 and 10.99 respectively, taking into account a human noise level of 10% and SBERT. Compared to a 100% accurate human annotator, this is an increase in manual efforts of 19.47%, 17.13%, 16.22%, 14.39%, 32.87%, and 23.29% respectively. Our results indicate that very high F1-scores (around 95 to 99%)

Table 5. Performance of human-in-the-loop classifiers with BERT encodings. Each cell shows the percentage of the most uncertain classification results that must be manually annotated to achieve a given F1-score at a given human noise level. F1-scores that cannot be achieved due to a high level of human misclassifications are marked with "-".

Classifier	App Store 89%	91%	.93%	95%	News 91%	93%	95%	97%	Hate Speech 89%	91%	93%	95%	
DT	74.87	79.16	83.51	88.45	76.34	81.48	86.80	92.16	70.30	75.83	81.26	86.57	
RF	36.70	41.40	47.12	53.47	21.49	26.78	32.96	42.37	28.78	34.15	41.16	50.23	
kNN	31.23	36.26	40.58	47.25	25.40	30.95	37.10	44.74	30.37	35.72	42.66	51.92	0% human noise
GNB	43.02	47.68	52.25	58.20	28.09	34.41	41.44	53.22	46.34	54.36	62.65	72.53	
SVM	23.65	27.78	32.23	37.80	12.69	17.10	22.79	28.92	19.06	23.56	29.57	38.17	
LR	18.49	22.65	27.82	33.64	8.89	12.79	17.30	23.46	17.72	22.48	28.53	37.25	
MLP	17.80	21.68	25.75	31.57	8.55	12.37	16.94	23.30	17.82	22.99	29.62	38.46	
MLP*	16.74	20.65	25.53	30.63	7.47	11.25	15.68	21.44	16.04	20.90	26.96	35.01	
B-MLP*	17.08	21.25	25.53	30.91	7.61	11.52	16.14	21.65	15.99	20.71	26.56	34.34	
DT	82.01	87.23	91.90	97.12	84.74	90.92	96.78	-	77.10	83.13	89.03	95.06	
RF	42.02	48.19	55.54	63.20	24.02	30.57	40.70	63.64	32.04	39.00	48.77	64.92	
kNN	35.67	40.52	47.78	54.66	28.42	35.42	44.15	59.21	33.89	41.06	51.25	68.77	
GNB	47.87	53.10	59.98	69.96	32.07	40.32	55.09	-	53.11	62.90	74.83	90.00	
SVM	26.03	31.10	36.86	47.87	13.91	19.09	26.08	37.63	20.73	26.21	34.57	50.07	5% human noise
LR	20.18	24.81	31.32	40.93	9.63	14.05	19.43	29.80	19.29	25.00	33.40	46.56	
MLP	19.40	23.62	29.41	38.58	9.27	13.53	18.98	28.81	19.45	25.76	34.64	49.41	
MLP*	18.02	22.50	28.19	35.92	8.07	12.46	17.43	26.71	17.58	23.23	31.16	45.05	
B-MLP*	18.68	23.19	28.69	35.95	8.30	12.76	18.07	26.94	17.50	23.12	30.77	43.38	
DT	91.49	97.47	-	-	97.10	-	-	-	85.17	92.06	99.03	-	
RF	47.28	55.60	64.99	-	27.60	37.59	-	-	36.87	47.80	71.12	-	
kNN	39.92	48.00	56.66	-	33.18	42.30	-	-	38.46	50.23	78.78	-	
GNB	53.88	61.83	-	-	38.06	-	-	-	62.02	7.57	98.13	-	
SVM	29.72	35.70	49.62	-	15.32	22.16	31.52	-	22.84	30.16	45.42	-	10% human noise
LR	22.81	29.66	40.77	-	10.43	15.40	22.66	-	21.43	28.74	41.92	-	
MLP	21.59	26.72	35.54	-	10.01	15.10	22.24	-	21.87	30.20	45.30	-	
MLP*	20.59	26.66	34.11	-	8.69	13.66	20.20	-	19.41	26.89	39.73	-	
B-MLP*	21.50	26.94	34.73	-	8.81	14.21	20.69	-	19.13	26.07	37.72	-	
DT	-	-	-	-	-	-	-	-	97.33	-	-	-	
RF	59.67	-	-	-	33.81	-	-	-	47.37	-	-	-	
kNN	48.03	-	-	-	41.36	-	-	-	49.54	-	-	-	
GNB	70.62	-	-	-	-	-	-	-	87.02	-	-	-	
SVM	33.26	54.01	-	-	17.30	26.32	-	-	26.07	39.70	-	-	15% human noise
LR	25.03	35.29	-	-	11.48	17.59	-	-	24.42	38.24	-	-	
MLP	23.28	31.20	-	-	10.93	17.01	-	-	24.93	39.20	-	-	
MLP*	22.65	31.54	-	-	9.57	15.00	32.39	-	22.02	32.54	-	-	
B-MLP*	22.90	31.13	-	-	9.74	15.62	-	-	22.10	31.88	-	-	

Table 6. Performance of human-in-the-loop classifiers with BERT encodings. Each cell shows the percentage of the most uncertain classification results that must be manually annotated to achieve a given F1-score at a given human noise level. F1-scores that cannot be achieved due to a high level of human misclassifications are marked with "-".

0% human noise

Classifier	Issues				Reuters				TREC			
	79%	81%	83%	85%	93%	95%	97%	99%	89%	91%	93%	95%
DT	58.97	62.92	66.89	70.76	86.35	89.92	93.85	97.79	79.67	83.33	87.10	90.46
RF	29.93	34.46	39.18	44.00	17.44	21.45	28.95	44.86	42.94	48.82	56.72	67.44
kNN	32.32	36.75	41.63	46.54	17.65	21.11	25.93	38.36	38.84	45.53	53.76	61.46
GNB	36.07	40.64	45.67	50.99	27.12	31.27	36.78	49.69	62.60	69.96	77.42	83.74
SVM	22.35	26.79	31.66	36.78	5.69	8.92	13.93	24.36	9.91	16.10	22.24	28.66
LR	20.61	25.06	29.68	34.60	4.50	7.66	13.05	22.54	8.33	13.74	20.09	26.85
MLP	21.07	25.51	30.44	35.50	5.55	8.52	13.19	23.84	9.11	13.17	19.35	25.87
MLP*	19.26	23.65	28.34	33.04	4.85	8.06	12.10	21.96	7.56	12.87	18.51	26.38
B-MLP*	19.42	23.97	28.61	33.42	5.25	7.99	12.03	21.04	8.30	14.01	19.52	27.25

5% human noise

Classifier	Issues				Reuters				TREC			
	79%	81%	83%	85%	93%	95%	97%	99%	89%	91%	93%	95%
DT	63.20	67.40	71.54	75.84	-	-	-	-	90.96	95.63	99.83	-
RF	32.44	37.46	42.66	47.98	21.27	39.26	-	-	56.89	73.52	96.77	-
kNN	34.99	39.98	45.53	50.58	21.22	29.21	-	-	38.84	45.53	53.76	61.46
GNB	39.19	44.50	50.14	56.49	33.29	-	-	-	78.43	88.51	97.11	-
SVM	24.29	29.26	34.64	40.28	6.62	11.84	-	-	13.17	21.37	31.45	-
LR	22.31	27.22	32.50	38.02	5.02	9.87	20.76	-	10.25	19.25	29.03	-
MLP	22.83	27.96	33.34	38.75	6.32	10.77	20.78	-	11.66	17.37	26.28	56.45
MLP*	20.87	25.76	30.86	36.02	5.87	9.52	18.06	-	9.95	17.07	28.09	48.96
B-MLP*	21.03	26.14	31.30	36.74	6.04	9.80	18.55	-	11.09	18.65	29.47	54.91

10% human noise

Classifier	Issues				Reuters				TREC			
	79%	81%	83%	85%	93%	95%	97%	99%	89%	91%	93%	95%
DT	67.85	72.38	76.90	81.43	-	-	-	-	-	-	-	-
RF	35.17	40.78	46.68	52.92	-	-	-	-	-	-	-	-
kNN	38.02	44.20	49.62	56.26	-	-	-	-	-	-	-	-
GNB	42.88	48.98	55.88	63.30	-	-	-	-	-	-	-	-
SVM	26.26	32.19	38.24	44.63	8.08	-	-	-	17.00	26.41	-	-
LR	24.19	29.73	35.59	41.98	6.04	-	-	-	11.66	23.42	-	-
MLP	24.75	30.68	36.58	42.67	7.41	-	-	-	12.20	21.91	-	-
MLP*	22.57	28.02	33.56	39.44	7.27	13.47	-	-	11.32	21.88	-	-
B-MLP*	22.89	28.40	34.24	40.36	7.22	13.47	-	-	12.00	25.74	-	-

15% human noise

Classifier	Issues				Reuters				TREC			
	79%	81%	83%	85%	93%	95%	97%	99%	89%	91%	93%	95%
DT	73.80	78.63	83.59	88.38	-	-	-	-	-	-	-	-
RF	38.70	45.03	51.96	59.47	-	-	-	-	-	-	-	-
kNN	42.17	48.56	55.91	64.68	-	-	-	-	-	-	-	-
GNB	47.88	55.82	64.50	72.91	-	-	-	-	-	-	-	-
SVM	28.88	35.54	42.84	50.81	-	-	-	-	32.49	-	-	-
LR	26.39	32.65	39.49	46.99	11.93	-	-	-	25.03	-	-	-
MLP	27.00	33.68	40.36	47.88	12.05	-	-	-	21.40	-	-	-
MLP*	24.51	30.54	36.85	44.08	9.84	-	-	-	20.19	-	-	-
B-MLP*	25.18	31.35	38.14	45.53	11.07	-	-	-	25.71	-	-	-

Table 7. Performance of human-in-the-loop classifiers with SBERT encodings. Each cell shows the percentage of the most uncertain classification results that must be manually annotated to achieve a given F1-score at a given human noise level. F1-scores that cannot be achieved due to a high level of human misclassifications are marked with "-".

Classifier	App Store				News				Hate Speech				Noise
	89%	91%	.93%	95%	91%	93%	95%	97%	89%	91%	93%	95%	
DT	73.12	78.04	82.76	87.73	72.70	78.98	84.84	90.88	66.28	72.66	78.70	84.80	0% human noise
RF	32.45	36.83	41.36	46.75	6.48	10.70	15.10	23.82	18.30	22.68	28.08	35.31	
kNN	27.35	31.35	36.23	41.96	2.07	5.30	9.43	15.39	19.70	23.14	27.65	34.28	
GNB	31.85	36.83	42.77	50.94	6.65	10.13	14.32	22.47	25.83	31.65	38.88	48.95	
SVM	19.31	23.37	27.82	33.26	4.34	8.58	12.76	19.21	9.72	14.01	19.21	26.76	
LR	17.55	21.21	25.69	31.04	3.15	6.68	10.95	16.51	9.28	13.24	18.19	25.00	
MLP	17.18	21.18	25.66	31.91	2.84	6.06	9.67	14.97	9.37	13.77	18.88	26.57	
MLP*	15.93	20.15	24.47	29.32	2.57	5.62	9.48	14.45	8.17	11.93	16.80	23.50	
B-MLP*	16.27	20.24	24.53	29.60	2.57	5.63	9.58	14.57	8.17	11.96	16.74	23.48	
DT	81.04	86.23	91.49	96.87	81.97	88.81	95.80	-	73.77	80.76	87.65	94.81	5% human noise
RF	36.14	41.36	47.43	57.01	7.04	11.61	17.86	36.09	20.01	25.36	32.27	44.16	
kNN	30.35	35.61	42.18	51.60	2.23	5.65	10.53	17.57	21.22	25.31	31.21	42.68	
GNB	35.36	41.86	51.19	64.08	7.08	10.93	16.16	40.73	28.31	35.95	46.34	66.19	
SVM	21.34	25.88	31.70	40.86	4.73	9.18	14.38	25.46	10.63	15.29	21.51	34.64	
LR	19.18	23.15	28.94	38.17	3.33	7.28	12.33	20.11	9.89	14.44	20.41	30.39	
MLP	18.99	23.53	30.38	38.45	3.05	6.51	10.80	17.70	10.17	15.08	21.76	33.45	
MLP*	17.30	22.06	27.03	35.70	2.76	5.98	10.33	16.91	8.72	12.96	18.67	28.49	
B-MLP*	17.58	22.12	27.16	35.67	2.74	6.02	10.66	17.37	8.87	13.17	18.82	28.63	
DT	91.21	97.50	-	-	95.75	-	-	-	82.63	90.86	98.65	-	10% human noise
RF	40.71	47.37	60.54	-	7.87	12.60	24.05	-	22.12	28.63	39.39	-	
kNN	34.89	42.15	54.47	-	2.43	6.18	12.40	27.46	22.87	28.16	38.48	-	
GNB	40.05	50.91	-	-	7.59	12.03	20.79	-	31.34	41.41	67.41	-	
SVM	23.44	29.22	37.83	-	5.55	9.99	16.91	-	11.31	16.89	25.43	-	
LR	21.09	26.69	34.04	-	3.61	8.07	13.56	-	10.63	15.90	24.02	-	
MLP	21.43	27.28	36.36	-	3.20	6.95	12.07	-	10.97	16.53	25.57	-	
MLP*	19.74	25.03	33.35	-	2.93	6.47	11.44	26.09	9.38	14.24	21.84	43.32	
B-MLP*	19.90	25.38	32.98	-	2.90	6.57	11.65	-	9.44	14.25	21.44	47.59	
DT	-	-	-	-	-	-	-	-	96.03	-	-	-	15% human noise
RF	48.19	-	-	-	8.56	13.84	-	-	25.39	35.64	-	-	
kNN	40.64	59.92	-	-	2.53	6.59	13.71	-	25.64	34.47	-	-	
GNB	52.35	-	-	-	8.07	12.79	-	-	37.87	-	-	-	
SVM	26.53	36.36	-	-	5.98	11.15	-	-	12.65	19.84	-	-	
LR	23.15	31.91	-	-	3.72	8.69	15.86	-	11.82	18.48	-	-	
MLP	23.90	33.67	-	-	3.43	7.61	13.89	-	12.18	19.06	-	-	
MLP*	21.68	28.44	-	-	3.07	6.98	12.80	-	10.19	16.16	29.11	-	
B-MLP*	22.22	29.13	-	-	3.03	7.04	12.73	-	10.15	16.06	30.04	-	

Table 8. Performance of human-in-the-loop classifiers with SBERT encodings. Each cell shows the percentage of the most uncertain classification results that must be manually annotated to achieve a given F1-score at a given human noise level. F1-scores that cannot be achieved due to a high level of human misclassifications are marked with "-".

	Issues				Reuters				TREC				
Classifier	79%	81%	83%	85%	93%	95%	97%	99%	89%	91%	93%	95%	
DT	60.17	63.94	67.76	71.60	80.33	86.32	91.57	97.33	80.11	83.23	87.37	90.76	
RF	32.36	37.26	42.14	47.32	4.11	7.38	14.67	30.60	35.79	42.24	49.73	58.33	
kNN	34.28	38.99	43.90	48.54	3.13	5.46	9.12	14.14	43.21	49.97	56.12	64.58	
GNB	31.42	35.52	39.96	44.73	5.78	8.80	13.12	21.73	34.38	41.60	50.60	59.78	0% human noise
SVM	17.14	21.94	26.96	31.73	0	1.16	4.46	11.79	5.95	10.89	16.50	24.63	
LR	16.68	21.16	26.02	31.00	0	1.23	4.36	8.87	6.22	10.99	16.73	24.36	
MLP	17.94	22.41	27.05	31.98	0	1.74	4.50	9.68	3.93	8.43	13.21	19.76	
MLP*	15.70	20.01	24.47	29.13	0	1.16	3.41	7.89	4.47	8.33	13.41	19.22	
B-MLP*	15.84	20.31	24.84	29.76	0	1.14	3.65	8.06	4.70	8.64	13.68	20.23	
DT	64.26	68.38	72.50	76.50	-	-	-	-	91.33	95.63	99.87	-	
RF	35.21	40.61	46.21	52.09	5.13	11.93	-	-	49.53	61.06	85.28	-	
kNN	37.17	42.51	47.59	54.22	3.46	6.57	12.63	-	55.75	68.38	85.72	-	
GNB	33.76	38.34	43.52	48.67	6.59	10.45	17.04	-	47.78	60.22	81.99	-	5% human noise
SVM	18.71	24.01	29.36	34.78	0	1.30	5.83	-	7.90	14.65	24.73	-	
LR	18.09	23.05	28.48	33.97	0	1.35	5.36	-	8.43	15.12	24.87	-	
MLP	19.41	24.31	29.58	34.95	0	1.93	5.46	-	5.21	10.99	17.57	42.78	
MLP*	16.97	21.61	26.47	31.08	0	1.32	4.02	-	5.95	11.29	18.85	-	
B-MLP*	17.16	21.92	26.99	32.44	0	1.30	4.20	-	6.72	12.33	18.72	-	
DT	68.92	73.28	77.59	81.85	-	-	-	-	-	-	-	-	
RF	38.80	44.70	50.95	57.67	6.99	-	-	-	-	-	-	-	
kNN	40.98	46.47	53.24	59.50	3.71	8.24	-	-	-	-	-	-	
GNB	36.47	41.68	47.26	53.62	7.73	13.58	-	-	-	-	-	-	10% human noise
SVM	20.36	26.28	32.18	38.45	0	1.37	-	-	8.53	18.85	-	-	
LR	19.60	25.25	31.22	37.46	0	1.67	7.31	-	9.14	20.53	-	-	
MLP	21.10	26.60	32.46	39.01	0	2.25	7.55	-	5.21	10.99	-	-	
MLP*	18.34	23.39	28.97	35.02	0	1.44	5.08	-	5.98	12.03	-	-	
B-MLP*	18.67	23.85	29.72	36.06	0	1.49	5.15	-	7.29	13.71	-	-	
DT	74.30	78.89	83.39	87.89	-	-	-	-	-	-	-	-	
RF	43.10	49.88	57.83	66.28	-	-	-	-	-	-	-	-	
kNN	45.08	52.38	59.78	68.60	5.85	-	-	-	-	-	-	-	
GNB	40.11	46.35	53.38	61.50	10.45	-	-	-	-	-	-	-	15% human noise
SVM	22.35	28.88	35.54	43.41	0	2.11	-	-	15.73	-	-	-	
LR	21.37	27.87	34.58	41.86	0	2.30	-	-	15.66	-	-	-	
MLP	22.97	29.20	35.76	43.54	0	3.37	-	-	8.43	-	-	-	
MLP*	19.93	25.50	31.83	39.10	0	1.65	-	-	10.48	-	-	-	
B-MLP*	20.28	26.11	32.76	39.96	0	1.97	-	-	11.93	-	-	-	

cannot be achieved in all human-in-the-loop classification settings. If human annotations are too noisy, the F1-score drops after a certain level of support. As less uncertain predictions are annotated more frequently by humans in larger workloads, accuracy decreases. This phenomenon occurs because noisy humans incorrectly annotate instances that the machine itself would have decided correctly, which reduces the overall accuracy of the semi-automatic classification results. SBERT encodings lead to higher F1-scores compared to BERT encodings across all noise levels. For example, on the Hate Speech dataset, SBERT encodings require on average 9.6, 12.0, 13.5 and 14% less manual efforts to achieve F1-scores of 89, 91, 93, 95% respectively. Furthermore, higher F1-scores can be reached using SBERT encodings which would be unobtainable using BERT encodings. For instance, an F1-score of 97% would not be reachable by a 15% noisy human on the News dataset using BERT while SBERT requires a manual effort of 12.8%. Overall, SBERT encodings reduce manual effort by ∼5% to ∼20%. However, for the App Store dataset, the differences between BERT and SBERT were small (∼1%).

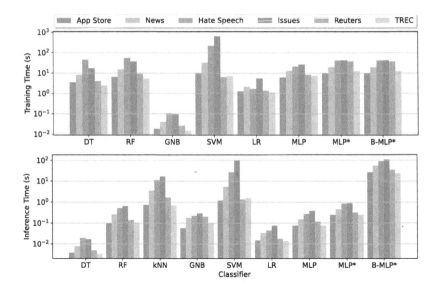

Fig. 2. Total training and inference time of the experiments using SBERT.

5.4   Runtime Investigation and Scalability

Figure 2 displays the training time of the classifiers using SBERT encodings. The classifiers are listed on the x-axis and the average training time in seconds is shown on the y-axis in logarithmic scale. The runtimes with BERT encodings are not reported because they cannot keep up with SBERT in terms of F1-score and provide less insight. For MLP, MLP*, B-MLP* and SVM, the training time increases by up to 53% when using BERT compared to SBERT. The differences were not significant when using DT,

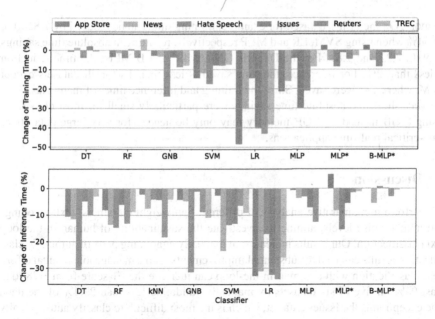

Fig. 3. Relative time change when using 8 GB of main memory compared to 4 GB using SBERT.

RF and NB. Also, the kNN is not included because it is a memory-based learning algorithm that does not require any training.

A GNB has the fastest training time with an average of ~0.1 seconds for 14999 instances (Issues). The LR has the second-shortest training time at 5.5 s. A DT, MLP, and RF perform much slower at 17.21, 26.08, and 36.78 s respectively. The dropout based-MLP* implementation took 40.54 s, almost 1.5 times as much as the MLP. MLP* and B-MLP* take the same time to train because they use the same training procedure. The SVM is the only classifier which shows an exponential increase in training time with respect to the size of the training data, ranging from 10.38 s for the App Store (size 2876) to 10.67 min for the Issues (size 14999) dataset. Thus, SBERT/BERT-based LR classifiers are time-saving and can be trained in a few seconds while obtaining a high F1-score with a human-in-the-loop.

We additionally assess the time needed to perform inference. The DT, RF, GNB, LR, MLP and MLP* classifiers take less than one second to infer the labels for 14999 instances (Issues). The kNN classifier is much slower with an inference time of 16.69 s. The inference time of an SVM and kNN grows exponentially in regard to the number of predicted texts. The SVM needs 1.20 s for the App Store and 93.85 s for the Issues dataset. The kNN classifier requires 0.73 s for the App Store and 17.00 s for the Issues dataset. Sampling-based Bayesian approximations require more time for inference, since multiple forward passes have to be carried out to approximate the condition class probabilities. By performing 100 forward passes, a Bayesian MLP takes 108.71 s (Issues).

Figure 3 shows the relative time savings in training and inference when using 8 GB of main memory compared to 4 GB. The LR, SVM and MLP benefit most from the extra memory. On the Issues dataset, for example, training time can be reduced by 7.8, 40.3, 29.94% when using SVM, LR and MLP respectively, resulting in absolute time savings of 50.0, 2.22 and 7.8 s. For the DT, RF, GNB, MLP and B-MLP* the time reduction is less than 2%. For inference, the time saved is less than 1 s for all datasets except SVM, where 12 s were saved. Since the training and inference times of many classifiers are very short, the absolute time savings were particularly small for most classifiers. Using 8 GB instead of 4 GB memory may only be needed for very large datasets or time-critical real-time applications.

6 Discussion

We perform a comparative analysis of different lightweight classifiers, text encodings and human noise levels, aiming to investigate the sustainability of human-in-the-loop text classification. Our results indicate that manually annotating parts of automatic classification results can lead to substantial improvements with a manageable manual effort. Text classification with a human-in-the-loop can increase the F1-score from $\sim$78 to at least 95% on five of six datasets by manually validating less than 29.4% of the data. The exception is the Issues data set, which is the most difficult to classify automatically in our evaluation with a comparatively low F1-score of 71%. Here F1-scores of 83% and 85% are achieved when 24.47% and 29.13% of the data are manually annotated. Which corresponds to an absolute F1-score improvement of 12.01 and 14.01%. Our results are particularly relevant for domains for which fully automatic text classifiers do not provide the required F1-score and therefore have to be performed purely manually instead. Although text classification can potentially always be done manually, many application areas are facing an overwhelming amount of data that exceeds human capabilities. Human-in-the-loop classification aims to overcome the accuracy limitations of purely automatic classification at the expense of human involvement. Human efforts are usually wasted when they are used for tasks that a cheap artificial model can do just as well. The effectiveness of human-in-the-loop comes from focusing human efforts on cases where an automatic classifier usually fails. Overall, the applicability of human-in-the-loop text classification depends on the need for more reliable classification results and the affordability of the human effort required to achieve them.

The findings of our experiments revealed large differences between different classification algorithms in terms of their suitability for human-in-the-loop text classification. We show that the quality of uncertainty estimates of simple classifiers such as Decision Trees, Gaussian Naive Bayes, Random Forest and k-Nearest Neighbor are fare less accurate compared to a Logistic Regression model, a Support Vector Machine or a Multilayer Perceptron, limiting their suitability for human-in-the-loop text classification. Only on the News dataset using SBERT encodings the kNN provides the best F1-scores. We also find that these simple models do not offer advantages over a Logistic Regression model, as they achieve a lower F1-score or require much more computational costs.

The Multilayer Perceptron and a Support Vector Machine provide similar or even stronger performance scores than Logistic Regression, but require much more computational resources. Although in our experiments, no classifier consistently outperforms the others, a Multilayer Perceptron with dropout attains the highest performance on average across all datasets. Overall, classifiers that obtain a higher F1-score purely automatically also require less effort to achieve an even higher F1-score when using a human-in-the-loop. Moreover, our results demonstrate that Bayesian modelling i.e. Monte Carlo Dropout [15], slightly improves the quality of uncertainty estimation but does not have a large impact on the resulting F1-score of the human-in-the-loop classification using a small MLP and SBERT or BERT encodings as text features. Since classifiers with the highest F1-score also report the best Brier scores, it is not necessary to use one classifier for uncertainty estimation and another classifier to provide the classification decision.

To enable fast or even real-time human-in-the-loop processing, a Logistic Regression model is the fastest approach for inference and training while providing decent initial and human in the loop performance. It requires only <5.6 and <3.3 seconds for training and inference on 14,998 data instances with 4 GB and 8 GB memory, respectively. A Support Vector Machine is less applicable due to its comparable slow training time and does not scale well for large datasets. A dropout-based Multilayer Perceptron has shown to perform better on average, but comes with higher total computational costs of <44 seconds for training and inference. Furthermore, we show that 4 GB of memory is suitable for the proposed classification environment and that more memory brings only minor improvements, especially using MLP* and B-MLP*.

We also demonstrate that humans and machines can work together to achieve even higher accuracy than their individual parts. Highly uncertain instances are most likely to be automatically misclassified, and even noisy human annotators have the potential to provide more accurate labels. By simulating different levels of annotation noise on various datasets, we demonstrate the performance of human-in-the-loop text classification in different domains and with different human performances. Practitioners must evaluate their own behavior to assess how much effort is worth investing in the loop. Our study provides guidelines to support practitioners choosing the most efficient classifier when strong classifiers are not applicable due to high computational costs and humans are willing to label part of the classification results.

Lightweight classifiers using SBERT clearly underperform state-of-the-art text classifiers such as end-to-end BERT [13]. For example, a fine-tuned BERT model achieved an F1-score of 93.46% [44] on the IMDB [36] dataset. However, BERT requires enormous computing resources and takes several hours to days to be fine-tuned on a CPU, if it is applicable at all. In comparison, our previous results show [4] that a Logistic Regression model applied for the same task using SBERT encodings takes a few seconds of training and inference on a CPU. Further, a Logistic Regression classifier attains an F1-score of 90.2%, which is a higher score than recent word embedding based approaches [20,21]. Manual labelling of 12.70% of the most uncertain predictions lead to an F1-score of 95%, which outperforms BERT. Thus, SBERT-based classifiers with a human in the loop are an alternative or even a replacement for BERT when training and inference need to be performed efficiently and the human effort can be arranged.

This paper explores human-in-the-loop classification with on-device training and inference. As an alternative to our approach, practitioners can also train classifiers on more powerful machines when available and then transfer the parameters to weak edge devices to maintain applicability and save computational costs. However, inference of state-of-the-art classifiers such as BERT on weak computational infrastructure, e.g. edge devices, is still very slow due to their high resource consumption. With our research, we are taking a more personalized approach where practitioners are capable of achieving strong classification performances on weak infrastructure. In doing so, we aim to support practitioners to rapidly extract the information they want from their text data by performing classification on their own workstations.

7   Conclusion and Future Work

The efficient integration of human domain experts can support a sustainable AI-based text classification. In our experiments we compare nine classifiers on six benchmark datasets when a specified amount of data is labelled by the expert. The collected data compares the achievable F1-score of different classifiers as well as the runtime required to perform the training and inference. We also compared SBERT vs. BERT embeddings and find that in every setting, SBERT performs better and equally sustainable if compared with BERT. Our research can be used as a foundation to develop a sustainable real-time text classification system with limited and predetermined human effort.

As future work, we will perform real-world tests of our uncertainty-based human-in-the-loop approach in a production setting. Furthermore, we plan to investigate the influence of the embeddings on the sustainability of the overall system.

References

1. Al-Jarrah, O.Y., Yoo, P.D., Muhaidat, S., Karagiannidis, G.K., Taha, K.: Efficient machine learning for big data: a review. Big Data Res. **2**(3), 87–93 (2015)
2. Amershi, S., Cakmak, M., Knox, W.B., Kulesza, T.: Power to the people: the role of humans in interactive machine learning. AI Mag. **35**(4), 105–120 (2014)
3. Andersen, J.S., Maalej, W.: Efficient, uncertainty-based moderation of neural networks text classifiers. In: Findings of the Association for Computational Linguistics: ACL 2022, pp. 1536–1546 (2022)
4. Andersen, J.S., Zukunft, O.: Towards more reliable text classification on edge devices via a human-in-the-loop. In: 2022 International Conference on Agents and Artificial Intelligence, vol. 2, pp. 636–646. SciTePress (2022)
5. Arnt, A., Zilberstein, S.: Learning to perform moderation in online forums. In: Proceedings IEEE/WIC International Conference on Web Intelligence (WI 2003), pp. 637–641. IEEE (2003)
6. Baram, Y., Yaniv, R.E., Luz, K.: Online choice of active learning algorithms. J. Mach. Learn. Res. **5**(Mar), 255–291 (2004)
7. Bishop, C.M.: Pattern Recognition and Machine Learning. Springer, New York (2006)
8. Blundell, C., Cornebise, J., Kavukcuoglu, K., Wierstra, D.: Weight uncertainty in neural network. In: International Conference on Machine Learning, pp. 1613–1622. PMLR (2015)
9. Brier, G.W.: Verification of forecasts expressed in terms of probability. Mon. Weather Rev. **78**(1), 1–3 (1950)
10. Corazza, M., Menini, S., Cabrio, E., Tonelli, S., Villata, S.: A multilingual evaluation for online hate speech detection. ACM Trans. Internet Technol. (TOIT) **20**(2), 1–22 (2020)

11. Cortes, C., DeSalvo, G., Mohri, M.: Learning with rejection. In: Ortner, R., Simon, H.U., Zilles, S. (eds.) ALT 2016. LNCS (LNAI), vol. 9925, pp. 67–82. Springer, Cham (2016). https://doi.org/10.1007/978-3-319-46379-7_5

12. Davidson, T., Warmsley, D., Macy, M., Weber, I.: Automated hate speech detection and the problem of offensive language. In: Proceedings of the International AAAI Conference on Web and Social Media, vol. 11 (2017)

13. Devlin, J., Chang, M.W., Lee, K., Toutanova, K.: BERT: pre-training of deep bidirectional transformers for language understanding. arXiv preprint arXiv:1810.04805 (2018)

14. Dudley, J.J., Kristensson, P.O.: A review of user interface design for interactive machine learning. ACM Trans. Interact. Intell. Syst. (TiiS) **8**(2), 1–37 (2018)

15. Gal, Y., Ghahramani, Z.: Dropout as a Bayesian approximation: representing model uncertainty in deep learning. In: International Conference on Machine Learning, pp. 1050–1059. PMLR (2016)

16. Geifman, Y., El-Yaniv, R.: Selective classification for deep neural networks. In: Proceedings of the 31st International Conference on Neural Information Processing Systems, pp. 4885–4894 (2017)

17. Green, B., Chen, Y.: Disparate interactions: an algorithm-in-the-loop analysis of fairness in risk assessments. In: Proceedings of the Conference on Fairness, Accountability, and Transparency, pp. 90–99 (2019)

18. Haering, M., et al.: Forum 4.0: an open-source user comment analysis framework. In: Proceedings of the 16th Conference of the European Chapter of the Association for Computational Linguistics: System Demonstrations, pp. 63–70 (2021)

19. Hastie, T., Tibshirani, R., Friedman, J.: The Elements of Statistical Learning: Data Mining, Inference, and Prediction. Springer, Heidelberg (2009). https://doi.org/10.1007/978-0-387-84858-7

20. He, J., et al.: Towards more accurate uncertainty estimation in text classification. In: Proceedings of the 2020 Conference on Empirical Methods in Natural Language Processing (EMNLP), pp. 8362–8372 (2020)

21. Hendrycks, D., Gimpel, K.: A baseline for detecting misclassified and out-of-distribution examples in neural networks. arXiv preprint arXiv:1610.02136 (2016)

22. Hernández-Lobato, J.M., Adams, R.: Probabilistic backpropagation for scalable learning of Bayesian neural networks. In: International Conference on Machine Learning, pp. 1861–1869. PMLR (2015)

23. Hingmire, S., Chougule, S., Palshikar, G.K., Chakraborti, S.: Document classification by topic labeling. In: Proceedings of the 36th International ACM SIGIR Conference on Research and Development in Information Retrieval, pp. 877–880 (2013)

24. Holzinger, A.: Interactive machine learning for health informatics: when do we need the human-in-the-loop? Brain Inform. **3**(2), 119–131 (2016). https://doi.org/10.1007/s40708-016-0042-6

25. Kallis, R., Di Sorbo, A., Canfora, G., Panichella, S.: Ticket tagger: machine learning driven issue classification. In: 2019 IEEE International Conference on Software Maintenance and Evolution (ICSME), pp. 406–409. IEEE (2019)

26. Karmakharm, T., Aletras, N., Bontcheva, K.: Journalist-in-the-loop: continuous learning as a service for rumour analysis. In: Proceedings of the 2019 Conference on Empirical Methods in Natural Language Processing and the 9th International Joint Conference on Natural Language Processing (EMNLP-IJCNLP): System Demonstrations, pp. 115–120 (2019)

27. Kendall, A., Gal, Y.: What uncertainties do we need in Bayesian deep learning for computer vision? In: Proceedings of the 31st International Conference on Neural Information Processing Systems, pp. 5580–5590 (2017)

28. Lai, C.C., Tsai, M.C.: An empirical performance comparison of machine learning methods for spam e-mail categorization. In: Fourth International Conference on Hybrid Intelligent Systems (HIS 2004), pp. 44–48. IEEE (2004)
29. Lang, K.: NewsWeeder: learning to filter netnews. In: Machine Learning Proceedings 1995, pp. 331–339. Elsevier (1995)
30. LeCun, Y., Bengio, Y., Hinton, G.: Deep learning. Nature **521**(7553), 436–444 (2015)
31. Lewis, D.D., Gale, W.A.: A sequential algorithm for training text classifiers. In: Croft, B.W., van Rijsbergen, C.J. (eds.) SIGIR 1994, pp. 3–12. Springer, London (1994). https://doi.org/10.1007/978-1-4471-2099-5_1
32. Lewis, D.D., Yang, Y., Rose, T.G., Li, F.: RCV1: a new benchmark collection for text categorization research. J. Mach. Learn. Res. **5**(Apr), 361–397 (2004)
33. Li, X., Roth, D.: Learning question classifiers. In: COLING 2002: The 19th International Conference on Computational Linguistics (2002)
34. Liu, Z., Chen, H.: A predictive performance comparison of machine learning models for judicial cases. In: IEEE Symposium Series on Computational Intelligence (SSCI), pp. 1–6. IEEE (2017)
35. Maalej, W., Kurtanović, Z., Nabil, H., Stanik, C.: On the automatic classification of app reviews. Requirements Eng. **21**(3), 311–331 (2016). https://doi.org/10.1007/s00766-016-0251-9
36. Maas, A., Daly, R.E., Pham, P.T., Huang, D., Ng, A.Y., Potts, C.: Learning word vectors for sentiment analysis. In: Proceedings of the 49th Annual Meeting of the Association for Computational Linguistics: Human Language Technologies, pp. 142–150 (2011)
37. Pavlopoulos, J., Malakasiotis, P., Androutsopoulos, I.: Deep learning for user comment moderation. In: Proceedings of the First Workshop on Abusive Language Online, pp. 25–35 (2017)
38. Platt, J.: Probabilistic outputs for support vector machines and comparisons to regularized likelihood methods. Adv. Large Margin Classif. **10**(3), 61–74 (1999)
39. Rasmussen, C.E., Williams, C.K.I.: Gaussian Processes for Machine Learning. MIT Press, Cambridge (2006)
40. Rattigan, M.J., Maier, M., Jensen, D.: Exploiting network structure for active inference in collective classification. In: Seventh IEEE International Conference on Data Mining Workshops (ICDMW 2007), pp. 429–434. IEEE (2007)
41. Reimers, N., Gurevych, I.: Sentence-BERT: sentence embeddings using Siamese BERT-networks. In: Proceedings of the 2019 Conference on Empirical Methods in Natural Language Processing. Association for Computational Linguistics (2019)
42. Sacha, D., Senaratne, H., Kwon, B.C., Ellis, G., Keim, D.A.: The role of uncertainty, awareness, and trust in visual analytics. IEEE Trans. Visual Comput. Graphics **22**(1), 240–249 (2015)
43. Sachan, D.S., Zaheer, M., Salakhutdinov, R.: Revisiting LSTM networks for semi-supervised text classification via mixed objective function. In: Proceedings of the AAAI Conference on Artificial Intelligence, vol. 33, pp. 6940–6948 (2019)
44. Sanh, V., Debut, L., Chaumond, J., Wolf, T.: Distilbert, a distilled version of BERT: smaller, faster, cheaper and lighter. arXiv preprint arXiv:1910.01108 (2019)
45. Schwartz, R., Dodge, J., Smith, N.A., Etzioni, O.: Green AI. Commun. ACM **63**(12), 54–63 (2020)
46. Shannon, C.E.: A mathematical theory of communication. ACM SIGMOBILE Mob. Comput. Commun. Rev. **5**(1), 3–55 (2001)
47. Siddhant, A., Lipton, Z.C.: Deep Bayesian active learning for natural language processing: results of a large-scale empirical study. In: Proceedings of the 2018 Conference on Empirical Methods in Natural Language Processing, pp. 2904–2909 (2018)

48. Stanik, C., Haering, M., Maalej, W.: Classifying multilingual user feedback using traditional machine learning and deep learning. In: 27th International Requirements Engineering Conference Workshops (REW), pp. 220–226. IEEE (2019)
49. Strubell, E., Ganesh, A., McCallum, A.: Energy and policy considerations for deep learning in NLP. In: Proceedings of the 57th Annual Meeting of the Association for Computational Linguistics, pp. 3645–3650 (2019)
50. Yang, Z., Dai, Z., Yang, Y., Carbonell, J., Salakhutdinov, R.R., Le, Q.V.: XLNet: generalized autoregressive pretraining for language understanding. Adv. Neural Inf. Process. Syst. **32** (2019)
51. Zanzotto, F.M.: Human-in-the-loop artificial intelligence. J. Artif. Intell. Res. **64**, 243–252 (2019)
52. Zhang, Q., Yang, L.T., Chen, Z., Li, P.: A survey on deep learning for big data. Inf. Fusion **42**, 146–157 (2018)

Author Index

Printed in the United States
by Baker & Taylor Publisher Services